THE QUALITY IMPROVEMENT HANDBOOK

Second Edition

Also available from ASQ Quality Press:

The Quality Toolbox, Second Edition
Nancy R. Tague

Root Cause Analysis: Simplified Tools and Techniques, Second Edition
Bjørn Andersen and Tom Fagerhaug

The Certified Manager of Quality/Organizational Excellence Handbook: Third Edition
Russell T. Westcott, editor

Quality Essentials: A Reference Guide from A to Z
Jack B. ReVelle

The Quality Improvement Glossary
Donald L. Siebels

The Path to Profitable Measures: 10 Steps to Feedback That Fuels Performance
Mark W. Morgan

Lean Kaizen: A Simplified Approach to Process Improvements
George Alukal and Anthony Manos

Simplified Project Management for the Quality Professional: Managing Small & Medium-Size Projects
Russell T. Westcott

Leadership for Results: Removing Barriers to Success for People, Projects, and Processes
Tom Barker

Everyday Excellence: Creating a Better Workplace through Attitude, Action, and Appreciation
Clive Shearer

Making Change Work: Practical Tools for Overcoming Human Resistance to Change
Brien Palmer

The Executive Guide to Improvement and Change
G. Dennis Beecroft, Grace L. Duffy, and John W. Moran

To request a complimentary catalog of ASQ Quality Press publications, call 800-248-1946, or visit our Web site at http://qualitypress.asq.org.

THE QUALITY IMPROVEMENT HANDBOOK

Second Edition

John E. Bauer, Grace L. Duffy,
and Russell T. Westcott, Editors

Quality Management Division
American Society for Quality

ASQ Quality Press
Milwaukee, Wisconsin

American Society for Quality, Quality Press, Milwaukee 53203
© 2006 by ASQ
All rights reserved. Published 2006
Printed in the United States of America
15 14 13 12   8 7 6 5 4

Library of Congress Cataloging-in-Publication Data

The quality improvement handbook / John E. Bauer, Grace L. Duffy, and
Russell T. Westcott, editors.—2nd ed.
　　p. cm.
　　Includes bibliographical references and index.
　　ISBN-13: 978-0-87389-690-0
　　1. Quality control—Handbooks, manuals, etc. 2. Quality assurance—
Handbooks, manuals, etc. I. Bauer, John E. II. Duffy, Grace L. III.
Westcott, Russ, 1927-
　　TS156.Q3Q355 2006
　　658.5′62—dc22   2006010039

ISBN-13: 978-0-87389-690-0
ISBN-10: 0-87389-690-4

Publisher: William A. Tony
Acquisitions Editor: Annemieke Hytinen
Project Editor: Paul O'Mara
Production Administrator: Randall Benson

ASQ Mission: The American Society for Quality advances individual, organization, and
community excellence worldwide through learning, quality improvement, and knowledge
exchange.

Attention Bookstores, Wholesalers, Schools, and Corporations: ASQ Quality Press books,
videotapes, audiotapes, and software are available at quantity discounts with bulk
purchases for business, educational, or instructional use. For information, please contact
ASQ Quality Press at 800-248-1946, or write to ASQ Quality Press, P.O. Box 3005,
Milwaukee, WI 53201-3005.

To place orders or to request a free copy of the ASQ Quality Press Publications Catalog,
including ASQ membership information, call 800-248-1946. Visit our Web site at
www.asq.org or http://qualitypress.asq.org.

Printed in the United States of America

 Printed on acid-free paper

Quality Press
600 N. Plankinton Avenue
Milwaukee, Wisconsin 53203
Call toll free 800-248-1946
Fax 414-272-1734
www.asq.org
http://qualitypress.asq.org
http://standardsgroup.asq.org
E-mail: authors@asq.org

Contents

List of Figures and Tables

Preface

The Quality Management Division (QMD) of the American Society for Quality (ASQ) continues to see organizational and process improvement being integrated into all areas of organization. This has resulted in a decrease in many of the traditional quality functions such as quality assurance, quality control, and quality audits. However, this move to integrate quality has led to an ever-increasing requirement for everyone in the organization to understand the basic principles of process control and process improvement.

ASQ introduced the *Certified Quality Improvement Associate* (CQIA) certification in 2000. This body of knowledge (BoK) was initially designed to address the non-traditional quality professional. It encompassed the basics of quality, teamwork, and continuous improvement. Over the past five years the CQIA has been strongly supported by the business community. Feedback from our customers resulted in a revision of the BoK, which in turn necessitated the second edition of this handbook.

The Voice of the Customer surveys for the BoK update identified three key areas for revision: value, problem solving, and decision making. This second edition addresses each of these key areas separately. It provides new material on identifying the value of teams, the specific process approaches for problem solving, and the different approaches for entering either problem-solving or decision-making pathways. A sample exam is included once again with new items for problem solving, value, and decision making.

The QMD sees the achievement of *Certified Quality Improvement Associate* as an important entry-level qualification for a career path toward the leadership and management of effective business systems. This path might ultimately culminate in certification as a *Certified Manager of Quality/Organizational Excellence.* Knowledge of quality basics, teamwork, and continuous improvement are the first steps in any successful career.

Once again, our division is very pleased to have three of our very knowledgeable members to act as the editors for this second edition:

- John E. Bauer
- Grace L. Duffy
- Russell T. Westcott

This handbook will be a valuable resource not only for those seeking certification but also for individuals wishing to increase their knowledge of basic quality information and tools.

G. Dennis Beecroft
Chair
Quality Management Division
American Society for Quality

Notes to the Reader

A BRIEF HISTORY OF QUALITY[1]

Although the history of quality goes back to ancient times, this short review starts with the current quality movement that had its beginning in the 1920s. The quality profession as we know it today began when Walter Shewhart of Bell Laboratories developed a system, *known as statistical process control,* for measuring variance in production systems. Statistical process control is still used to help monitor consistency and diagnose problems in work processes. Shewhart also created the Plan—Do—Check—Act (PDCA) cycle, which applies a systematic approach to improving work processes. When the PDCA cycle is applied consistently, it can result in continuous process improvement.

During World War II, the U.S. War Department hired Dr. W. Edwards Deming, a physicist and U.S. Census Bureau researcher, to teach statistical process control to the defense industry. Quality control and statistical methods were considered to be critical factors in a successful war effort. Unfortunately, most of the companies in the United States stopped using these statistical tools after the war.

The U.S. occupation forces in Japan invited Deming to help Japan with its postwar census. He was also invited to present lectures to business leaders on statistical process control and quality. The Japanese acceptance and use of Dr. Deming's techniques had a profound positive effect on the economy of Japan.

Two other American experts, Dr. Joseph Juran and Armand Feigenbaum, also worked with the Japanese. Both Deming and Juran, a former investigator at the Hawthorne Works experiments, drew on Shewhart's work and recognized that system problems could be addressed through three fundamental managerial processes—planning, control, and improvement—and that satisfying the customer's needs was important. Feigenbaum stressed the need to involve all departments of a company in the pursuit of quality, something he called *total quality control.* The Japanese expanded Juran's customer concept to include internal customers, those people within the organization who depend on the output of other workers.

Kaoru Ishikawa, a Japanese engineer and manager, enlarged Feigenbaum's ideas to include all employees, not just department managers, in the total-quality-control concept. Ishikawa also helped to create *quality circles,* small teams of managers, supervisors, and workers trained in statistical process control, the PDCA cycle, and group problem solving. Applying these techniques created a flow of new ideas for improvement from everyone in the organization and continuous small improvements that led to better performance. The quality circles were the original model for our current process improvement teams. By the 1970s, most large Japanese companies had adopted what Ishikawa called *companywide quality control* (CWQC), resulting in a perception that Japan produced world-class quality products.

The Japanese success prompted American organizations to embrace the teachings of Deming, Juran, Feigenbaum, and other quality "gurus" and to apply their successful quality management techniques in many types of business. Beginning in the mid 1980s, American organizations began to experience improved quality results and enhanced customer satisfaction.

In 1987, the criteria for the first Malcolm Baldrige National Quality Award were published. At the same time, ISO 9001, Quality Systems—Model for quality assurance in design, development, production, installation, and servicing was published. These documents have resulted in profound changes in the way the quality profession operates.

By the end of 2004, 150-plus countries were using the ISO 9000 standards and more than 670,000 quality system certificates had been issued. Many industry-specific quality management system documents have evolved from ISO 9000.

More than 2 million copies of the Malcolm Baldrige National Quality Award criteria have been distributed, and many state and local quality award programs have developed their own criteria based on the national award criteria. Although very few organizations actually apply for the national award, thousands use the criteria to evaluate and improve their quality management systems. Health-care and education versions of the award criteria have been published in the last few years, further expanding the applicability and value of the criteria.

STRUCTURE OF THE BOOK

The content of this book is structured to follow the BoK to be used in preparation for taking the Certified Quality Improvement Associate (CQIA) examination given by the American Society for Quality (ASQ). Though the content coincides with the sequence of the BoK, each chapter stands alone, and the chapters may be read in any order. Where appropriate, supplemental reading suggestions are provided.

DIVERSITY

The use of quality and continual improvement is no longer considered the sole property of manufacturing or the traditional engineering and production environment. Most professionals entering the workforce today are required to analyze situations, identify problems, and provide solutions for improved performance. Improving the organization is everyone's job. Teamwork is critical, requiring the participation of members of all backgrounds, nationalities, educational levels, and career aspirations.

An attempt has been made to balance the use of personal pronouns as well as introduce examples from a variety of organizations. The use of the term *orga-*

nization means that the content is considered generic—applicable to any type of entity. Where the term *company* is used, the content is more applicable to a "for-profit" enterprise.

READERS

This handbook was written for any person in any organization in which quality is a primary commitment and knowledge of quality fundamentals is a prerequisite to participation in building and maintaining that commitment. The handbook is also for any CQIA aspirant striving to achieve the first step in becoming a certified quality practitioner.

ADDITIONAL PRACTICE SUPPLEMENT—APPENDIX E

Many texts written to support entry-level practitioners include practice test items to help readers reinforce their learning. A sample 100-item test included with this text (Appendix E) addresses the materials covered in the BoK for the *Certified Quality Improvement Associate* (CQIA).

A sample test is provided on CD-ROM, along with tables giving cross-references to the suggested reference materials as well as the BoK. Answers to the questions in the sample test are also provided. Some readers may choose to use this test material to prepare to take the CQIA examination.

Because of ASQ examination rules, no questions or answers to questions may be brought into the room where the examination is given. This handbook, the suggested reference materials, and other references, such as notes from a course, may be brought into the examination room subject to inspection by the examination proctor.

The CQIA BoK, presented in Appendix A, indicates the number of questions that will be asked about each major topic and the maximum cognitive level to which the questions may be asked. The levels are derived from Bloom's taxonomy.[2] The levels are:

1. Remember (Knowledge)

2. Understand (Comprehension)

3. Apply (Application)

4. Analyze (Analysis)

5. Evaluate (Evaluation)

6. Create (Synthesis)

In addition to the content supporting the BoK, the CQIA aspirant is expected to be familiar with the ASQ Code of Ethics, which is presented in Appendix B.

AVAILABILITY OF REFERENCE MATERIALS

All of the texts referenced here, with the exception noted on page xiv, should be readily available from normal book sources, many from ASQ Quality Press. A Web site search will add a plethora of additional information.

Some of the text is derived from U.S. government publications that are no longer in print or are no longer available to the public. The U.S. government is an excellent source of government quality-related materials that are available for downloading.[3]

---

[1]Juran, J. M., ed. *A history of managing for quality.* Milwaukee, WI: ASQC Quality Press, 1995.

[2]Bloom, B. S., ed. *Taxonomy of educational objectives: The classification of educational goals, Handbook I, Cognitive domain.* New York: Longmans, Green, 1956. Additional information about Bloom's taxonomy may be obtained from http://www.coun.uvic.ca/learn/program/hndouts/bloom.html.

[3]Office of the Secretary of Defense's Quality Management Office Web site at http://www.odam.osd.mil/qmo/library.htm.

Acknowledgments

The editors would like to thank those who contributed to this effort. Ms. Brenda Harrell of Charleston, South Carolina, provided some of the graphics and a good bit of the typing. Ms. Maria Stoletova of the Vladimir Regional NGO Family Protection Center, Vladimir, Russia, compiled much of the Quality Glossary when she was an exchange fellow at Carnegie Mellon University, Pittsburgh, Pennsylvania, during 2000/2001.

We also recognize all those ASQ Quality Management Division members who have provided ideas for this text. Many of the application examples are real situations in which the editors have had the opportunity of working with quality improvement professionals in our daily activities. The concepts in this handbook work. Producing it has been a true team effort.

A final acknowledgment is due for Jeanne M. Bauer, John G. Duffy, and the late Jeanne M. Westcott for providing loving support and enduring many disruptions in schedules and family activities.

Part I
Quality Basics

Look beneath the surface, let not the quality nor its worth escape thee.

Marcus Aurelius

We are what we repeatedly do. Excellence, then, is not an act, but habit.

Aristotle

Quality is about making products that don't come back for customers that do.

Margaret Thatcher

Chapter 1

A. Terms, Concepts, and Principles

1. QUALITY

> Define and know how to use this term
> correctly. (Apply)
>
> **CQIA BoK 2006**

There are many definitions of quality, such as the following:

- Quality is a subjective term for which each person has his or her own definition. In technical usage, quality can have two meanings: (1) the characteristics of a product or service that bear on its ability to satisfy stated or implied needs, and (2) a product or service free of deficiencies.[1]

- Quality is the degree to which a set of inherent characteristics fulfills requirements.[2]

- Quality is conformance to requirements.

- Quality is fitness for use.

- Quality is meeting customer expectations.

- Quality is exceeding customer expectations.

- Quality is superiority to competitors.

- Quality—I'll know it when I see it.

In addition to these various meanings, quality may also be viewed from several dimensions:

- Characteristics such as reliability, maintainability, and availability

- Drivers of quality, such as standards

- Quality of design versus quality of conformance

- Quality planning, control, and improvement

- Little q and big Q (product or functional quality versus improvement of all organizational processes)

- Quality as an organizational strategy

Many other quality-related terms are defined in Appendix C, Quality Glossary.

The two quality management system models most frequently used by quality professionals are (1) the Baldrige National Quality Program Criteria for Performance Excellence,[3] and (2) the ISO 9000:2000 family of quality management system standards.[4] These quality models provide an insight into the components of a quality management system and define quality as it is practiced today.

2006 Baldrige National Quality Program: Criteria for Performance Excellence (Business Version)

1 Leadership

1.1   Senior Leadership

1.2   Governance and Social Responsibilities

The *Leadership* category examines how your organization's senior leaders guide and sustain your organization's governance and how your organization addresses its ethical, legal, and community responsibilities.

2 Strategic Planning

2.1   Strategy Development

2.2   Strategy Deployment

The *Strategic Planning* category examines how your organization develops strategic objectives and action plans. Also examined are how your chosen strategic objectives and action plans are deployed and changed if circumstances require, and how progress is measured.

3 Customer and Market Focus

3.1   Customer and Market Knowledge

3.2   Customer Relationships and Satisfaction

The *Customer and Market Focus* category examines how your organization determines the requirements, needs, expectations, and preferences of customers and markets. Also examined is how your organization builds relationships with customers and determines the key factors that lead to customer acquisition, satisfaction, loyalty, and retention, and to business expansion and sustainability.

4   *Measurement, Analysis, and Knowledge Management*

4.1   Measurement, Analysis, and Review of Organizational Performance

4.2   Information Management

The *Measurement, Analysis, and Knowledge Management* category examines how your organization selects, gathers, analyzes, manages, and improves its data, information, and knowledge assets. Also examined is how your organization reviews its performance.

5   *Human Resource Focus*

5.1   Work Systems

5.2   Employee Learning and Motivation

5.3   Employee Well-Being and Satisfaction

The *Human Resource Focus* category examines how your organization's work systems and employee learning and motivation enable all employees to develop and utilize their full potential in alignment with your organization's overall objectives, strategy, and action plans. Also examined are your organization's efforts to build and maintain a work environment and employee support climate conducive to performance excellence and personal and organizational growth.

6   *Process Management*

6.1   Value-creation processes

6.2   Support processes and operational planning

The *Process Management* category examines the key aspects of your organization's process management, including key product, service, and organizational processes for creating customer and organizational value and key support processes. This category also encompasses all key processes and all work units.

7   *Results*

7.1   Product and Service Outcomes

7.2   Customer-Focused Outcomes

7.3   Financial and Market Outcomes

7.4   Human Resource Outcomes

7.5   Organizational Effectiveness Outcomes

7.6   Leadership and Social Responsibility Outcomes

The *Results* category examines your organization's performance and improvement in all key areas—product and service outcomes, customer satisfaction, financial and marketplace performance, human resource outcomes, operational performance, and leadership and social responsibility. Performance levels are examined relative to those of competitors and other organizations providing similar products and services.

In recent years the Baldrige National Quality Program has been expanded to include criteria covering health-care and educational organizations. The program will expand further in 2007 to cover not-for-profit organizations. Information on these newer programs is available at *http://www.quality.nist.gov*.

ANSI/ISO/ASQ Q9000:2000 Quality Management Systems Principles

A *quality management principle* is a comprehensive and fundamental rule or belief for leading and operating an organization; it is aimed at continually improving performance over the long term by focusing on customers while addressing the needs of all other stakeholders. There are eight quality management principles that form the basis of current international quality management requirements. These principles are paraphrased as follows:

1. *Customer Orientation.* Organizations must focus on understanding their customers' needs and requirements. Successful organizations try to anticipate and exceed the customers' expectations.

2. *Leadership.* Organizations need strong leaders to establish common goals and direction. Effective leaders establish open environments in which all employees can participate in meeting their organization's goals.

3. *Involvement.* People are the most important part of any organization. Managers must ensure that employees at all levels of the organization can fully participate and use all their skills to make the organization successful.

4. *Process Management.* The most successful organizations understand that they must manage all their activities as processes.

5. *System Management.* Successful organizations understand that their many individual processes are interrelated and that, in addition to being managed individually, they must be managed within an overall system.

6. *Continual Improvement.* Continual improvement is the key to long-term success and high performance. Successful managers recognize that processes must be reviewed and improved continuously to ensure that their organization stays competitive.

7. *Fact-Based Decisions.* Organizations that base their decisions on factual data are more likely to make the correct decision than those that do not.

8. *Close Supplier Relationships.* Organizations that partner and work closely with their suppliers ensure that both the organization and the suppliers are better able to achieve success.

A side-by-side review of the Baldrige and ISO 9000:2000 quality models reveals many similarities. They both stress strong organizational leadership; a focus on customers; the development and involvement of the organization's people; gathering, analyzing, and using information to make decisions; and process management. Together these characteristics define quality as it is practiced in many successful organizations.

2. QUALITY PLANNING

> Understand a quality plan and its purpose
> for the organization as a whole and who in
> the organization contributes to its
> development. (Understand)
>
> **CQIA BoK 2006**

Quality planning is the process of developing a master plan linked to organizational strategy, goals, and objectives that pertain to the quality of products or services to be delivered to customers. The quality plan includes key requirements, performance indicators, and commitment of resources to ensure that customer needs are met.

Although it is separate from the three phases of organizational planning (strategic, tactical, and operational), quality planning is dependent on the decisions and processes established by management during these phases. Key quality requirements and performance indicators must be established in the design, development, and implementation of all products and services for final customer delivery. Quality initiatives must be understood in their relation to all three levels of the organization: strategic planning, tactical planning, and operational planning.

Strategic planning deals with developing the long-range strategies of the organization, including:

- The organization's basic goals and objectives
- External customers' needs and expectations
- The needs and expectations of internal stakeholders (employees, shareholders, and so on)
- Risks that must be taken into account
- Regulatory requirements
- Competitors' capabilities
- Business systems needed to operate the organization effectively and efficiently

Tactical planning (sometimes called action or project planning) deals with translating strategic objectives into actionable activities that must occur, on a short-term basis, to support the achievement of the strategic plans. These are the measurable steps and events that result from the downward deployment of the strategic plans.

Operational planning deals with developing day-to-day operating procedures that ensure the quality of individual products and services. Operational plans address areas such as:

- Resources needed to develop and create the organization's products and services

- Materials and supplies required for creating and delivering the products and services

- Knowledge and skills required of employees

- Processes and procedures required to create the organization's products and services

- Unique tools or equipment required

- Documentation (specifications, standards, drawings, visual aids, and so on) required

- Examination, inspection, or testing requirements

- Administrative support and follow-up for customer communication

- Records required to document the creation of the organization's products and services

- Process improvement methods to continually improve the organization's deliverables

Quality planning: At the day-to-day level, meeting a specific customer's requirements sometimes requires a "quality plan" for an individual contract or purchase order. To develop such a working plan means looking at the particular order and determining the resources (time, materials, equipment, process steps, skills, and so on) that will be required to complete the individual transaction to the customer's satisfaction and provide an adequate return on the resource investment. This type of quality plan is usually completed as part of the process that organizations use to give quotes on new or repeat work for their customers.

Overall, a consistent planning, monitoring, and reviewing approach is required for organizations using established quality systems based on criteria such as the Baldrige National Quality Program or the ISO 9001:2000 standard. The approach taken by an organization becomes the guiding policy in producing a valued product or service that remains competitive in the marketplace. The planning must include:

- A comprehensive focus on customer needs and expectations

- Support of quality goals and strategies by upper management

- A balance of resources between short-term and long-term requirements, including capital expenditures, training, and continuous improvement

- Ongoing interpretation of long-term goals into tactical and operating plans

- Development of processes for evaluation and process improvement

- Integration of quality activities into the daily work of the front-line associates

3. THE IMPORTANCE OF EMPLOYEES

> Understand employee involvement and
> employee empowerment and understand
> the benefits of both concepts, distinguish
> between involvement and empowerment.
> (Understand)
>
> **CQIA BoK 2006**

The two predominant quality models (Baldrige and ISO 9000) stress the importance of the participation of all employees in an organization's quality efforts. Organizations work to motivate and enable their employees to develop and utilize their full potential in support of the organization's overall goals and objectives. Organizations also work to build and maintain work environments that support their employees and create a climate conducive to performance excellence and personal and organizational growth. People at all levels are the essence of any organization, and empowering them to fully use their abilities and to be fully involved in the organization's processes benefits the organization.

Empowerment means that employees have the authority to make decisions and take actions in their work areas without prior approval, within established boundaries. Allowing employees to work as active members of process improvement teams is one way to empower them to fully use their collective wisdom and decision-making skills. But they must also be given the training, tools, materials, equipment, processes, and procedures to accomplish their individual tasks. Providing these critical resources shows employees that the organization truly values their minds, not just their bodies.

Each employee must recognize that the outputs of his or her individual activities provide the inputs to the next person's process. Employee involvement allows employees the right to participate in decision making at some level, provides the necessary skills to accomplish the required task, and carefully defines responsibilities and authority. Employee involvement also provides recognition and rewards for accomplishments and enables communication with all levels of the organization's structure.

Managers must do more than just tell employees that they have the authority to participate fully in processes. They must also relinquish some of their authority and show by their actions that they expect full employee involvement and that they support actions taken by employees and decisions made by them to further the organization's goals and objectives. Giving employees the authority to act also gives them responsibility and accountability for what they do. To fully participate, employees must understand the organization's mission, values, and systems.

It is also important to understand the difference between *job enlargement* and *job enrichment*. Enlarging a job means expanding the variety of tasks performed by an employee. Enriching a job means increasing the worker's responsibilities and authority in work to be done. Two examples are as follows:

*In addition to staffing a customer-transaction window, a bank teller's job is
expanded to tidying-up the tables used by customers to fill out forms and also
ensuring that all brochure displays are restocked.* (job enlargement)

*A waitperson's job is increased in scope to include helping the cook in deciding
on the next day's menu.* (job enrichment)

Organizations sometimes have formal suggestion systems that allow employees to
provide input on problems and suggestions on how to improve existing processes.
Many of these suggestion systems are tied to incentives or rewards for suggestions
that are implemented.

4. SYSTEMS AND PROCESSES

> Define a system and a process; distinguish
> between a system and a process;
> understand the interrelationship between
> process and system; and know how the
> components of a system (supplier, input,
> process, output, customer, and feedback)
> impact the system as a whole. (Analyze)
>
> **CQIA BoK 2006**

A system can be defined as a set of interrelated or interacting processes. A process
is a set of interrelated or interacting activities that transforms inputs into outputs.
For example:

*The quality audit process uses various inputs (trained auditors, procedures,
employee interviews, checklists, and so on) to develop an output (the audit
report) that is used to improve the organization's overall quality management
system. The quality management system is composed of many individual
processes that interact with each other and contribute to improving the
organization's overall performance.*

Using a system of interrelated processes to manage an organization is called a
process approach to management, or simply *process management.* The process management approach is based on the ability of an organization to identify all its
processes, recognize the inputs and outputs of each process, document the
processes so they can be easily implemented, identify who the owners of each
process are, implement the processes, measure the outcomes of the implementation, and continually improve the efficiency and effectiveness of the processes. The
objectives of an organization are achieved more efficiently when related resources
and activities are managed as processes and when the individual processes work
together to form an integrated management system.

Processes can be divided into various categories:

- Product/service development processes deal with how the organization:
  - Designs new and improved products and services
  - Changes old products and services to meet new customer requirements
  - Incorporates improvements in technology
  - Anticipates customers' future needs
- Product/service production processes deal with how the organization:
  - Produces products and services in the most efficient and economical way
  - Ensures that the products and services meet all technical requirements
  - Delivers the products and services in the time frame required by the customer
  - Uses customer and employee feedback
- Business processes deal with how the organization:
  - Accounts for its resources
  - Develops and uses measures of performance
  - Continually improves its operations
  - Trains, evaluates, and rewards its employees

Process documentation might include these components:

1. A short, simple description of the process and its purpose
2. A description of the process's starting and ending activities
3. A list of inputs required at the process starting points and who provides the inputs, or the process supplier
4. A list of outputs at the process ending point and who receives the outputs, or the process customer
5. A flowchart of the process; that is, a process map identifying the interfaces of the process with other functions of the organization
6. Identification of the process owner, establishing clear responsibility, authority, and accountability for managing the process
7. The measurements used to identify that the process has been completed successfully
8. A statement of the overall capability of the process

Using the process approach to management leads to more predictable results, better use of resources, prevention of errors, shorter cycle times, and lower costs, as well as a better understanding of the capability of processes and more predictable outputs.

The Baldrige and ISO models encourage the use of a process and system approach to management. They also stress the importance of integrating different business processes, such as design, production, quality, packaging, and shipping, into one interlinked system. All processes have inputs and outputs. The inputs into a process being worked on usually come as outputs from another process, and the outputs of the process being worked on usually serve as the inputs to another process. For example:

> Parts manufactured and inspected to meet customer requirements are sent to the packaging department for preparation for shipment. The packaged parts are sent to the shipping department for transfer to a transportation company. The outputs of the manufacturing and inspection processes are inputs to the packaging process. The outputs of the packaging process are inputs to the shipping process. These interrelationships must be understood by managers to develop an efficient overall system.

This business methodology, sometimes called a *system of processes* or a *process approach,* is critical to the efficient and effective operation of modern organizations. Also critical to this methodology is the concept that all processes generate data (information) that must be "fed back" to other interrelated processes. Information about a deficient product found at inspection must be "fed back" to the manufacturing process so that corrective action can be taken to cure the process defect that created the deficient product.

SIPOC Analysis

Process improvement efforts are often focused on removing a situation that has developed in which a process is not operating at its normal level. However, much of continual improvement involves analyzing a process that may be performing as expected, but where a higher level of performance is desired. A fundamental step to improving a process is to understand how it functions from a process management perspective. This can be understood through an analysis of the process to identify the supplier-input-process-output-customer linkages (see Figure 1.1).

It begins with defining the process of interest, and listing on the right side the outputs that the process creates that go to customers, who are also listed. Suppliers and what they provide to enable the process (the inputs) are similarly shown

Figure 1.1 SIPOC diagram.

on the left side. Once this fundamental process diagram is developed, two additional items can be discussed: (1) measures that can be used to evaluate performance of the inputs and outputs, and (2) the information and methods necessary to control the process.

5. VARIATION

Understand the concept of variation and common and special cause variation. (Understand)

CQIA BoK 2006

Variations are differences, usually minor, from the designed and expected outputs of a process. Some variation is found in all processes. The key to controlling processes is to control variation as much as possible.

All variation has some cause. Knowing the causes of variation is important in order to determine the actions that must be taken to reduce the variation. It is most important to distinguish between *special cause* variation and *common cause* variation.

Special cause variation results from unexpected or unusual occurrences that are not inherent in the process. As an example:

> *A new school bus driver is on her way to pick up her first student in the morning when the engine stalls because of a fuel-line leak.*

This occurrence was not inherent in the student pick-up process. Special causes of variation account for approximately 15 percent of the observed variation in processes. They are usually very easy to detect and correct. No major modifications to the process are required. These special causes are sometimes called *assignable causes*, because the variation they result in can be investigated and assigned to a particular source.

Common cause variation results from how the process is designed to operate and is a natural part of the process. As an example:

> *A school bus driver starts her route of assigned streets on time, makes her required stops, and arrives at the school nine minutes later than usual but within the overall time allowance of her schedule. She experienced a slowdown due to the timing of traffic lights.*

Common causes of variation account for approximately 85 percent of the observed variation in processes. When the process is in control, as it was in the school bus example, there is no need to take action. Common causes are sometimes called *system causes* or *chance causes*, because the variations they result in are inherent in the system.

Making minor adjustments to a process because of perceived common cause variation is called *tampering*. Tampering can drive a process into further variation due to unnecessary changes being made to a stable process because of a perceived special cause that is actually a common cause.

Process owners should recognize that the special cause variations in production or quality within manufacturing or service processes can usually be detected and removed by the individuals operating the process and that the common cause variations usually require management action to change some inherent feature of the process. This is sometimes called the "85/15 rule," recognizing that management is responsible for providing the necessary inputs to correct the majority of variation problems, that is, *common causes*.

One of the first goals of successful organizations is to concentrate on developing reliable processes. A *reliable process* is one that produces the desired output each time with very little variation. Once reliable processes are established and the system becomes stable, the next goal is to continually improve the process (further reduce variation) to produce output that is even better able to meet customer requirements.

Many processes, particularly long-term, high-quantity production processes, lend themselves to the use of *statistical process control* (SPC). SPC is a method of monitoring a process during its operation in order to control the quality of the products or services while they are being produced rather than relying on inspection of the products or services after completion. SPC involves gathering information (data) on the product or service as it is being created, graphically charting the information on one of several types of control charts, and following the progress of the process to detect unwanted variation.

Once a process is under control and shows very little variation, process capability studies can be run to calculate the maximum capability of the process. Once a process is running near its maximum capability, making any additional changes to the process is usually not economical.

Notes

1. Siebels, Donald L. *The Quality Improvement Glossary.* (Milwaukee, WI: ASQ Quality Press, 2004).
2. ASQ. *ANSI/ISO/ASQ Q9000:2000, Quality Management Systems—Fundamentals and Vocabulary,* December 2000.
3. National Institute of Standards and Technology. *Baldrige National Quality Program: Criteria for Performance Excellence.* (Gaithersburg, MD: National Institute of Standards and Technology, Technology Administration, United States Department of Commerce.) The criteria are available in three categories: business, health care, and education. The program is administered by ASQ. One copy of the criteria, any category, is available free of charge. Contact NIST: telephone 301-975-2036; fax 301-948-3716, e-mail *nqp@nist.gov,* or Web site *http://www.baldrige.nist.gov.* Bulk copies are available from ASQ: telephone 800-248-1946, fax 414-272-1734, e-mail *asq@asq.org,* or Web site *http://www.asq.org.* Call ASQ for pricing. (The criteria changes yearly. The version cited in this book is the 2006 criteria.)
4. ASQ. *ANSI/ISO/ASQ Q9000:2000, Quality Management Systems—Fundamentals and Vocabulary, ANSI/ISO/ASQ Q9001:2000, Quality Management Standards—Requirements,* and *ANSI/ISO/ASQ Q9004:2000, Quality Management Standards—Guidelines for Performance Improvements.* (Milwaukee, WI: ASQ, 2000). Available from ASQ:

telephone 800-248-1946, fax 414-272-1734, e-mail *asq@asq.org,* or Web site *http://www.asq.org.* Available in print form, for downloading (PDF), and in English and Spanish. Call ASQ for pricing.

Additional Resources

American National Standards Institute. *ANSI/ISO/ASQ Q9000:2000.* (Milwaukee, WI: ASQ Quality Press, 2000). (The series consists of ISO 9000, ISO 9001, and ISO 9004.)

Juran, J. M., and A. B. Godfrey, eds. *Juran's Quality Handbook* (5th ed.). (New York: McGraw-Hill, 1999).

National Institute of Standards and Technology. *Baldrige National Quality Program: Criteria for Performance Excellence.* (Gaithersburg, MD: NIST, 2006).

Naval Leader Training Unit. *Introduction to Total Quality Leadership.* (Washington, DC: U.S. Department of the Navy, 1997).

Navy Total Quality Leadership Office. *Handbook for Basic Process Improvement.* (Washington, DC: U.S. Department of the Navy, 1996).

Westcott, Russell T., ed. *The Certified Manager of Quality/Organizational Excellence Handbook* (3rd ed.). (Milwaukee, WI: ASQ Quality Press, 2006).

Part I
Quality Basics (cont.)

Chapter 2
B. Benefits of Quality
C. Quality Philosophies

Quality is not the exclusive province of engineering, manufacturing, or, for that matter, services, marketing, or administration. Quality is truly everyone's job.

John R. Opel (IBM)

Defects are not free. Somebody makes them, and gets paid for making them.

Everybody here has a customer. And if he doesn't know who it is and what constitutes the needs of the customer . . . then he does not understand his job.

Inspection with the aim of finding the bad ones and throwing them out is too late, ineffective, and costly. Quality comes not from inspection but from improvement of the process.

People work in the system. Management creates the system.

A company cannot buy its way into quality—it must be led into quality by top management.

W. Edwards Deming

Chapter 2

B. Benefits of Quality

Understand how improved process,
product and/or service quality will benefit
any function, area of an organization, or
industry. Understand how each
stakeholder (e.g., employees, organization,
customers, suppliers, community) benefits
from quality and how the benefits may
differ for each type of stakeholder.
(Understand)

CQIA BoK 2006

High quality affects all of an organization's stakeholders. Employees, the organization itself, customers, suppliers, and the community benefit from strong quality performance.

EMPLOYEES

Quality benefits the employees involved in producing high-quality products and services by enhancing their feeling of accomplishment in knowing they have done their jobs to the best of their ability. It also strengthens the security of their position by ensuring continued work to meet the demands of satisfied customers. High-quality products and services sometimes demand higher prices, which can result in higher wages. Well-documented quality systems and processes make the employee's job easier and less frustrating, reduce errors, and allow employees to grow because they are given ready access to the information they need to acquire the skills and knowledge to succeed. By participating in the development of the organization's processes, employees can see their experience, skills, and ideas being put to use for the benefit of everyone in the organization. Accurate, complete documentation reduces errors. And with instant access, documentation allows unplanned problems to be dealt with quickly and safely. Well-informed employees have less risk of on-the-job injuries. Employees benefit from the positive organizational culture that exists in a high-quality organization. The reputation, prestige, and image of a high-quality organization make it easier to recruit new employees and play an important part in employee job satisfaction. Satisfied employees are less likely to want to move on to other organizations.

THE ORGANIZATION

Quality benefits the organization because it represents the productive and profitable use of the organization's resources. Processes that generate high-quality products and services result in lower costs from repair, rework, and warranty actions. High quality can lead to repeat orders from current customers, and it often enables an organization to win an enhanced reputation and additional orders in the market.

When there is a lack of quality it can not only result in losing the current order but also damage the supplier's reputation and result in loss of future orders. It's widely believed that one dissatisfied customer will tell at least 20 other people how poor your organization's product or service is, and the loss of future orders could be substantial. The lack of a quality system can create the need for extensive rework, repair, and warranty actions. These actions add extra costs and delays and reduce the productivity of the system. When components are scrapped or services have to be repeated, it is not only the time and material cost that is lost but also the cost of all the work done on the product or service (the added value) up to the point at which it is scrapped. Poor quality costs money. Good quality may cost money, too, but in most cases the costs of poor quality exceed those of good quality.

According to a survey sponsored by the Automotive Industry Action Group (AIAG) and the ASQ Automotive Division, "Companies certified to QS 9000, the past automotive industry version of ISO 9000, estimated their average certification cost at $118,100 per site, while they estimated their benefit was $304,300 per site."[1]

Good quality can be a very powerful marketing tool. Recognition by third-party sources can enhance an organization's ability to market its products and services in ways that competitors can't. Here's an example from a recent automotive advertisement:

> Over the past few years, Buick has steadily and quietly been improving its vehicles to where last year it received the highest ranking among domestic manufacturers for quality from JD Power and Associates. Buick's Regal, which comes in either the LS or more elaborate GS trim, has benefited from this move to quality, which begins with the versatile 3.8 liter V-6 fuel-injection workhorse engine that powers several models.

A high-quality organization can focus on continuous improvement—assessing what's happening in the organization and preventing bad product and service quality—rather than just reacting to problems and cases of customer dissatisfaction. This proactive style of management will result in a much more profitable organization than a style that only reacts to problems. It greatly increases the probability of the organization's survival.

CUSTOMERS

Customer satisfaction has been defined as *meeting or exceeding the customers' requirements for product and service features, price, timeliness, and performance.* Quality benefits the customer by increasing customer satisfaction. Fewer defects mean that the customer will be more satisfied. Higher service quality will also make the customer's experience much more pleasant.

Customers dealing with an organization that has a strong quality program will have fewer complaints because they are being supplied a product or service from better-trained staff following clearer processes and thus making fewer errors. As the organization progressively reduces the time it is forced to devote to correcting mistakes, it can turn to streamlining its processes to make them more cost-effective and more customer-friendly. Customers will trust the organization more because they know that it takes quality seriously and gives a better level of service.

Every organization has customers. Quality organizations differentiate themselves from their competitors by providing their customers with high levels of personalized customer service. It's easier and much less costly to retain current satisfied customers than to develop new ones.

Though increased sales and growing profits are generally seen as an accurate measurement of success, customer retention may be the most important measurement of all. High-quality organizations build long-term customer relationships. Evidence has shown that it usually costs more to obtain a new customer than to retain an existing customer.

A number of organizations, both public and private, measure customer satisfaction. One of the most prominent measures is the American Customer Satisfaction Index (ACSI), a national economic indicator of customer satisfaction with the quality of goods and services available to consumers in the United States. The index is produced through a partnership of which the American Society for Quality is a member. The results of the surveys are posted on the ACSI Web site *http://www.theacsi.org.*

SUPPLIERS

Quality organizations work closely with their suppliers and share information to ensure that the suppliers fully understand the organization's requirements and that the organization knows the capabilities of their suppliers. Suppliers' sales, marketing, and service personnel know what the organization needs and can communicate with the appropriate personnel at their customers' facilities to resolve potential problems before they become serious concerns.

Suppliers benefit from working with quality organizations because of the close partnerships that the organizations and the suppliers establish to accomplish their mutual goals. Good supplier–organization partnerships tend to have a common set of characteristics, including:

- Reduced cost of inspections

- Less-frequent customer audits

- Open sharing of organization and supplier quality information

- Frequent visits to both the organization's and the supplier's facilities to ensure mutual understanding of each party's relative responsibilities

- Supplier shipments of materials directly to the organization's production line for immediate use

- Decreased expenses from cost sharing

- Reduced risk to the organization because of its ability to use the supplier's knowledge and skills to improve its product or service

THE COMMUNITY

The individual communities in which high-quality organizations operate share in the benefits just mentioned. Successful employees, organizations, and suppliers are taxpayers. They contribute to the community by stabilizing the economy. Think of the many communities and regions that have been devastated by the failure of organizations and industries. The quality, productivity, and competitiveness of high-quality organizations directly affect the viability of the communities they occupy.

Communities are very aware of the benefits of having high-quality organizations. Many state and local government jurisdictions provide incentives, including training and consulting, for organizations to fully develop their potential and to assist employees in gaining the necessary training and skills to work in the highly competitive environment of today's economy.

QUALITY BENEFITS TO SOCIETY AS A WHOLE

Everyone can help make communities better places in which to live and work. The process of improvement requires proactive participation by all members of the community: technical societies, neighborhood associations, government agencies, religious organizations, educational institutions, corporations, and businesses.

In many locations, community quality councils provide a forum for improving the quality of life in communities and regions through the use of total quality management (TQM) principles. TQM principles are a major step forward in manufacturing organizations and, more recently, in service industries. The next step involves society itself. Applying improvement principles to a community is a leading-edge concept in the quality movement.

Quality brings other factors into play, such as vision, leadership, and lifelong learning. It is important because it gives people the opportunity to cooperate and gives their enterprises the means to strive for excellence. The essential ingredient for community improvement is a network of civic and government entities focused on quality and improvement principles. The benefit of propagating quality and improvement techniques and principles through a community quality council is that success does not cost the citizens their jobs—truly a win-win situation.

Successful experiences in life are almost always the result of careful planning and thorough preparation. People are using quality principles in their communities, providing a pragmatic, holistic approach to making fundamental improvements in the way community problems are addressed. Their experiences are lessons that can be shared for the benefit of all.

Many state and local governments also sponsor quality awards, usually based on the Baldrige National Quality Program criteria, to encourage organizations to advance the level of the quality management processes in their respective communities.

C. Quality Philosophies

> Understand each of these philosophies
> and how they differ from one another.
> (Remember)
>
> **CQIA BoK 2006**

Philosophy is defined in *Webster's Dictionary* as "a critical examination of the grounds for fundamental beliefs." A *quality philosophy* has been defined as "a system of fundamental or motivating principles that form a basis for action or belief." A quality philosophy should reflect how an organization acts in its day-to-day business operations. It should reflect the organization's ideas, values, principles, attitudes, and beliefs. The organization's quality philosophy sets the cultural background in which the organization operates. The philosophy should focus on improving the organization and helping it grow to meet its full potential.

A quality philosophy will be the background for developing the organization's mission, goals, objectives, and strategic plans and will assist the organization's employees in understanding what is expected of them. With these documents, employees can work in an environment with guidelines for understanding and responding to day-to-day variables in their work experiences.

A philosophy with a strong focus on quality requires managers to develop well-defined management systems with an emphasis on process management. In developing a quality philosophy, managers need to focus on:

- What their customers consider the most important quality characteristics of the organization's products and services

- What their customers', other stakeholders', and society's needs and expectations are

- What ethical principles should govern how the organization operates

- How the quality philosophy affects the overall operation of the organization's other management systems (financial, health and safety, environmental, and so on)

- What statutory, regulatory, and technical specification requirements affect the organization's operations

- Which of the currently available quality tools should be used in developing and supporting the organization's quality management system

The principles for modern quality management have evolved over the past 50+ years based on the work of a number of experts who are sometimes referred to as "quality gurus." These experts have developed a number of theories and principles that assist organizations in developing their own quality philosophies.

The following is an encapsulated review of the work of three prominent quality gurus: Dr. W. Edwards Deming, Dr. Joseph M. Juran, and Philip B. Crosby. Brief information is also provided on several other quality gurus who have influenced the practice of quality in recent times.

1. DR. W. EDWARDS DEMING

William Edwards Deming was born on October 14, 1900, in Sioux City, Iowa. His family then moved to several other locations, ending up in Powell, Wyoming. Deming attended the University of Wyoming, earning a bachelor's degree in engineering in 1921. He went on to receive a master's degree in mathematics and physics from the University of Colorado in 1925, and he earned a doctorate in physics from Yale University in 1928. During the summers of 1925 and 1926, he worked for the Western Electric Company's Hawthorne plant in Chicago. It was at Hawthorne that he met Walter A. Shewhart and became interested in Shewhart's work to standardize the production of telephone equipment. After receiving his PhD, Deming went to work for the U.S. government. He applied Shewhart's concepts to his work at the National Bureau of the Census. Routine clerical operations were brought under statistical process control in preparation for the 1940 population census. This led to sixfold productivity improvements in some processes. As a result, Deming started to run statistical courses to explain his and Shewhart's methods to engineers, designers, and others in the United States and Canada.

In 1938, he published a technical book[2] and taught courses on the use of his statistical methods. The beneficial effects of Deming's programs, such as reductions in scrap and rework, were seen during World War II. However, his techniques were generally abandoned after the war as emphasis shifted to producing quantities of consumer goods to alleviate the shortages that had been experienced during wartime.

After World War II, Deming was invited to Japan as an advisor to the Japanese census. He became involved with the Japanese Union of Scientists and Engineers (JUSE) after its formation in 1946. As a result, Deming's name became known and JUSE invited him to lecture to the Japanese on statistical methods. In the early 1950s he lectured to engineers and senior managers, including in his lectures ideas now regarded as part of modern quality principles. In 1956, Deming was awarded the Shewhart medal by the American Society for Quality. Four years later, Deming's teachings were widely known in Japan, and the emperor awarded him the Second Order of the Sacred Treasure.

In the late 1970s, Deming started to work with major American organizations. However, his work was relatively unknown in the United States until June 1980, when NBC aired a documentary entitled "If Japan Can, Why Can't We?" Following this exposure, he became well known and highly regarded in the quality community. Deming's first popular book, *Out of the Crisis*, was published in 1986. The following year, he was awarded the National Medal of Technology in America. Dr. Deming died in 1993 at the age of 93.

Deming's Philosophies

Deming's teachings reflected his statistical background. He encouraged managers to focus on variability and to understand the difference between special causes and common causes.

Deming's writings, teachings, and work also extended beyond statistical methods. He encouraged organizations to adopt a systematic approach to problem solving, which later became known as the Deming cycle, or the Plan—Do—Study—Act (PDSA) cycle. He also pushed senior managers to become actively involved in their companies' quality improvement programs. Work done by Deming and his followers in the United States and elsewhere has attempted to make major changes in the style of Western management.

Dr. Deming taught that management should have a full understanding of his philosophies in order to achieve sustainable progress in an organization. He constantly improved and refined his ideas, and he also used the ideas of others. He is considered by many to be the father of the modern quality revolution.

In his landmark 1986 book *Out of the Crisis*, Dr. Deming delineated a "chain reaction" philosophy: improve quality → decrease costs → improve productivity → increase market share with better quality, lower price → stay in business → provide more jobs. In the book, he discussed management's failures in planning for the future and foreseeing problems. These shortcomings create waste of resources, which in turn increases costs and ultimately affects the prices to customers. When customers do not accept paying for such waste, they go elsewhere, resulting in loss of market for the supplier. See Figure 2.1.

In the introduction to *Out of the Crisis*, Deming wrote about the need for an entirely new structure, from the foundation upward, to achieve the needed transformation and replace the typical American reconstruction or revision approach. He proposed a new structure in his renowned 14 points of management. The 14 points include creating a constant purpose for the organization, eliminating reliance on inspection, constantly improving systems, increasing training, and instituting leadership. The complete text of the 14 points is available on the Massachusetts Institute of Technology Center for Advanced Education Services Web site at *http://caes.mit.edu/deming/14-points.html*.

In *Out of the Crisis*, Deming also discussed the seven "deadly diseases," which include lack of constancy of purpose, focus on short-term profits, management that is too mobile, and excessive medical and legal costs.

Deming's System of Profound Knowledge

In 1993, in his final book, *The New Economics for Industry, Government, and Education*, Deming outlined his *system of profound knowledge*. This is the knowledge needed for transformation from the present style of management to one of optimization. Deming's system of profound knowledge includes management's need to understand systems, to have knowledge of statistical theory and variation, to plan based on past experience, and to have an understanding of psychology.

The Deming Chain Reaction

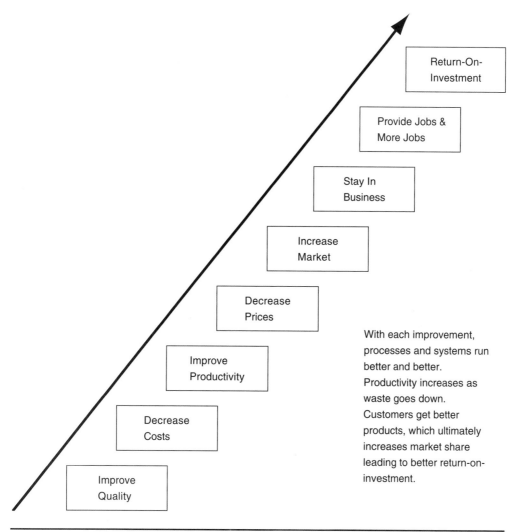

Figure 2.1   Deming's "Chain Reaction."
Adapted from *Out Of The Crisis*, W. Edwards Deming. Cambridge, MA: MIT, Center for Advanced Engineering Study, 1986.

2. DR. JOSEPH M. JURAN

Joseph Moses Juran was born to a poor family in Braila, Romania, in December 1904. Five years later his father Jakob left Romania for America. By 1912, he had earned enough money to bring the rest of the family to join him in Minnesota. The younger Juran did well in school and showed a high level of proficiency in math and science; in fact, he did so well that he was able to skip the equivalent of four grade levels. In 1920, he enrolled at the University of Minnesota, the first member of his family to pursue higher education. By 1925, he had received a BS in electrical engineering and began working with Western Electric in the inspection department of the famous Hawthorne Works in Chicago. In 1926, he was selected from a group of 20 trainees to become one of two engineers for the Inspection Statistical Department, one of the first such divisions created in American industry. By 1937, Juran was the chief of industrial engineering at Western Electric's home office in New York. During World War II, Juran received a temporary leave of absence from Western Electric to assist the U.S. government with the war effort. During that time, he served in Washington, D.C., as an assistant administrator for the Office of Lend-Lease Administration. He and his team improved the efficiency of the process, eliminating excessive paperwork and thus hastening the arrival of supplies to the United States' overseas friends. Juran did not return to Western Electric. Rather, he chose to devote the remainder of his life to the study of quality management. As early as 1928, Juran had written a pamphlet entitled "Statistical Methods Applied to Manufacturing Problems." By the end of the war, he was a well-known and highly regarded statistician and industrial engineering theorist. After he left Western Electric, Juran became the chairman of the Department of Administrative Engineering at New York University, where he taught for many years. In 1951, the first *Juran Quality Control Handbook* was published and led him to international eminence. Still a classic standard reference work for quality managers, it is now in its fifth edition.

The Japanese Union of Scientists and Engineers invited Juran to come to Japan to teach them the principles of quality management as they rebuilt their economy after World War II. He arrived in 1954 and conducted seminars for top and middle-level executives. His lectures had a strong managerial flavor and focused on planning, organizational issues, management's responsibility for quality, and the need to set goals and targets for improvement. He emphasized that quality control should be conducted as an integral part of management control. In 1979, Juran founded the Juran Institute to better facilitate broader exposure of his ideas. The Juran Institute is today one of the leading quality management consultancies in the world. In 1981, Juran received the Second Order of the Sacred Treasure award from Emperor Hirohito for "the development of quality control in Japan and the facilitation of U.S. and Japanese friendship."

His 12 books have collectively been translated into 13 languages. He has received more than 30 medals, honorary fellowships, and awards from 12 different countries. Dr. Juran, who continued working to promote quality management into his 90s, is now semiretired.

Juran's Philosophies

Juran teaches a project-by-project, problem-solving, team method of quality improvement in which upper management must be involved. He believes that quality does not happen by accident; it must be planned. And he asserts that quality improvements come from a project-by-project approach.

Juran's book *Planning for Quality* is perhaps the definitive guide to Juran's current thoughts and his structured approach to companywide quality planning. Juran teaches that quality planning is the first step in a three-level approach to quality management within the organization. Along with planning comes quality control, which involves assessing quality performance, comparing performance with established goals, and closing the gap between actual performance and stated goals. Juran sees the third level—quality improvement—as an ongoing and continual process that includes the establishment of the organizational infrastructure necessary to make cyclical quality improvements. He recommends using teams and project-by-project activities to maintain a continual effort toward both incremental and breakthrough improvement. Juran sees quality planning as part of the *quality trilogy* of quality planning, quality control, and quality improvement.

His key points in implementing organization-wide quality planning include identifying customers and their needs; establishing optimal quality goals; creating measurements of quality; planning processes capable of meeting quality goals under operating conditions; and producing continuing results in improved market share, premium prices, and reduction of error rates in an office or factory.

Juran's more recent work involves creating an awareness of the quality crisis, establishing a new approach to quality planning, training, assisting companies to replan existing processes to avoid quality deficiencies, and establishing mastery within companies over the quality planning process, thus avoiding the creation of new chronic problems. In the fifth edition of *Juran's Quality Handbook,* the contrast between the concepts of "Big Q" and "little q" is displayed in a table: "little q" views quality as a technological matter, whereas "Big Q" relates to quality as a business concern.[3]

Dr. Juran believes that the majority of quality problems are the fault of poor management rather than poor workmanship on the shop floor. In general, he believes that management-controllable defects account for over 80 percent of all quality problems.

He was the first to incorporate the human aspect of quality management, which is now embraced within the concept of total quality management. Juran's process of developing his ideas was gradual. Top management involvement, the need for widespread training in quality, the definition of quality as fitness for use, the project-by-project approach to quality improvement, the distinction between the "vital few" and the "useful many," and the *trilogy* (quality planning, quality control, and quality improvement)—these are the ideas for which Juran is best known.

3. PHILIP B. CROSBY

Philip B. Crosby was born in Wheeling, West Virginia, on June 18, 1926. He served two tours in the U.S. Navy, separated by attendance at Western Reserve University.

He worked as a technician in the quality department for the Crosley Corporation from 1952 to 1955. He then moved to the Martin-Marietta facility in Mishawaka, Indiana, where he was a reliability engineer on a government missile program. Later Crosby moved to the Martin-Marietta facility in Orlando, Florida, as a quality manager. During his time at the Orlando facility, he created the "zero defects" concept. In 1965, he began working for ITT. During his 14 years as corporate vice president for ITT, he worked with many ITT subsidiary manufacturing and service divisions around the world, implementing his philosophy.

In 1979, he founded Philip Crosby Associates (PCA). PCA taught management courses on how to establish a quality improvement culture. Large corporations such as GM, Chrysler, Motorola, Xerox, and many other organizations worldwide came to PCA to understand quality management. The courses were taught in many languages in locations around the world.

Mr. Crosby's first book, *Quality Is Free*, sold over 2 million copies and has been translated into 15 languages. Many organizations around the world began their quality improvement activities because of the popularity of *Quality Is Free* and because of Crosby's reputation for clear and to-the-point advice. Much of *Quality Is Free* is devoted to the concept of zero defects, which is a way of explaining to employees the idea that everything should be done right the first time, that there should be no failures or defects in work outputs.

Crosby left PCA in 1991 and founded Career IV. In 1997, he purchased PCA and established Philip Crosby Associates II, a consultancy that now operates in over 20 countries around the world.

He published his second best seller, *Quality Without Tears*, in 1984, and he is also the author of *The Art of Getting Your Own Sweet Way*. More recently, he has published a group of three management books: *Running Things*, *The Eternally Successful Organization*, and *Leading: The Art of Becoming an Executive*.

Philip B. Crosby died in August 2001.

Crosby's Philosophies

According to Crosby, quality is conformance to requirements, and it can only be measured by the price of nonconformance. This approach means that the only standard of performance is zero defects.

Cost of quality refers to all costs involved in the prevention of defects, assessment of process performance, and measurement of financial consequences. Management can use cost of quality to document variations against expectations and to measure efficiency and productivity. Crosby believed that tracking cost of quality takes the business of quality out of the abstract and brings it sharply into focus as cold hard cash.

Crosby claimed that all nonconformances are caused—they don't appear without reason. Anything that is caused can be prevented. Therefore, organizations should adopt a quality "vaccine" to prevent nonconformance and save money. The three ingredients of the vaccine are determination, education, and implementation.

The Points, or Steps to Quality Improvement

The points that Crosby considered essential involve the following ideas:[4]

- Management commitment
- Education and training
- Measurements
- Cost of quality
- Quality awareness
- Corrective action
- Zero defects
- Goal setting
- Recognition

Crosby's points offer a way to implement the quality improvement process in an organization. They are management tools that evolved from a conviction that an organization's quality improvement policy should be defined, understood, and communicated in a practical manner to every member of the organization.

Crosby's perception of a continuing successful organization embraces the ideas that everyone in the organization routinely performs their tasks right the first time, that the organization continues to grow and prosper, that new offerings to customers are created as needed, that change is viewed as an opportunity, and that the people in the organization enjoy working there.

The Four Absolutes of Quality Management

Crosby articulated four absolutes of quality management as the basic concepts of a quality improvement process. The essence of these absolutes is contained in the following statements:

1. Conformance to requirements is the only definition of quality

2. What causes quality is prevention, not appraisal

3. Zero defects is the only acceptable performance standard

4. The price of nonconformance is how quality should be measured

Crosby is best known for his concepts of *do it right the first time* and *zero defects*. He considered traditional quality control, acceptable quality limits, and waivers of substandard products to represent failure rather than assurance of success. He believed that because many organizations have policies and systems that allow deviation from what is actually required, the organizations lose vast amounts of revenue by doing things wrong and then doing them over again. He estimated the loss to be 20 percent of revenues for manufacturing companies and up to 35 percent of revenues for service organizations.

DR. ARMAND V. FEIGENBAUM

Armand V. Feigenbaum was born in New York City in 1920. He attended Union College and Massachusetts Institute of Technology (MIT), graduating in 1951 with a PhD in engineering. The first edition of his book *Total Quality Control* was completed while he was still a doctoral student at MIT. *Total Quality Control* has been published in more than a score of languages, including French, Japanese, Chinese, Spanish, and Russian, and is widely used throughout the world as a foundation for quality control practice. A 40th anniversary edition was published in 1991.

Feigenbaum worked for the General Electric Company from 1942 until 1968. He was worldwide director of manufacturing operations and quality control at General Electric from 1958 to 1968, when he left to found General Systems Company with his brother Donald.

Feigenbaum was elected to the National Academy of Engineering of the United States in 1992. The citation presented at his election read, "For developing concepts of 'total quality control,' and for contributions to 'cost of quality' and quality systems engineering and practice."

He was the founding chairman of the International Academy for Quality and is a past president of the American Society for Quality, which presented him with the Edwards Medal and the Lancaster Award for his international contribution to quality and productivity. In 1988, the U.S. secretary of commerce appointed Feigenbaum to the first Board of Overseers of the Malcolm Baldrige National Quality Award Program.

Feigenbaum is considered by many to be the originator of total quality control. He argued for a systematic or total approach to quality, requiring the involvement of all functions, not just manufacturing, in the quality process. The idea was to build in quality at an early stage rather than inspecting and controlling quality after the fact.

Feigenbaum's Philosophies

In his teachings, Feigenbaum strove to move away from the then primary concern with technical methods of quality control to quality control as a business method. He emphasized the administrative viewpoint and considered human relations to be a basic issue in quality control activities. Individual methods, such as statistics and preventive maintenance, are seen only as segments of a comprehensive quality control program. He defined quality control as "an effective system for coordinating the quality maintenance and quality improvement efforts of the various groups in an organization so as to enable production at the most economical levels which allow for full customer satisfaction."

He stated that quality does not mean "best" but "best for the customer use and selling price." The word *control* in the term *quality control* represents a management tool that includes setting quality standards, appraising conformance to the standards, acting when standards are violated, and planning for improvements in the standards.

Dr. Feigenbaum emphasized in his work that total quality programs are the single most powerful tool for organizations and companies today. For quality programs to work, organizational management must assume the responsibility of making the leadership commitment and contributions that are essential to the growth of their respective organizations.

DR. KAORU ISHIKAWA

Kaoru Ishikawa was born in 1915 and graduated in 1939 from the Engineering Department of Tokyo University, having majored in applied chemistry. In 1947, he was made an assistant professor at the university. He obtained his doctorate of engineering and was promoted to professor in 1960. He has been awarded the Deming Prize and the Nihon Keizai Press Prize, the Industrial Standardization Prize for his writings on quality control, and the Grant Medal from the American Society for Quality Control in 1971 for his education program on quality control. He died in April 1989.

Ishikawa is best known as a pioneer of the "quality circle" movement in Japan in the early 1960s. In a speech at a convention to mark the 1000th quality circle in Japan in 1981, he described how his work took him in this direction: "I first considered how best to get grassroots workers to understand and practice quality control. The idea was to educate all people working at factories throughout the country but this was asking too much. Therefore I thought of educating factory foremen or on-the-spot leaders in the first place."

In 1968, Ishikawa produced a nontechnical quality analysis textbook for quality circle members. The book, *Guide to Quality Control,* was subsequently translated into English in 1971, with a second edition published by the Asian Productivity Organization in 1986. He subsequently published *What Is Total Quality Control? The Japanese Way,* which was again translated into English (Prentice Hall, 1985).

Ishikawa's Philosophies

In his teachings, Ishikawa emphasized good data collection and presentation. He is best known for his promotion of the use of quality tools such as the Pareto diagram to prioritize quality improvements and the cause-and-effect (Ishikawa or fishbone) diagram.

Ishikawa saw the cause-and-effect diagram, like other tools, as a device to assist groups or quality circles in quality improvement. As such, he emphasized open group communication as critical to the construction of the diagrams. These Ishikawa diagrams are useful as systematic tools for finding, sorting out, and documenting the causes of variation of quality in production and for organizing mutual relationships between them.

Dr. Ishikawa is associated with the companywide quality control movement that started in Japan in the years 1955 to 1960, following the visits of Deming and Juran. Under this system, quality control in Japan was characterized by companywide participation, from top management to lower-ranking employees. Quality control concepts and methods were used for problem solving in the production process, for incoming material control and new product design control, for analysis to help top management decide policy and verify that policy was being carried out, and for solving problems in sales, personnel, labor management, and clerical departments. Quality audits, internal as well as external, formed part of this activity.

DR. GENICHI TAGUCHI

Dr. Genichi Taguchi was born in 1924. After service in the Astronomical Department of the Navigation Institute of the Imperial Japanese Navy in 1942 to 1945, he worked in the Ministry of Public Health and Welfare and the Institute of Statistical Mathematics, Ministry of Education. He learned much about experimental design techniques from the prize-winning Japanese statistician Matosaburo Masuyama, whom he met while working at the Ministry of Public Health and Welfare. This also led to his early involvement as a consultant to Morinaga Pharmaceuticals and its parent company, Morinaga Seika.

In 1950, Taguchi joined the newly founded Electrical Communications Laboratory of the Nippon Telephone and Telegraph Company. He stayed for more than 12 years, during which he began to develop his methods. While working at the Electrical Communications Laboratory, he consulted widely in Japanese industry. As a result, Japanese companies, including Toyota and its subsidiaries, began applying Taguchi methods extensively from the early 1950s. His first book, which introduced orthogonal arrays, was published in 1951.

From 1954 to 1955, Taguchi was a visiting professor at the Indian Statistical Institute. During this time, he met the well-known statisticians R. A. Fisher and Walter A. Shewhart. In 1957/1958, he published his two-volume book, *Design of*

Experiments. His first visit to the United States was in 1962 as a visiting research associate at Princeton University, during which time he visited the AT&T Bell Laboratories. Also in 1962, he was awarded his PhD by Kyushu University.

In 1964, Taguchi became a professor at Aoyama Gakuin University in Tokyo, a position he held until 1982. In 1966, he and several coauthors wrote *Management by Total Results*. At this stage, Taguchi's methods were still essentially unknown in the West, although applications were taking place in Taiwan and India. In this period and throughout the 1970s, most applications of his methods were on production processes; the shift to product design occurred in the last decade.

In the early 1970s, Taguchi developed the concept of the *quality loss function*. He published two other books in the 1970s as well as the third (current) edition of *Design of Experiments*. He won the Deming Application Prize in 1960 and the Deming Award for Literature on Quality in 1951 and 1953.

In 1982, Taguchi became an advisor at the Japanese Standards Association. In 1984, he again won the Deming Award for Literature on Quality.

Taguchi's Philosophies

Taguchi methods are concerned with the routine optimization of product and process prior to manufacture rather than reliance on the achievement of quality through inspection. Concepts of quality and reliability are pushed back to the design stage, where they really belong. The method provides an efficient technique to design product tests prior to entering the manufacturing phase. However, it can also be used as a troubleshooting methodology to sort out pressing manufacturing problems.

In contrast to Western definitions, Taguchi worked in terms of quality loss rather than quality. This is defined as "loss imparted by the product to society from the time the product is shipped." This loss includes not only the loss to the company through costs of reworking or scrapping, maintenance costs, downtime due to equipment failure, and warranty claims, but also the costs to the customer through poor product performance and reliability, leading to further losses to the manufacturer as its market share falls. Taking a target value for the quality characteristic under consideration as the best possible value of this characteristic, Taguchi associated a simple quadratic loss function with deviations from this target. The loss function showed that a reduction in variability about the target leads to a decrease in loss and a subsequent increase in quality.

Taguchi methodology is fundamentally a prototyping method that enables the engineer or designer to identify the optimal settings to produce a robust product that can survive manufacturing time after time, piece after piece, in order to provide the functionality required by the customer. Two major features of the Taguchi methodology are that it was developed and is used by engineers rather than statisticians, thus removing most of the communication gap and the problems of language traditionally associated with many statistical methodologies, and that the methodology is also tailored directly to the engineering context.

DR. WALTER A. SHEWHART

Walter A. Shewhart was born in New Canton, Illinois, on March 18, 1891. He received his bachelor's and master's degrees from the University of Illinois and his

PhD in physics from the University of California at Berkeley in 1917. He taught at the Universities of Illinois and California, and he briefly headed the Physics Department at the Wisconsin Normal School in LaCrosse.

Shewhart spent most of his early professional career as an engineer at Western Electric (1918–1924) and later worked at Bell Telephone Laboratories, where he served as a member of the technical staff from 1925 until his retirement in 1956. He lectured on quality control and applied statistics at the University of London, at Stevens Institute of Technology, at the graduate school of the U.S. Department of Agriculture, and in India.

Called upon frequently as a consultant, Dr. Shewhart served the War Department, the United Nations, and the government of India, and he was active with the National Research Council and the International Statistical Institute. He served for more than 20 years as the first editor of the *Mathematical Statistics* series published by John Wiley and Sons. He is considered by many to be the father of statistical quality control. Dr. Shewhart died on March 11, 1967, in Troy Hills, New Jersey.

Shewhart's Philosophies

Shewhart's most important book, *Economic Control of Quality of Manufactured Product,* was published in 1931 and is considered by many to be the origin of the basic principles of quality. The book was considered by statisticians to be a landmark contribution to the effort to improve the quality of manufactured goods. Shewhart reported that variations existed in every facet of manufacturing but that variation could be understood through the application of simple statistical tools, such as sampling and probability analysis. Many of his writings were published internally at Bell Laboratories. One of these was the historic memorandum of May 16, 1924, in which he proposed the *control chart* to his superiors.

Shewhart's techniques taught that work processes could be brought under control by determination of when a process should be left alone and when intervention was necessary. He was able to define the limits of random variation that occur in completing any task and said that intervention should occur only when the set limits have been exceeded. He developed control charts to track performance over time, thereby providing workers with the ability to monitor their work and predict when they were about to exceed limits and possibly produce scrap.

Shewhart also wrote *Statistical Method from the Viewpoint of Quality Control* in 1939 and published numerous articles in professional journals. His work in sampling and control charts attracted the interest of and influenced others working with quality problems, most notably W. Edwards Deming and Joseph M. Juran.

Shewhart's idea for the Plan—Do—Check—Act cycle was used extensively by Deming and others to help management quality improvement projects. The cycle involves planning what you want to do, doing it, studying the results, making corrections, and then starting the cycle again.

SUMMARY

Dr. Deming emphasized statistical process control and uniformity and dependability at low cost. "Work smarter, not harder," he said. Dr. Juran stresses the human elements of communication, organization, planning, control, and coordination, and says that problems should be scheduled for solution. Mr. Crosby, who introduced the concept of zero defects, argued that quality is conformance to requirements and that prevention is the best quality management technique.

All three of these quality management experts agree that quality means meeting customer requirements and that increased productivity is the result of quality improvement. They all advocate management commitment and employee involvement to improve systems and avoid problems, identification of the most critical problems, use of statistics and other problem-solving tools, and the focus of all activities on the customer.

It is important to understand that the philosophies of Deming, Juran, Crosby, and the many other quality and management "gurus" are starting points to the development of an organization's quality philosophy. Each organization has unique products, services, cultures, and capabilities. The philosophies of the gurus can help an organization get started, but management, working with all the organization's stakeholders, must develop a philosophy that fits the unique needs of the organization. No one philosophy is totally correct or incorrect. All must be studied and used in the context of how they apply to each individual organization.

Additional information about each of the mentioned gurus may be found by doing a Web site search using their full names.

QUALITY MODELS

For the quality profession, 1987 was a very significant year. During 1987, two events occurred that dramatically changed the way many quality professionals operate. The first was the publication of the original *Malcolm Baldrige National Quality Award Criteria* (now called the *Baldrige National Quality Program*). The second was the publication of the first edition of the *ISO 9000 series* of quality management system requirements and guideline documents. Both events have resulted in the establishment of hundreds of thousands of documented quality management systems based on the models outlined in the two publications. The following is a brief review of the two models.

The Baldrige Quality Award Program

The Malcolm Baldrige National Quality Award was created by Public Law 100–107 and signed into law on August 20, 1987. The award is named for Malcolm Baldrige, who served as secretary of commerce from 1981 until his tragic death in a rodeo accident in 1987. His managerial excellence contributed to long-term improvement in the efficiency and effectiveness of government.

The quality award program was established to assist organizations in the United States to improve quality and productivity by:

- Helping to stimulate American companies to improve quality and productivity for the pride of recognition while obtaining a competitive edge through increased profits

- Recognizing the achievements of those companies that improve the quality of their goods and services and provide an example to others

- Establishing guidelines and criteria that can be used by business, industrial, governmental, and other organizations in evaluating their own quality improvement efforts

- Providing specific guidance for other American organizations that wish to learn how to manage for high quality by making available detailed information on how winning organizations were able to change their cultures and achieve eminence

The awards are given to recognize organizations based in the United States for their achievements in quality and business performance and to raise awareness about the importance of quality and performance excellence as a competitive edge. The award is not given for specific products or services. In 1998, the president and the U.S. Congress approved legislation that made education and health-care organizations eligible to participate in the award program. Up to three awards may be given annually in each of five categories: manufacturing, service, small business, health-care, and education.

Though the Baldrige Award and its recipients form the very visible centerpiece of the U.S. quality movement, a broader national quality program has evolved around the award and its criteria. A report, *Building on Baldrige: American Quality for the 21st Century,* by the private Council on Competitiveness said, "More than any other program, the Baldrige Quality Award is responsible for making quality a national priority and disseminating best practices across the United States." The U.S. Commerce Department's National Institute of Standards and Technology (NIST) manages the Baldrige National Quality Program in close cooperation with the private sector. The American Society for Quality assists in administering the award program under contract to NIST.

The Baldrige performance excellence criteria are a framework that any organization can use to improve overall performance. Seven categories make up the award criteria. Comparisons of the Baldrige Award Criteria for each of the three major segments are listed in Table 2.1.

The award program promotes quality awareness, recognizes quality achievements of U.S. organizations, and provides a vehicle for sharing successful strategies. The Baldrige Award Criteria focus on results and continuous improvement. They provide a framework for designing, implementing, and assessing a process for managing all business operations.

In recent years the Baldrige National Quality Program has been expanded to include criteria covering educational and health-care organizations. The program will be expanded further in 2007 to cover nonprofit organizations. Information on these newer programs is available at *http://www.quality.nist.gov/.*

The criteria are used by thousands of organizations of all kinds for self-assessment and training and as a tool to develop performance and business processes. Almost 2 million copies have been distributed since the first edition in 1988, and heavy reproduction and electronic access multiply that number many times.

For many organizations, using the criteria results in better employee relations, higher productivity, greater customer satisfaction, increased market share, and improved profitability. Studies by NIST, universities, business organizations, and the U.S. General Accounting Office have found that investing in quality principles and performance excellence pays off in increased productivity, satisfied employees and customers, and improved profitability—for both customers and investors. For example, NIST has tracked a hypothetical stock investment in Baldrige Award winners and applicants receiving site visits. The studies have shown that these companies significantly outperform the Standard & Poor's 500.

Table 2.1 Comparisons of Baldrige Award Criteria.

Baldrige National Quality Program—2006 Criteria Categories

Manufacturing Services and Small Business	Health Care	Education
1. Leadership 1.1 Senior Leadership 1.2 Governance and Social Responsibilities	1. Leadership 1.1 Senior Leadership 1.2 Governance and Social Responsibilities	1. Leadership 1.1 Senior Leadership 1.2 Governance and Social Responsibilities
2. Strategic Planning 2.1 Strategy Development 2.2 Strategy Deployment	2. Strategic Planning 2.1 Strategy Development 2.2 Strategy Deployment	2. Strategic Planning 2.1 Strategy Development 2.2 Strategy Deployment
3. Customer and Market Focus 3.1 Customer and Market Knowledge 3.2 Customer Relationships and Satisfaction	3. Focus on Patients, Other Customers, and Markets 3.1 Patient, Other Customers, and Health Care Market Knowledge 3.2 Patient and Other Customer Relationships and Satisfaction	3. Student, Stakeholder, and Market Focus 3.1 Student, Stakeholder, and Market Knowledge 3.2 Student and Stakeholder Relationship and Satisfaction
4. Measurement, Analysis, and Knowledge Management 4.1 Measurement, Analysis, and Review of Organizational Performance 4.2 Information and Knowledge Management	4. Measurement, Analysis, and Knowledge Management 4.1 Measurement, Analysis, and Review of Organizational Performance 4.2 Information and Knowledge Management	4. Measurement, Analysis, and Knowledge Management 4.1 Measurement, Analysis, and Review of Organizational Performance 4.2 Information and Knowledge Management
5. Human Resource Focus 5.1 Work Systems 5.2 Employee Learning and Motivation 5.3 Employee Well-Being and Satisfaction	5. Human Resource Focus 5.1 Work Systems 5.2 Staff Learning and Motivation 5.3 Staff Well-Being and Satisfaction	5. Faculty and Staff Focus 5.1 Work Systems 5.2 Faculty and Staff Learning and Motivation 5.3 Faculty and Staff Well-Being and Satisfaction

Continued

Table 2.1 Comparisons of Baldrige Award Criteria. *(Continued)*

Baldrige National Quality Program—2006 Criteria Categories

Manufacturing Services and Small Business	Health Care	Education
6. Process Management	6. Process Management	6. Process Management
6.1 Value Creation Processes	6.1 Health Care Processes	6.1 Learning-Centered Processes
6.2 Support Processes and Operational Planning	6.2 Support Processes and Operational Planning	6.2 Support Processes and Operational Planning
7. Results	7. Results	7. Results
7.1 Product and Service Outcomes	7.1 Health Care and Service Delivery Outcomes	7.1 Student Learning Outcomes
7.2 Customer-Focused Outcomes	7.2 Patient- and Other Customer-Focused Outcomes	7.2 Student and Stakeholder-Focused Outcomes
7.3 Financial and Market Outcomes	7.3 Financial and Market Outcomes	7.3 Budgetary, Financial, and Market Outcomes
7.4 Human Resource Outcomes	7.4 Human Resource Outcomes	7.4 Faculty and Staff Outcomes
7.5 Organizational Effectiveness Outcomes	7.5 Organizational Effectiveness Outcomes	7.5 Organizational and Effectiveness Outcomes
7.6 Leadership and Social Responsibility Outcomes	7.6 Leadership and Social Responsibility Outcomes	7.6 Leadership and Social Responsibility Outcomes

Additional information on the award is available at the Baldrige National Quality Program Web site, *http://www.quality.nist.gov.*

ISO 9000 Series

ISO 9000 is a series of international standards first published in 1987 by the International Organization for Standardization (ISO), Geneva, Switzerland. Organizations can use the standards to help determine what is needed to maintain an efficient quality management system. For example, the standards describe the need to have an effective quality system, to ensure that measuring and testing equipment is calibrated regularly, and to maintain an adequate record-keeping system, as well as many other elements of a complete quality management system.

The ISO 9000 family of standards represents an international consensus on good management practices that ensure that an organization has a system that can deliver a product or services that meet the customer's quality requirements. The ISO 9000 series is a set of standardized requirements and guidelines for a quality management system applicable to any type of organization, regardless of what the organization does, how big it is, and whether it's in the private or public sector.

Under the ISO 9000 approach, organizations establish written quality management systems based on the quality elements listed in the ISO 9000 requirement documents. Once the quality management system has been documented and is in regular use, the organization can have an independent third-party registrar do an audit to assess the system to determine whether it, in fact, meets the requirements of the ISO 9000 standard. If the written quality management system meets the standard and is operating as written, the registrar will certify the quality management system as meeting ISO 9000 requirements and will register the organization on an international list of organizations that have met the quality management system standard.

The 2000 edition of the ISO 9000 family has a quality assurance model against which organizations can be certified: ISO 9001. The series also contains two additional documents. The three documents are:

- *ISO 9000:2000, Quality management systems—Fundamentals and vocabulary.* This document gives the basic quality management principles upon which the new series is based and defines the fundamental terms and definitions used in the ISO 9000 family.

- *ISO 9001:2000, Quality management systems—Requirements.* This document is the requirement standard that outlines the quality management system elements that must be addressed to meet customer and applicable regulatory requirements. It is the only standard in the ISO 9000 family against which third-party certification can be granted.

- *ISO 9004:2000, Quality management systems—Guidelines for performance improvements.* This document provides guidance for the use of ISO 9001 to attain continual improvement of the quality management system in order to ensure customer satisfaction.

Because the 2000 edition of the ISO 9000 family contains only one quality management systems model—ISO 9001—the organization itself determines which elements of the standard apply to its business operations and develops a quality management system to meet those applicable requirements. Registrars will then indicate on the certificates issued to each organization what the scope of the registration is and any quality management elements of ISO 9001 that have been excluded.

The ISO 9001 standard lays out requirements in broad, general terms. Each company must interpret them within the context of its own business and develop its own quality management system (QMS) to comply. A brief outline of key requirements follows:

- Quality management system—addresses:
  - Identifying and sequencing processes
  - Monitoring, measuring, and analyzing processes
  - Documenting the QMS: quality manual, procedures, instructions, records
  - Controlling documents and records
- Management responsibility—addresses:
  - Top management's evidence of commitment to the QMS: communicating, quality policy, quality objectives, management reviews, availability of resources
  - Top management's support of a customer focus
  - Quality planning
  - Responsibility of a management representative
- Resource management—addresses:
  - Providing resources
  - Ensuring competence, awareness, and training of human resources
  - Providing suitable infrastructure and work environment
- Processes for producing products and services ("product realization")—addresses:
  - Planning for product realization
  - Requirements for customer-related processes
  - Requirements for designing and developing product
  - Purchasing processes
  - Controlling production and service
  - Controlling devices used for monitoring and measuring
- Processes for measurement, analysis, and improvement—addresses:
  - Monitoring and measuring relative to:
    - Satisfaction of customers
    - Auditing the QMS
    - Monitoring, measuring, and controlling product
  - Analyzing data
  - Continually improving (corrective and preventive action)[5]

An estimated 500,000+ ISO 9001 certificates have been issued worldwide. ISO 9001 certificates have been issued in more than 150 countries around the world.

In recent years, ISO has begun publishing International Workshop Agreements (IWAs) to establish the use of ISO 9000 in different communities of practice. Examples are:

- *IWA 1:2005—Quality Management Systems—Guidelines for process improvements in health service organizations*

- *IWA 4:2005—Quality management systems—Guidelines for the application of ISO 9001:2000 in local government*

Additional information about the ISO 9000 family of quality management standards can be found at the International Organization for Standardization Web site, *http://www.iso.ch/iso/en/ISOOnline.frontpage.*

Notes

1. Economou, M. "Quality's not costly." *Manufacturing Engineering* 120, no. 3 (Dearborn, MI: Society of Manufacturing Engineers, 1998): 20.
2. Deming, W. E. *Statistical Adjustment of Data.* (New York: John Wiley and Sons, 1938, 1943; Dover, 1964).
3. Juran, J. M., and A. B. Godfrey, eds. *Juran's Quality Handbook* (5th ed.). (New York: McGraw-Hill, 1999), table 2.1.
4. Derived from Crosby, P. B. *Quality Is Free.* (New York: McGraw-Hill, 1979), and also, *Quality Without Tears* (New York: New American Library, 1984).
5. Adapted from Westcott, R. T., ed. *The Certified Manager of Quality/Organizational Excellence Handbook* (3rd ed.). (Milwaukee, WI: ASQ Quality Press, 2006).

Additional Resources

Crosby, P. B. *Quality Is Free: The Art of Making Quality Certain.* (New York: McGraw-Hill, 1979).
———. *Quality Without Tears: The Art of Hassle-free Management.* (New York: New American Library, 1984).
Deming, W. E. *Out of the Crisis.* (Cambridge: MIT Center for Advanced Engineering Study, 1986).
———. *The New Economics for Industry, Government, and Education.* (Cambridge: Massachusetts Institute of Technology, 1993).
Federal Quality Institute. *Federal Total Quality Management Handbook.* (Washington, DC: U.S. Office of Personnel Management, 1990).
Feigenbaum, A. V. *Total Quality Control* (3rd ed., rev.). (New York: McGraw-Hill, 1991).
Ishikawa, K. *Guide to Quality Control* (2nd ed., rev.). (Tokyo: Asian Productivity Organization, 1986).
———. *What Is Total Quality Control? The Japanese Way.* (New York: Prentice-Hall, 1985).
Juran, J. M. *Management of Quality.* (4th ed.). (Wilton, CT: Juran Institute, 1986).
———. *Juran on Planning for Quality.* (New York: The Free Press, 1988).
Juran, J. M., and A. B. Godfrey, eds. *Juran's Quality Handbook* (5th ed.). (New York: McGraw-Hill, 1999).
Latzko, W. J., and D. M. Saunders. *Four Days with Dr. Deming: A Strategy for Modern Methods of Management.* (Reading, MA: Addison-Wesley, Longman, 1995).
Naval Leader Training Unit. *Introduction to Total Quality Leadership.* (Washington, DC: U.S. Department of the Navy, 1997).
Westcott, R. T., ed. *The Certified Manager of Quality/Organizational Excellence Handbook* (3rd ed.). (Milwaukee, WI: ASQ Quality Press, 2006).

Part II
Teams

Time after time, team members set what they feel are challenging but realistic goals for themselves, and once the program gets rolling, they find that they are not only meeting but also exceeding their goals. This is something that rarely happens if goals are set for the team, rather than by the team.

Mark Shepherd (Texas Instruments)

Chapter 3

A. Understanding Teams

1. PURPOSE

> Understand the definition of a team, when to use a team and for how long. (Apply)
>
> **CQIA BoK 2006**

The Definition of Team

- A team is a group of individuals organized to work together to accomplish an objective
- A team is a group of two or more people who are equally accountable for the accomplishment of a task and specific performance goals
- A team is a small number of people with complementary skills who are committed to a common purpose
- A team combines individuals' knowledge, experience, skills, aptitude, and attitude to achieve a synergistic effect

A team is *not:*

- An organizational work unit that is not functioning as a team; however, a team may be comprised of members of a work unit
- An informal gathering of people, a crowd
- Members of a club, association, or society that is not functioning as a team

- Top management of an organization, even though they may be referred to as the "management team," unless they truly function as a team

- A staff meeting, conference, seminar, educational course, unless functioning as a team

Teams may be initiated for a variety of purposes, some of which are to:

- Improve a process—for example, a cycle-time-reduction team

- Complete a project—for example, a relocation task force to relocate a manufacturing plant

- Conduct a study of a best practice—for example, a benchmarking team

- Solve a problem—for example, a hospital "tiger team" to hunt for the cause of fatalities

- Produce a special event—for example, a team to plan, organize, and conduct an employee recognition evening

- Investigate a discrepancy—for example, a team to determine the root cause of inventory shrinkage

- Participate in a competitive sport—for example, an organization's softball team

A team is appropriate when:

- Achieving an objective involves (or should involve) more than one organizational function. For example, a team to improve the procurement process might involve members from purchasing, materials management, finance, production, and key suppliers.

- Some degree of isolation from the mainstream work is desirable in order to focus on a specific objective or problem—for example, a team to launch a year-long project to implement a quality management system.

- Specially trained and experienced people are "on call" when a specific need arises. Three examples are: a "proposal response team" that is quickly assembled to address a request for proposal from a potential customer/client; a material review board that assembles when there is nonconforming product to review and determine disposition; and an in-plant volunteer fire brigade.

How long a team remains active in a functioning mode depends upon several factors, such as:

- The nature of the purpose of the team

- An anticipated or predetermined time span

- Available resources

- The progress being made by the team

- The value of the planned outcomes

- The effectiveness of the team itself

One fault that may occur with a team is when it remains in effect after its purpose and objectives are met. Two examples are:

1. A company has a policy that states that process improvement teams should meet for 14 weeks for any given improvement effort (regardless of circumstances).

2. A project team continues to find reasons to meet long after the original project has been completed. (Members like the comradeship. Some members may fear returning to their regular work after a long hiatus.)

2. CHARACTERISTICS AND TYPES

> Recognize characteristics and types of teams and how they are structured; know how teams differ and how they are similar; know which type of team to use in a given situation. (Apply)
>
> **CQIA BoK 2006**

Natural Team

A natural team (such as a work group, department, or function) is made up of persons who have responsibility for a specific process or function and who work together in a participative environment. Unlike the process improvement team, which is discussed next, the natural team is neither cross-functional nor temporary. The team leader is generally the person responsible for the function or process performed within the work area. The natural team is useful in involving all employees in a work group in striving for continual improvement. Starting with one or two functions, successful natural teams can become role models for expansion of natural teams throughout an organization. A natural team example follows:

> *The information technology (IT) department serves all the functions within the 4,000-person Mars Package Delivery's countrywide operations. The IT department's work units (technical system maintenance, application systems design and programming, data entry, computer operations, data output, customer service—internal, technology help desk, and administration) function as an internal team. Selected representatives from each work unit meet weekly to review the IT department's performance and to initiate corrective and preventive actions.*

Improvement Teams

Process improvement teams, or PITs, as they are typically called, focus on creating or improving specific business processes. A PIT may attempt to completely reengineer a process or may work on incremental improvements (see Incremental and

Breakthrough Improvement in Chapter 6). If attempting a breakthrough, the team is usually cross-functional in composition, with representatives from a number of different functions and with a range of skills related to the process to be improved. A PIT working on incremental improvements is often composed of persons having a functional interest in improving a portion of the overall process, such as representatives from a specific functional work unit. Two examples follow:

BPC, which manufactures a flexible packaging product, periodically convenes a "cycle-time-reduction team" (CTRT) under the leadership of a pressroom supervisor, with four or five operators from the supervisor's pressroom. A trained facilitator helps to bring about the team's formation and keep the meeting process on track during the one-hour-a-week meetings. Each CTRT defines its objectives and the procedures and tools to be used to improve its process. The CTRT typically meets for 10 to 12 weeks, and it may disband earlier if its objectives have been met. Pressrooms rotate so that only one CTRT is functioning at any one time. A technical trainer as necessary provides training, either for members new to improvement tools or for the whole team when a new tool or technique is needed. The CTRT may call upon anyone in the company to provide needed information. At BPC, it is considered a privilege to be invited to join a CTRT.

At A&H, a provider of group accident and health insurance in the southwestern United States, originators of significant process improvement suggestions (with an estimated savings of $100,000 per year or more) are invited to participate in a PIT to address their suggestions. A trained facilitator is assigned to help with team formation and team process issues. A&H finds that this approach not only recognizes and rewards those with suggestions, but also stimulates involvement in the suggestion system. The synergy of the PITs often results in savings exceeding the original estimates.

A variation used in many fast-paced organizations is the *kaizen blitz* or *kaizen event*. This accelerated team approach intensely focuses on achieving improvements in a three-day to five-day time frame. Reducing cycle time and waste and increasing productivity are examples in which improvements of as much as 70 percent have been reported.

Cross-Functional Teams

PITs that are focused more on the overall process within the whole organization as it impacts many functions are cross-functional in the composition of their members. This is especially so if the objective of the PIT is to develop a breakthrough improvement (see Chapter 6).

In some organizations, cross-functional teams carry out all or nearly all of the functions. In such cases, the organization resembles a matrix- or project-type organization. In attempting to eliminate internal competition among functional groups, organizations have adopted cross-functional teams for many areas, such as product design. Examples include the following:

Macho Motors, a leading manufacturer of off-road service vehicles, integrates its marketing, engineering, production, support services, shipping, and customer service functions into product families. Employing quality function deployment tools and concurrent engineering-production techniques, each family (cross-functional team) works together to meet customers' needs. Representatives from each family meet quarterly to share process improvement information.

The employees own Williams Air Service, a regional air passenger service firm. Nearly everyone, from the airline's president to the people staffing the check-in counter, are trained to rotate jobs in performing passenger check-in, baggage handling, fueling, flight attendant functions, and clerical functions. Only the pilots, mechanics, and the bookkeeper have specialized functions not delegated to other personnel. The entire airline is a cross-functional team.

The smaller the organization, the more likely employees are to work together, often doing each other's designated jobs as the need arises. Each employee "wears many hats." In recent times, larger organizations have come to recognize the value of smaller, cross-functional entities. In a fast-paced economy, these more flexible organizations can often move more swiftly than larger competitors to reconfigure themselves and their products and services to meet changing needs.

Project Teams

A project team is formed to achieve a specific mission. The project team's objective may be to create something new, such as a facility, product, or service, or to accomplish a complex task, such as to implement a quality management system certified to ISO 9001:2000 requirements, or to upgrade all production equipment to be computer-controlled. Typically, a project team employs full-time members, on loan, for the duration of the project. The project team operates in parallel with the primary organizational functions. The project team may or may not be cross-functional in member composition, depending upon its objectives and competency needs. Often the project leader is the person to whom the ultimate responsibility for managing the resulting project outcome is assigned. An example is as follows:

Abel Hospital, a community health-care organization of 250 employees, has established a task force (project team) to select a site and design and build a new hospital to replace the existing 112-year-old facility. New governmental regulations make a new facility imperative. The "Must Build It" (MBI) project team includes representatives from each hospital department, an external consulting firm, an architectural design firm, and a legal firm. A full-time facilitator-consultant provides team training and facilitates meetings. The team leader is the former assistant director of Abel Hospital and will likely assume the role of director when the present director retires (coincidental with the planned occupation of the new facility). The MBI has a three-year window in which to complete the facility and move the existing services and patients. Care is taken to conduct team building and provide training in the tools and techniques the team members will need, especially project planning and management. Team members have been replaced in their former positions until the project is completed. The MBI is located in a rental site that is removed from the present premises of Abel Hospital. The MBI leader provides weekly project status reports to senior management and quarterly project summary presentations to the board of directors.

Self-Directed Teams

Self-directed (self-managed) teams are groups of employees authorized to make a wide range of decisions about how they will handle issues regarding safety, quality, scheduling of work, work allocation, setting of goals, maintenance of work standards, equipment maintenance, and resolution of conflicts. Often called high-performance work teams, these teams offer employees a broader spectrum of responsibility and ownership of a process. Often the team members select the team leaders; sometimes leadership is rotated among members. Two examples are as follows:

> *Med Plastics has structured its new manufacturing operations for medical devices on the principles of cell manufacturing and self-managed teams. Each cell manufactures one complete category of products. Within a cell, each operator is fully trained to perform all operations. Self-led and making their own decisions, the members of the teams in each cell determine how and when to rotate tasks and are responsible for the quality of the products shipped.*

> *District 4 of Alabaster County's K–12 educational system allows the editorial offices of each of the three high schools' student newspapers to manage its own operations, within the rules and regulations of the district. Each school's newspaper office is responsible for recruiting its own student staff, selecting its editor, arranging for team and technical training, allocating assignments, and producing a high-quality student newspaper. Each newspaper office has adopted some unique approaches to managing its operations. The achievements of the student newspaper offices are publicized in local community media. Awards for significant contributions are given annually, sponsored by the Alabaster Chronicle.*

Because of the level of empowerment afforded, careful planning and training is key to a successful self-directed team. The most success usually occurs when a new business or process is initiated. Transforming a traditional work culture to self-management is a lengthy process and is prone to serious workforce turmoil.

Virtual Teams

Virtual teams are groups of two or more persons who are usually affiliated with a common organization and have a common purpose but are not necessarily employees. The nature of the virtual team is that its members conduct their work either partly or entirely via electronic communication. Virtual teams are a hybrid in that they may or may not be cross-functional in terms of competencies. These teams may or may not be partly or entirely self-managed. Typically, the virtual team is geographically dispersed, often with individual members working from their homes. For example:

> *A virtual team of three members of ASQ's Quality Management Division—one member in Pennsylvania, one in Florida, and one in Connecticut—wrote this book.*

3. VALUE

> Understand how a team's work relates to
> the organization's key strategies and the
> value of using different types of teams.
> (Understand)
>
> **CQIA BoK 2006**

A key principle is that no team should be formed unless its purpose (mission) and objectives can be traced upward in supporting the organization's strategies and plans.

This alignment with organizational strategies, goals, and objectives should be shown through measurements directly related to the customer requirements of the company. Tools such as the Balanced Scorecard, Voice of the Customer, House of Quality, customer or employee surveys, and focus groups are all effective vehicles for documenting the ultimate value of the team's work within the organization. Further, teams should be capable of demonstrating value. Every team, regardless of type, should plan to address one or more of the following purposes or missions:

- Fulfilling a mandate (law, regulation, owners' requirements)
- Producing a favorable benefits-to-cost ratio
- Providing a return on investment (ROI) equal to or greater than an alternative project
- Improving customer satisfaction and retention
- Meeting or exceeding competitive pressures
- Introducing new processes, products, or services
- Improving a process (cycle-time reduction, cost saving/avoidance, reduce waste)
- Increasing organization's core competencies
- Building an effective and efficient workforce
- Involving key suppliers and customers in improvement initiatives
- Enhancing the organization's reputation for delivering quality products/services

Chapter 4

B. Roles and Responsibilities

Identify major team roles and the attributes
of good role performance for champions,
sponsors, leaders, facilitators, timekeepers,
and members. (Understand)

CQIA BoK 2006

ROLE RESPONSIBILITIES

Of the seven roles described in Table 4.1, those of timekeeper and scribe are the
only ones that are optional, depending upon the mission of the team. Though the
remaining five roles are essential, they may be combined in a variety of ways.
However, the most crucial roles for the success of the team, once it is formed, are
those of the team leader and the facilitator. The team leader is responsible for the
content, the work done by the team. The facilitator is responsible for ensuring that
the process affecting the work of the team is the best for the stage and situation the
team is in.

The need for a trained facilitator depends on whether:

- The team has been meeting for some time and is capable of resolving
  conflicting issues

- A new member has been added, thus upsetting established relationships

- A key contributor to the group has been lost

- Other disturbing factors such as lack of adequate resources, the threat of
  project cancellation, or a major change in requirements

Table 4.1   Roles, responsibilities, and performance attributes.

Role Name	Responsibility	Definition	Attributes of Good Role Performance
Champion	Advocate	The person initiating a concept or idea for change/improvement.	• Is dedicated to seeing it implemented • Holds absolute belief it is the right thing to do • Has perseverance and stamina
Sponsor	Backer; risk taker	The person who supports a team's plans, activities, and outcomes.	• Believes in the concept/idea • Has sound business acumen • Is willing to take risk and responsibility for outcomes • Has authority to approve needed resources • Will be listened to by upper management
Team leader	Change agent; chair; head	A person who: • Staffs the team or provides input for staffing requirements • Strives to bring about change/improvement through the team's outcomes • Is entrusted by followers to lead them • Has the authority for, and directs the efforts of, the team • Participates as a team member • Coaches team members in developing or enhancing necessary competencies • Communicates with management about the team's progress and needs • Handles the logistics of team meetings • Takes responsibility for team records	• Is committed to the team's mission and objectives • Has experience in planning, organizing, staffing, controlling, and directing • Is capable of creating and maintaining channels that enable members to do their work • Is capable of gaining the respect of team members; serves as a role model • Is firm, fair, and factual in dealing with a team of diverse individuals • Facilitates discussion without dominating • Actively listens • Empowers team members to the extent possible within the organization's culture • Supports all team members equally • Respects each team member's individuality
Facilitator	Helper; trainer; advisor; coach	A person who: • Observes the team's processes and team members' interactions and suggests process changes to facilitate positive movement toward the team's goals and objectives • Intervenes if discussion develops into multiple conversations • Intervenes to skillfully prevent an individual from dominating the discussion or to engage an overlooked individual in the discussion • Assists the team leader in bringing discussions to a close • May provide training in team building, conflict management, and so forth	• Is trained in facilitating skills • Is respected by team members • Is tactful • Knows when and when not to intervene • Deals with the team's process, not content • Respects the team leader and does not override his or her responsibility • Respects confidential information shared by individuals or the team as a whole • Will not accept facilitator role if expected to report to management information that is proprietary to the team • Will abide by the ASQ Code of Ethics

Continued

Table 4.1   Roles, responsibilities, and performance attributes.   *(Continued)*

Role Name	Responsibility	Definition	Attributes of Good Role Performance
Timekeeper	Gatekeeper; monitor	A person designated by the team to watch the use of allocated time and remind the team members when their time objective may be in jeopardy.	• Is capable of assisting the team leader in keeping the team meeting within the predetermined time limitations • Is sufficiently assertive to intervene in discussions when the time allocation is in jeopardy • Is capable of participating as a member while still serving as a timekeeper
Scribe	Recorder; note taker	A person designated by the team to record critical data from team meetings. Formal "minutes" of the meetings may be published and distributed to interested parties.	• Is capable of capturing on paper, or electronically, the main points and decisions made in a team meeting and providing a complete, accurate, and legible document (or formal minutes) for the team's records • Is sufficiently assertive to intervene in discussions to clarify a point or decision in order to record it accurately • Is capable of participating as a member while still serving as a scribe
Team members	Participants; subject matter experts	The persons selected to work together to bring about a change/improvement, achieving this in a created environment of mutual respect, sharing of expertise, cooperation, and support.	• Are willing to commit to the purpose of the team • Are able to express ideas, opinions, and suggestions in a nonthreatening manner • Are capable of listening attentively to other team members • Are receptive to new ideas and suggestions • Are even-tempered and able to handle stress and cope with problems openly • Are competent in one or more fields of expertise needed by the team • Have favorable performance records • Are willing to function as team members and forfeit "star" status

Obviously, the team member role is also important, but it is somewhat less critical than those of team leader and facilitator. Supplementing the team with "on-call" experts can often compensate for a shortfall in either the number of members or members' competencies. Selected members must willingly share their expertise, listen attentively, and support all team decisions.

The selection of a team member to serve as a timekeeper may be helpful, at least until the team has become more adept at self-monitoring its use of time. When a timekeeper is needed, the role is often rotated, giving consideration to whether the selected member has a full role to play in the deliberations at a particular meeting.

For some team missions for which very formal documentation is required, a scribe or notetaker may be needed. This role can be distracting for a member whose full attention is needed on the topics under discussion. For this reason, an assistant, not a regular member of the team, is sometimes assigned to "take the minutes" and publish them. Care should be taken not to select a team member for this role solely on the basis of that team member's sex or position in the organization.

All team members must adhere to expected standards of quality, fiduciary responsibility, ethics, and confidentiality. (See Appendix B, ASQ Code of Ethics.) It is imperative that the most competent individuals available are selected for each role. See Table 4.1 for the attributes of good role performance.

Very frequently, a team must function in parallel with day-to-day assigned work and with the members not relieved of responsibility for the regularly assigned work. This, of course, places a burden and stress on the team members. The day-to-day work and the work of the team must both be conducted effectively. The inability to be two places at one time calls for innovative time management, conflict resolution, and delegation skills on the part of the team members.

Several roles within a team may be combined, depending upon the size of the team and its purpose. Following are some examples:

- The team has begun to function smoothly and the team leader has become more skilled under the guidance of a facilitator. It is decided that the facilitator is no longer needed.

- A three-person team self-selects the person who originated and sold the idea to management (the champion) as team leader.

- A cross-functional performance improvement team of eight persons elects to rotate the team leader role at two-week intervals.

- A departmental work group (natural team) rotates timekeeper and scribe roles at each meeting so as not to discriminate based on gender, job held, age, schooling, and so forth.

- The backer of the project team serves as the team leader because the project is confined to his or her area of responsibility.

- Specialists, such as a material-handling systems designer or a cost accountant, are periodically requested to temporarily join a team as needed.

TEAM SIZE

Though an ideal team size may be five members, team size will vary depending on the:

- Purpose for the team—its mission
- Size and complexity of the task that the team is to perform
- Size of the organization in which the team will be formed
- Type of team
- Duration of the team's work and the frequency of its meetings
- Degree of urgency for the outcomes of the team's efforts
- Resource constraints, such as funding, availability of appropriate personnel, facilities, and equipment
- Team management constraints, such as minimum and maximum number of team members needed to achieve the team's mission
- Organizational culture—organizational policies and practices
- Predominant managing style of the organization to which the team reports
- Regulatory requirements
- Customer mandates

When a whole function or department works as a natural team, the team size is the number of persons in the department. If three persons band together to operate a charter air-taxi service and they work as a team, then the team is the three persons. When a cross-functional project team is formed to design and build a new shopping center, the team could be very large and could comprise a number of smaller teams within the larger entity. In a municipal public library, when a PIT is formed to reduce retrieval and re-shelving cycle times, it is likely to be cross-functional but limited to one representative from each function within the process cycle and constrained by the availability of staff.

TEAM MEETINGS

The structure of team meetings depends on the team's purpose, its size, its duration, its projected outcomes, and the degree of urgency of results required. Teams may range from having no formal meetings to having frequent scheduled meetings with extensive agendas and formal minutes. Certain rules and regulations as well as client requirements may specify the extent of meetings to be held.

A company whose quality management system is certified under the ISO/TS16949 Automotive standard is expected to conduct periodic design reviews (meetings) as a product is being developed. Evidence that such reviews have been conducted and documented is examined. Failure to comply could place the certification in jeopardy.

In a typical formal team meeting, the team leader arranges for an agenda to be prepared and sent to all team members. The agenda states the time, place, and intent of the meeting. Additional material may be attached as premeeting reading for participants to prepare themselves for discussion. In some cases, the agenda states the role of each team member, why his or her input is needed, and decisions that must be made relative to the topics for the meeting. The logistics of obtaining the meeting venue and equipping the meeting room is the responsibility of the team leader, but the task is often delegated to an assistant.

All team members have a responsibility to assist the team in reaching consensus when differences of opinion arise, yet also to challenge assumptions that could endanger the outcome of the team. Further, each member must respect and cooperate with others on the team.

Inasmuch as a team should function as a process, a team meeting process self-assessment, Figure 4.1, can be a useful tool to critique the overall effectiveness of a

Circle a number to represent your perception of the team's process in this meeting.

We had no agenda or we did not follow the agenda we had.	*TEAM ON TRACK* 1 2 3 4 5 6 7 8 9 10	An agenda was distributed in advance of the meeting and we followed it exactly.
Members who were supposed to attend didn't show. Others straggled in late.	*ATTENDANCE AND PROMPTNESS* 1 2 3 4 5 6 7 8 9 10	All expected members attended and arrived on time. The meeting started at the scheduled time.
Some members tended to dominate and others did not participate.	*PARTICIPATION* 1 2 3 4 5 6 7 8 9 10	Member participation was evenly balanced; everyone contributed to decisions and openly discussed ideas.
More than one person talked at a time; disruptive remarks were made; side conversations occurred. Overall disrespect of person speaking was evident.	*LISTENING* 1 2 3 4 5 6 7 8 9 10	One person talked at a time; others helped clarify and build on ideas; all were attentive to person speaking. Respect for one another was evident.
No attempt was made to redirect the team to the agenda or to encourage balanced participation.	*SHARED LEADERSHIP* 1 2 3 4 5 6 7 8 9 10	Both the team leader and team members intervened to keep the team focused on the agenda and to stimulate participation when needed.
When conflicts arose, chaos resulted. Differences of opinion were allowed to escalate to inappropriate behavior and lack of adequate resolution.	*CONFLICT MANAGEMENT* 1 2 3 4 5 6 7 8 9 10	The energies involved with differing opinions were directed toward understanding conflicting views and seeking consensus.
Team decisions were inferior to what individuals would have produced. There was no attempt to summarize main ideas/decisions or future actions/responsibilities.	*RESULTS* 1 2 3 4 5 6 7 8 9 10	Team expertise and decisions were superior to individual judgments. Main ideas/decisions were summarized, and action assignments were made at end of meeting.
Team was totally ineffective in achieving its purpose for this meeting.	*OVERALL RATING* 1 2 3 4 5 6 7 8 9 10	Team was totally effective in achieving its purpose for this meeting. All agenda items were addressed or properly tabled for the next meeting.

Figure 4.1 Team meeting process self–assessment.

team meeting. The value lies in having each team member and the facilitator complete the assessment and then having the group as a whole discuss the results, reach consensus, and set one or more improvement objectives for the next meeting.

Circle a number to represent your perception of the team's process in this meeting.

TEAM LEADER AS COACH

Leaders frequently complain about employees, saying they have poor work habits, have little respect for authority, require constant supervision, arrive late and leave early, lack drive and initiative, want more money for less work—the list goes on. "If only they were more motivated" is the common lament. The fact is that most people start a new job already motivated. Something makes them want to take the job in the first place. It's what happens to employees after they take the job that demotivates them. To lead people better, a team leader needs to become an effective coach.

A basic principle is that one person cannot "motivate" another. Motivation comes from within and is a consequence of one's environment. This environment may consist of past experiences, the present situation, competency to do the job, knowledge of what's expected by management, working conditions, whether and how recognition is received, the degree to which decisions and suggestions are allowed and accepted, the degree to which one feels empowered to act on behalf of the business, perception of management's actions (for example, punishing), opportunity to develop and make more money, conditions outside of work, and personal health. Each person has a unique set of needs that vary depending on circumstances and that, if fulfilled, will tend to make them feel motivated. An effective leader can provide an environment in which an employee feels motivated. To do this, consider the "6 Rs":

1. *Reinforce.* Identify and positively reinforce work done well.

2. *Request information.* Discuss team members' views. Is anything preventing expected performance?

3. *Resources.* Identify needed resources, the lack of which could impede quality performance.

4. *Responsibility.* Customers make paydays possible; all employees have a responsibility to the customers, both internal and external.

5. *Role.* Be a role model. Don't just tell; demonstrate how to do it. Observe learners' performances. Together, critique the approach and work out an improved method.

6. *Repeat.* Apply the previous principles regularly and repetitively.

Coaching is an ongoing process. But it doesn't have to be a burden. Following these action steps to shape behavior will help a team leader to become an effective, quality-driven coach:

• Catch team members doing something right and positively reinforce the good behavior in that specific situation.

• Use mistakes as learning opportunities.

- Reward team members who take risks in changing, even if they sometimes fail.

- When discussing situations, sit next to the team member. Respond with "I see/understand."

- Acknowledge the team member's reason for action, but don't agree to it if it's inappropriate.

- When giving performance feedback, reveal reactions after, not before, describing the behavior needing change.

- Encourage members to make suggestions for improving. Always give credit to the member making the suggestion.

- Treat team members with even more care than other business assets.

POTENTIAL PERILS AND PITFALLS OF TEAMS

- The purpose of the team is not linked to the organization's strategic direction and goals.

- Management commitment and personal involvement are nonexistent or inadequate.

- The environment for the team is hostile or indifferent.

- Assigned members lack the needed competence (knowledge, skills, experience, aptitude, and attitude).

- Training for team members is not made available or is inadequate for the tasks to be done.

- Team leadership is inadequate to lead the team in meeting its objectives.

- Team building is nonexistent or inadequate.

- Team facilitation is nonexistent or inadequate.

- Team ground rules are nonexistent or inadequate.

- Team process is ignored or improperly managed.

- Members are not behaving as a team.

- Team members are unsure of what's expected of them.

- Recognition and reward for work done well is nonexistent or inappropriate.

- Adequate resources are not provided (support personnel, facilities, tools, materials, information access, and funding).

- Conflicts between day-to-day work and work on the team have not been resolved.

- The team cannot seem to move beyond the "storming" stage.

- Team members constantly need to be replaced.

- Team members show little respect for one another's competency.
- The decision to form a team is not the best approach for the situation.
- The team leader is reluctant to give up absolute control and unquestioned authority.
- Day-to-day operations perceive the team as a potential threat.
- The union resists team formation.
- The team, if self-directed, lacks the training and knowledge to handle situations that may be off-limits, such as hiring/firing and compensation.
- Planning the process and managing the process by which the team will operate has been done poorly, if at all.
- The team leader does not understand two primary concepts: how to lead a team and how to manage the team process.
- The team is allowed to continue beyond the time when it should have been disbanded.
- Team members have been selected involuntarily.
- The basis for team member selection is not consistent with the goals and objectives and the expected outcomes of the team.
- Team members' roles and organizational levels in day-to-day operations are carried into team activities, upsetting the "all are equal" environment desired.
- The team assumes an unauthorized life of its own.
- The team fails to keep the rest of the organization apprised of what it's doing and why.
- Team members are cut off from their former day-to-day functions, losing opportunities for professional development, promotions, and pay raises.
- The size of the team is inappropriate for the intended outcome—too limited or too large.
- The team's actions are in violation of its contract with the union or in violation of labor laws and practices.

WHAT MAKES A TEAM WORK?

- All team members agree on the expected outputs and outcomes of the team.
- Each member is clearly committed to the goals and objectives of the team and understands why he or she is on the team.
- Each member fully accepts the responsibilities assigned and makes an overall commitment to help with whatever needs to be done to ensure the team's success.

- Members agree to freely ask questions and openly share their opinions and feelings, with no hidden agendas and with respect for other team members.

- Information is not hoarded or restricted. Each member has access to what is needed, and when it is needed, to get the work accomplished.

- Building and maintaining trust is of paramount importance to the team's successful achievement of its purpose.

- Every member feels he or she can make a difference with his or her contribution.

- Management is committed to supporting the team's decisions, as is each team member.

- Conflict within the team, when properly managed, produces a win–win outcome.

- The team maintains a dual focus: its process as a team and its anticipated outcomes.

- Serving on the team can increase a member's expertise and reputation but should never be a detriment to his or her personal development (such as promotional opportunities, compensation increases, and training to maintain job skills).

Chapter 5

C. Team Formation and Group Dynamics

1. INITIATING TEAMS

> Apply the elements of launching a team: clear purpose, goals, commitment, ground rules, schedules, support from management, and team empowerment. (Apply)
>
> **CQIA BoK 2006**

The underlying principles pertaining to launching most any team are as follows:

- There must be a clearly understood purpose for having the team. This purpose must be communicated to all individuals and organizations potentially impacted by the work of the team.

- The team must be provided with or generate a mission statement and a clear goal—the expected outcome of the team's efforts. The mission and the goal must support the organization's strategic plans.

- The team must document objectives, with time lines and measurement criteria, for the achievement of the goal.

- The team must have the support of management, including the needed resources to achieve the team's objectives.

- The team must be given or define for itself the ground rules under which it will operate.

- The team must be empowered, to the extent allowed by the sponsor, to perform its scheduled activities.

- The team must build into its plans a means for interim measurement of progress and the means for improving its performance.

- The team must commit to achieving its mission, goals, and objectives.

- The sponsor must provide a mechanism for recognizing both the efforts and the outcomes of the team's activities.

Guidelines for Team Formation

- A formal charter may be appropriate. The charter could include:

  - The purpose for the team and overall outcome anticipated

  - The sponsor

  - Approval to launch the team (including release of funding)

  - Criteria for team member selection

  - Methodology and technology to be used

  - Degree of autonomy granted and team member empowerment boundaries

  - Any constraints pertinent to the team's work and conduct

  - A start and complete time (as applicable)

- Techniques and tools of project planning and management will be used as applicable.

- A tracking, measuring, and reporting procedure will be implemented.

- Risk assessment criteria will be established, contingency plans made, and periodic assessments conducted.

- Means will be put in place to recognize, reinforce, and reward the team for work done well.

2. SELECTING TEAM MEMBERS

> Know how to select team members who have appropriate skill sets and knowledge (e.g., number of members, expertise, and representation). (Apply)
>
> **CQIA BoK 2006**

The basis for a strong, successful team is careful selection of its members. See Table 4.1 for the attributes of good role performance.

Team members are often selected because of their knowledge and past achievements. Membership choices for smaller and shorter-duration teams are frequently based on informal referrals. Some instruments and formal methods may be employed in staffing larger and longer-duration teams, especially when candidates are unknown to the sponsor or team leader.

In our fast-paced environment, most organizations seek team leaders who are both visionary and flexible—team leaders who can inspire an eclectic, high-performance group of followers. Needed are team leaders who can coach as well as cajole, captain as well as crew, control as well as collaborate, criticize as well as commend, confess as well as confront, consummate as well as concede, create as well as conform—these and others are attributes of a flexible leader. Although they may help, neither charisma nor superiority (in terms of position, education, longevity, or political clout) should be the primary criterion for choosing a potentially effective team leader.

A floundering project team formed to design and implement a substantive information technology project failed to reach any of its first-year goals, other than spending the $100,000 (1970 time period) allocated for the project. The small team of three, augmented by personnel from a software design firm, was led by a person who had in-depth knowledge of present systems, the organization, and the principal people in the organization. He had been with the company his entire working career and was within two years of retirement when first assigned. A systems analyst and an accomplished computer programmer were the other in-house team members.

When the CEO became concerned that nothing visible was occurring, he ordered that a new project manager be assigned with the directive to find out what was going on and then recommend either continuance with restructuring or abandonment. The new project manager assessed the situation and confirmed that the three project incumbents had sufficient expertise, with help from the software house, to complete the project with a one-year extension and with additional funding.

The recommendation was approved, and the now-four-person team proceeded under new direction. Formal project management practices were instituted, and a tight time line with interim milestones and clear objectives for the work were established. Measurements and monitoring were instituted along with weekly progress reviews. Much of the earlier work had to be discarded. Assurances had to be obtained for the analyst and the programmer to ensure their reentry to their former work units when the project was completed. The contract with the software house had to be renegotiated, with penalty clauses for nonconformances. Working conditions for the team were improved. Means for recognizing their contribution were created.

Relieved of his project manager responsibility, the former leader poured newfound energy and his extensive knowledge into the detailed design of the system, eager to retire with a success. Ensured of their jobs after the project was completed, the analyst and the programmer committed to making the project successful.

The key to the successful completion of the project, 10 months later, was due in large part to the new team leader's attributes, some of which were similar to those noted earlier.

Ideally, a profile of what attributes are sought for each member of a team establishes the criteria for guiding selection. Résumés of candidates and records of past performance are reviewed, and interviews of potential members are conducted. Instruments may augment member selection, such as:

- The Myers-Briggs Type Indicator (MBTI) is an instrument for assessing personality "type" based on Carl Jung's theory of personality preferences. The test results, analyzed by a trained practitioner, can aid in structuring either the diversity or the similarity desired in a potential team. Four bipolar scales, as follows:

(E) Extroverted	or	(I) Introverted
(S) Sensing	or	(N) Intuitive
(T) Thinking	or	(F) Feeling
(J) Judging	or	(P) Perceiving

form 16 possible styles, for example:

ENFP, INTJ, ISFJ . . .

- The DiSC profiling instrument, based on William Marston's theories, measures characteristic ways of behaving in a particular environment. The DiSC dimensions are: Dominance, Influence, Steadiness, and Conscientiousness.

- A KESAA factors analysis is a method for capturing and analyzing the factors that are important for performing a specific job or task. The factors are: Knowledge, Experience, Skills, Aptitude, and Attitude.[1]

In addition to the composition of the team, another key consideration for its success is whether the team will function as an autonomous parallel organization or as an adjunct to the daily operation of the organization. The standalone team is often located away from the parent organization and is also sometimes exempt from some of the restrictive rules of the parent organization. Members of such a team are typically on temporary assignment to the team and do not carry their former daily responsibilities with them to the new assignment. When the team must function while at the same time members retain day-to-day responsibilities, conflicts can arise over which activity takes precedence. If such conflicts are not carefully handled, team effectiveness can be compromised.

"Pills-are-us," a cross-functional PIT in a small community hospital, was established to find ways to reduce the time it took to obtain medications from the hospital's pharmacy. The nine-person team, consisting of nurses from each of the larger departments, was to meet for one hour once a week "until they found a way to substantially reduce the cycle time."

From the outset, the team was plagued with absences and late arrivals. Each absent or tardy nurse had legitimate reasons for his or her behavior. Regardless, team effectiveness suffered and the team dragged on without an end in sight.

Repeatedly, the team leader attempted to get department heads to help resolve the conflict, but their concerns were elsewhere.

Finally, the team's sponsor, a vice president, stepped up to his responsibility and convened a meeting of department heads to reaffirm their commitment and reach agreement as to how their nurses' participation would be handled. Priorities were established, resource-sharing agreements were reached, and supervisors were advised of the decisions. Project team participation now had its assigned priority and the appropriate management commitment to back it up. The team members—the nurses—were relieved of the decision as to which "master" to serve first and under what conditions.

3. TEAM STAGES

> Describe the classic stages of team evolution (forming, storming, norming, and performing). (Understand)
>
> **CQIA BoK 2006**

Teams move through four stages of growth as they develop maturity over time.[2] Each stage may vary in intensity and duration.

Stage 1: Forming

The cultural background, values, and personal agenda of each team member come together in an environment of uncertainty. New members wonder, "What will be expected of me? How do I, or can I, fit in with these people? What are we really supposed to do? What are the rules of the 'game,' and where do I find out about them?" Fear is often present but frequently denied. Fear may be about personal acceptance, possible inadequacy for the task ahead, and the consequences if the team fails its mission. These fears and other concerns manifest themselves in dysfunctional behaviors such as:

- Maneuvering for a position of status on the team
- Undercutting the ideas of others
- Degrading another member
- Trying to force one's point of view on others
- Bragging about one's academic credentials
- Vehemently objecting to any suggestion but one's own
- Abstaining from participation in discussions
- Distracting the work by injecting unwanted comments or trying to take the team off track
- Retreating to a position of complete silence

Because of the diversity of some teams, there may be a wide variety of disciplines, experience, academic levels, and cultural differences among the members. This can result in confusion, misunderstanding of terminology, and language difficulties. A technique for moving the team through this stage is to clearly state and understand the purpose of the team, identify the roles of the members, and establish criteria for acceptable behavior ("norms").

Stage 2: Storming

In this stage, team members still tend to think and act mostly as individuals. They struggle to find ways they can work together, and sometimes they belligerently resist. Each member's perspective appears to be formed from his or her own personal experience rather than based on information from the whole team. Uncertainty still exists, defenses are still up, and collaborating is not yet the accepted mode of operation. Members may be argumentative. They frequently test the leader's authority and competence. Members often try to redefine the goal and direction of the team and act as individual competitors.

Stage 3: Norming

At this stage, true teamwork begins. Members shift from dwelling on their personal agendas to addressing the objectives of the team. Competitiveness, personality clashes, and loyalty issues are sublimated, and the team moves toward willingness to cooperate and openly discuss differences of opinion. The leader focuses on process, promoting participation and team decision making, encouraging peer support, and providing feedback. A potential danger at this stage is that team members may withhold their good ideas for fear of reintroducing conflict.

Stage 4: Performing

Now the members, functioning as a mature and integrated team, understand the strengths and weaknesses of themselves and other members. The leader focuses on monitoring and feedback, letting the team take responsibility for solving problems and making decisions. The team has become satisfied with its processes and is comfortable with its working relationships and its resolution of team problems. The team is achieving its goals and objectives. However, reaching this stage does not guarantee smooth waters indefinitely.

Typically, a team moves through these four stages in sequence. However, a team may regress to an earlier stage when something disturbs its growth. The addition of a new member may take a team back to stage 1 as the new member tries to become accepted and the existing team members "test" the newcomer. Loss of a respected member may shift the apparent balance of power so that the team reverts to stage 2. A change in scope or the threat of the cancellation of a team's project may divert the team to an earlier stage to redefine direction. Exposure of an individual team member's manipulation of the team can cause anger, retrenchment to silence, or a push to reject the offending member, along with a jump back to stage 1.

Some teams find difficulty in sustaining stage 4 and oscillate between stages 3 and 4. This may be a matter of inept team leadership, unsupportive sponsorship, less-than-competent team members, external factors that threaten the life of the team's project, or a host of other factors.

Big Risk, an insurer of off-road construction and pleasure vehicles, has a strategic plan to reduce administrative expenses by 30 percent over the next three years. In support of this goal, the vice president of administration sponsors a project: a claim-processing team (CPT) to reduce the claim-processing cycle time (mission) from three weeks to four days within one year. A team leader is selected. She gathers data and estimates savings of $250,000 per year and an estimated project cost of $25,000.

The CPT members are selected from functions affected by any potential change. A facilitator is retained to conduct team-building training and to guide the team through its formative stages until it reaches a smooth-functioning level of maturity. The CPT prepares a project plan, including monthly measurement of progress, time usage, and costs. The vice president of administration (sponsor) approves the plan. The CPT fine-tunes its objectives, determines ground rules, and allocates the tasks to be performed. The project is launched.

The CPT reviews its progress weekly, making any necessary adjustments. The CPT presents a monthly summary review to the vice president of administration, giving the status of time usage, costs, and overall progress toward the goal. Any problems requiring the vice president's intervention or approval are discussed (such as the need for more cooperation from the manager of field claims adjusters or the need to contract for the services of a computer systems consultant).

The CPT completes the process reengineering and successfully implements the changes. A formal report and presentation are presented to the senior management. The outcomes of the CPT are publicized (recognition). The CPT is disbanded.

4. TEAM BARRIERS

> Understand the value of conflict, know how to resolve team conflict, define and recognize groupthink and how to overcome it, understand how poor logistics and agendas as well as lack of training become barriers to a team. (Analyze)
>
> **CQIA BoK 2006**

Conflict among team members can occur at any of the stages but is more likely to surface during the "forming" and "storming" stages. Conflict can, and does, occur in cooperative as well as competitive relationships. It is a part of human life. Conflict is inevitable—make it work for the team.

Authors Schmidt and Tannenbaum list five stages of the evolution of conflict:[3]

1. Anticipation
2. Conscious but unexpressed difference
3. Discussion
4. Open dispute
5. Open conflict

The team leader, with guidance from a facilitator, if needed, can help transform a conflict into a problem-solving event by:

- Welcoming differences among team members
- Listening attentively with understanding rather than evaluation
- Helping to clarify the nature of the conflict
- Acknowledging and accepting the feelings of the individuals involved
- Indicating who will make the final decision
- Offering process and ground-rule suggestions for resolving the differences
- Paying attention to sustaining relationships between the disputants
- Creating appropriate means for communication between the persons involved in the conflict

A commonly used instrument for assessing individual behavior in conflict situations is the Thomas-Kilmann Conflict Mode Instrument.[4] This instrument assesses behavior on two dimensions: assertiveness and cooperativeness. These dimensions are then used to define three specific methods for dealing with conflicts: avoiding–accommodating, competing–collaborating, and compromising.

"Conflict is common and useful. It is a sign of change and movement. Conflict is neither good nor bad. The effort should not be to eliminate conflict but to refocus it as a productive rather than destructive force. Conflict can be a vital, energizing force at work in any team."[5] Therefore, if conflict is approached as an opportunity to learn and move forward it really isn't a barrier, it's more an enabler.

Active listening is a key attribute for team leaders in managing conflict. Active listening is used to:

- Reduce defensiveness
- Help others feel understood
- Defuse emotional situations
- Build rapport and trust
- Help to focus energy on problem solving

Active listening involves two steps:

1. Accept what the individual is saying (which does not imply agreement) and his or her right to say it

2. Offer your understanding of both the content of what was said and the feelings you observe and hear, giving no unsolicited advice

Groupthink

In the team-selection process, as well as when the team is functioning day-to-day, care must be taken to avoid groupthink. Groupthink occurs when most or all of the team members coalesce in support of an idea or a decision that hasn't been fully explored, or one on which some members secretly disagree. The members are more concerned with maintaining friendly relations and avoiding conflict than in becoming engrossed in a controversial discussion.

Actions to forestall groupthink may include:

- Brainstorming alternatives before selecting an approach

- Encouraging members to express their concerns

- Ensuring that ample time is given to surface, examine, and comprehend all ideas and suggestions

- Developing rules for examining each alternative

- Appointing an "objector" to challenge proposed actions

Other Barriers

- *Logistics* is defined as a process involving planning, implementing, and controlling an efficient, cost-effective flow and storage of raw materials, in-process inventory, finished goods, and related information from point of origin to point of consumption for the purpose of conforming to customer requirements.[6] Breakdowns in the planning and implementing phases can substantially and negatively impact the work of a team. For example:

  HandiWare, a manufacturer of household tools designed especially for women, has assembled its first team to design, procure, and install an exhibit at an upcoming home show. The team completes the exhibit design on schedule, procures the needed materials to assemble the exhibit, and arranges for the shipping to and erection of the exhibit at the site—all on schedule.

  The HandiWare salespeople arrive at the site to set up, but the exhibit does not. Phone calls and e-mails finally confirm the exhibit is on a truck four states away and heading even farther away. The sales team cobbles together a makeshift exhibit that fails to portray the quality products they wish the consumers to buy.

  A postexhibition lessons learned debriefing concludes that:

  - *No risk assessment had been done*
  - *No contingency plans were made based on potential scenarios*
  - *No exhibition-savvy person was involved in the planning*
  - *No attempt had been made to query other, more experienced exhibitors*
  - *No representative of the HandiWare exhibition team had been invited to sit in on the design team*
  - *The exhibit design was beautifully and cost-effectively designed, and was never used*

- Agendas (hidden and otherwise) are another common barrier. If a team member is hiding a purpose for participating that conflicts with the mission and objectives of the team, it can result in a dysfunctional team. Such hidden agendas may be politically motivated or motivated for self-gain.

  Also, a member who continually disrupts the work of the team with behavior that is offensive to other members can cause rebuffs, resentment, and/or retaliation. Some such people seek to:

  - Get personal attention
  - Gain control of the team
  - Disrespect the team leadership
  - Take the team "off-track"
  - Destroy the team environment

  It is vital that the team leaders, perhaps with assistance from the facilitator, deal with these agendas as soon as detected. Best scenario: a brief, straight-to-the-point talk with the individual, away from the team, resulting in a positive behavior change. Worst scenario: the person becomes belligerent, resists attempts to correct the disruptive behavior, and requires disciplinary action, even removal from the team.

- Lack of training is yet another common barrier. Lack of the "soft" or interpersonal skills as well as lack of skills in the use of appropriate tools can impede a team's progress. Unless team members have had previous experience on teams, it is wise to provide training on teamwork and team dynamics. A team should strive to move through the stages of team development in as effective a way as possible. It usually pays to spend the effort, time, and expense to carefully train the team members for the roles they will be asked to fulfill.

With most adults, just-in-time training works well. This means that skill training takes place immediately before the trainee will use the skill.

5. DECISION MAKING

> Understand and apply different decision models (voting, consensus, etc.) (Apply)
>
> **CQIA BoK 2006**

Definitions

Decision making is a process for analyzing pertinent data to make the optimum choice. *Decisiveness* is the skill of selecting a decision and carrying it through.

> *Some readers, fans of the Star Trek television program, may recall the decision process of the captain of the Starship Enterprise. He considered the input (data and a recommendation) from his subordinate officers, made a decision, and ordered: "Make it so."*

The Decision Making Process

1. Clearly state the decision purpose

2. Establish the criteria (basis for decision and results required)

3. Assess criteria for those criterions that would be acceptable and measurable (identify the desirable criteria in order of priority)

4. Create a list of alternatives to consider, and collect data about each

5. Assess the alternatives (relate each alternative solution back to the criteria and eliminate those that are unacceptable, weigh and prioritize remaining alternatives)

6. Conduct a risk analysis of the remaining alternatives (what could go wrong?)

7. Assess the risks (probability and seriousness of impact)

8. Make the decision (a decision with manageable and acceptable risk)

Decision Making Styles

- Top-down (The boss makes the decisions.)

- Consultative (Top-level people solicit input from lower levels.)

- Proactive consultative (Lower-level people propose ideas and potential decisions to the top level for final decision.)

- Consensus (Intelligence and alternatives are widely discussed in the team. When everyone agrees they can support a single decision, without opposition, it is considered final.)

- Delegation

  - Delegation with possible veto (Top-level retains right to reject decision made at a lower level.)

  - Delegation with guidelines (Lower levels may make decisions within established constraints.)

  - Total delegation (Lower levels are free to make decisions however they wish.)

- Voting (Each team member has a vote. Each member stating his or her rationale for his or her vote may expand this method. Voting is acceptable for fairly unimportant decisions. It is fast but lacks the rigor necessary for critical and more complex decisions.)

Attributes of a Good Decision

The decision:

- Represents the optimum in operational feasibility

- Involves a minimum of undesirable side effects and trade-offs

- Is technically free from flaws

- Delineates specific action commitments

- Is within the capacity of the affected people to comprehend and execute

- Is acceptable to those involved

- Is supportable with the resources that can be made available

- Includes provision for alignment, audit, and measurement

Considerations

- Fact-finding is often confused with decision making. Technical questions can be answered with a "yes or no" or a "Go or no go" decision. There are no alternatives; the answer is right or wrong.

- Decision making is selecting the most effective action from among less favorable actions.

- Decisions can be no better than the intelligence supporting them.

- Determine the dollar value of decision-making intelligence and then determine what a better decision is worth.

- Decision making is a process rather than a single act.

- Good team leaders don't make decisions; they manage decision makers and decision making.

- No team leader in today's world knows enough to make major decisions without help from others.

- Good decision makers hold off decisions until they are needed, but they do think about decisions they will make, and they don't delay the gathering of intelligence.

- A decision made today may be totally inappropriate in tomorrow's changed environment.

Notes

1. Westcott, Russell T. *Simplified project management for the quality professional.* (Milwaukee, WI: ASQ Quality Press, 2005), pp. 79–81.
2. Defined by Tuckman, B. W. Developmental sequence in small groups. *Psychological Bulletin 63*, no. 6 (November–December, 1965): 384–99.
3. Schmidt, W., and R. Tannenbaum. Management of differences. *Harvard Business Review* (November–December 1960).
4. Thomas, Kenneth W., and Ralph H. Kilmann. *Thomas-Kilmann conflict mode instrument.* (Tuxedo, NY: XICOM Inc.).
5. Beecroft, G. Dennis, Grace L. Duffy, and John W. Moran, eds. *The executive guide to improvement and change.* (Milwaukee, WI: ASQ Quality Press, 2003).
6. Adapted from the Council of Logistics Management.

Additional Resources

Bauer, Robert W., and Sandra S. Bauer. *The team effectiveness survey workbook.* (Milwaukee, WI: ASQ Quality Press, 2005).

Beecroft, G. Dennis, Grace L. Duffy, and John W. Moran, eds. *The executive guide to improvement and change.* (Milwaukee, WI: ASQ Quality Press, 2003).

Bens, Ingrid, M., ed. *Facilitation at a glance!* (Salem, NH: GOAL/QPC, 1999).

Dreo, Herb, Pat Kunkel, and Thomas Mitchell. *The virtual teams guidebook for managers.* (Milwaukee, WI: ASQ Quality Press, 2003).

Evans, J. R., and W. M. Lindsay. *The management and control of quality.* (5th ed.). (Cincinnati: South-Western College Publishing, 2002).

GOAL/QPC and Joiner Associates. *The team memory jogger.* (Salem, NH: GOAL/QPC, 1995).

Hartzler, Meg, and Jane E. Henry. *Team fitness: A how-to manual for building a winning work team.* (Milwaukee, WI: ASQ Quality Press, 1994).

Hicks, R. F., and D. Bone. *Self-managing teams.* (Los Altos, CA: Crisp Publications, 1990).

Hitchcock, D. *The work redesign team handbook: A step-by-step guide to creating self-directed teams.* (White Plains, NY: Quality Resources, 1994).

Juran, J. M., and A. B. Godfrey, eds. *Juran's quality handbook* (5th ed.). (New York: McGraw-Hill, 1999).

McDermott, Lynda C., Nolan Brawley, and William W. Waite. *World class teams: Working across borders.* (New York: John Wiley & Sons, 1998).

Parker, Glenn M. *Cross-functional teams: Working with allies, enemies & other strangers.* (San Francisco: Jossey-Bass Publishers, 1994).

Plunkett, Lorne C., and Guy A. Hale. *The proactive manager: The complete book of problem solving and decision making.* (New York: John Wiley & Sons Inc., 1982).

Scholtes, Peter R., Brian L. Joiner, and Barbara J. Streibel. *The team handbook* (3rd ed.). (Madison, WI: Joiner Associates, 2003).

Westcott, Russell T. *Simplified project management for the quality professional.* (Milwaukee, WI: ASQ Quality Press, 2005).

Westcott, Russell T., ed. *The certified manager of quality/organizational excellence handbook* (3rd ed.). (Milwaukee, WI : ASQ Quality Press, 2006).

Part III
Continuous Improvement

Quality improvement must be included in the corporate yearly strategy.

H. James Harrington (IBM)

If you think you are going to be successful running your business in the next 10 years the way you [did] in the last 10 years, you're out of your mind. To succeed, we have to disturb the present.

Roberto Goizueta (Coca-Cola)

Even if accurate data are available, they will be meaningless if they are not used correctly. The skill with which a company collects and uses data can make the difference between success and failure.

Masaaki Imai, *Kaizen: The Key to Japan's Competitive Success*

The largest room in the world is room for improvement.

Anonymous

You can observe a lot by watching.

Yogi Berra

Chapter 6

A. Incremental and Breakthrough Improvement

> Understand how process improvement can
> identify waste and non-value-added
> activities. Understand how both
> incremental and breakthrough
> improvement processes achieve results.
> Know the steps required for both types of
> improvement. Recognize which type of
> improvement approach is being used in
> specific situations. Know the similarities
> and differences between the two
> approaches. (Understand)
>
> **CQIA BoK 2006**

There are two fundamental philosophies relative to improvement. Improvement may be achieved on a gradual basis, taking one small step at a time. A dramatically different concept is practiced by proponents of breakthrough improvement, a "throw out the old and start anew" approach frequently referred to as *process reengineering*. Both approaches have proven to be effective depending on the circumstances, such as the size of the organization, the degree of urgency for change, the degree of acceptability within the organization's culture, the receptivity to the relative risks involved, the ability to absorb implementation costs, and the availability of competent people to effect the change.

INCREMENTAL IMPROVEMENT

For example:

> Assume that a team is formed in the order fulfillment department of a magazine publisher to find ways to reduce the processing time for new subscriptions. The team will likely be seeking small steps it can take to improve the processing time. When a change is implemented and an improvement is confirmed, the team may meet again to see whether it can make further time reductions.

This approach of incremental improvement may be in use throughout an organization.

Masaaki Imai made popular the practice of *kaizen*,[1] a strategy for making improvements in quality in all business areas. Kaizen focuses on implementing small, gradual changes over a long time period. When the strategy is fully utilized, everyone in the organization participates. Kaizen is driven by a basic belief that when quality becomes ingrained in the organization's people, the quality of products and services will follow. Key factors are the initiation of operating practices that lead to the uncovering of waste and non-value-added steps, the total involvement of everyone in the organization, extensive training in the concepts and tools for improvement, and a management that views improvement as an integral part of the organization's strategy. In a serious problem situation, an intensified approach may be used, called *kaizen blitz*. For example:

> MedElec, a manufacturer of switches used in medical diagnostic equipment, was faced with the potential of losing its six largest customers. The threat, due to mounting numbers of missed delivery dates, caused significant delays in the entire supply chain. Employing a facilitator, MedElec initiated a five-day kaizen blitz, with representatives from every department and management. The objective of the session was to find and implement ways to not only shorten the delivery cycle but also prevent any future late deliveries. Ultimately, the goal was to initiate an unconditional guarantee policy for on-time shipments to the company's customers.
>
> Following extensive training, the team members gathered and analyzed performance data, pinpointed the root causes of delays, and prioritized the problem areas. Then they systematically addressed each problem in order of priority, first dealing with those problems for which solutions could be immediately implemented. For each solution, a careful review ensured that no additional problems would be created once the solution was initiated. The team then took the solutions back to their work areas and began implementation of the changes.

The following steps, which follow a Plan—Do—Check—Act sequence, are typically taken in incremental improvement:

1. Select the process or subprocess to be process-mapped

2. Define the process

   a. Inputs to the process, including suppliers

   b. Outputs from the process

    c. Users/customers to whom outputs are directed

    d. Requirements of users/customers

    e. Constraints (such as standards, regulations, and policies)

3. Map out the principal flow (the main flow without exceptions)

4. Add the decision points and alternative paths

5. Add the check/inspection points and alternative paths

6. Analyze the process flow to identify:

    a. Non-value-added steps

    b. Redundancies

    c. Bottlenecks

    d. Inefficiencies

    e. Deficiencies

7. Prioritize problems:

    a. Quantify the results of each problem

    b. Identify the impact each problem has on the overall process

    c. Subject the problems to Pareto analysis and identify the most important problem

8. Redo the map to remove a primary problem

9. Do a desktop "walk-through" with persons who are involved with the process

10. Modify the process map as needed (and modifications will be needed!)

11. Review changes and obtain approvals

12. Institute changes

13. Review results of changes

14. Make needed changes to documented procedures

15. Repeat the process for the next-most-important problem area

The individuals responsible for the process may make incremental improvements. However, depending on organizational policies and procedures, appropriate approvals may be required. Also, there should be concern for interactions with other processes that take place before and after the process being changed. More typically, a team from the work group involved initiates incremental changes. If the organization has a suggestion system in place, care must be taken to ensure that conflict of interest does not result.

BREAKTHROUGH IMPROVEMENT

Taken to its extreme, breakthrough improvement may encompass totally reengineering an entire organization.[2] This usually means literally ignoring how the organization is structured and how it currently produces and delivers its products and services. It's a "start from a clean sheet of paper" approach. The subject of much criticism and a number of notable failures, this approach has gained an unsavory reputation. Unfortunately, many organizations have grabbed at this approach as a way to drastically cut costs, most significantly by reducing the number of their employees.

In these organizations with a quest to cut back (on everything), the basic tenets of the reengineering approach were either ignored or sublimated. A few of the most important factors to be considered include the need for:

- Careful understanding of the organization's culture and management's commitment to change (especially when positions are threatened)

- A well-communicated policy and plan for the disposition of people displaced by the changes

- A well-communicated plan for the transition (for example, whether the changes just mean more work for the employees left behind)

- Means for dealing with the psychological trauma inherent in downsizing (such as the guilt felt about being a survivor, the loss of friends, and the anger of terminated or transferred employees)

- Means for addressing the potential for sabotage, intentional or unintentional (such as lethargy, loss of interest in the job, retaliation, a careless attitude, and so forth)

Given the small number of real successes in totally reengineering an entire company all at once, a more limited approach has emerged, typically called *process reengineering*. Using process reengineering, a team examines a given process, such as complaint handling. It may take a macro look at how complaints are now handled, just to gain a sense of the situation. Then, starting with a clean sheet of paper (and perhaps based on information gained from benchmarking), the members of the team devise a new (and hopefully better) process approach without resorting to how the present process operates. The resultant process design is a *breakthrough*. Achievement of the breakthrough presumes that the team participants are able to shed their biases and their ingrained notions of how things have always been done. For example:

> *State University realizes that its student enrollment process is cumbersome to administer and frustrating for new students. A cross-functional process improvement team is formed with a charter to "completely overhaul" the enrollment process.*
>
> *The team members undergo training in the concepts of process reengineering and the tools they may need. Up front, they identify the primary*

subprocesses that must be considered: student applications (review, selection, and notification), payment processing, student loans, new student orientation, class assignments, dormitory assignments, special requirements (security issues, dietary needs, and disability accommodations), document completion, data entry, data processing, and report preparation. They then generate a macro-level process flowchart showing the interaction of these subprocesses. A brainstorming session, followed by a multivoting activity, uncovers a host of ideas on how some of the subprocesses can be improved and a priority for addressing the ideas and how the ideas can be prioritized. As the team progresses, it becomes apparent that almost all of the data required to initiate student enrollment can be captured on a single document prepared by the expectant enrollee in machine-readable format. From this document, students selected for enrollment can be sent a bar-coded identification card that can be used throughout the enrollment process and subsequently for ongoing transactions throughout the academic year. Upon arrival on enrollment day, the student presents the bar-coded card to a computer terminal that generates a printout of the student's class and dormitory assignments and any special requirements. The equipment needed to handle the enrollment-day processing is "on loan" from other university processes, such as the cafeteria and the school store. This major breakthrough reduces the number of administrators needed to staff tables on enrollment day. It also eliminates the long wait times in lines and the crowding for forms and places to fill out the forms. Essentially, the only table requiring staff, assuming a well-designed system, is one to handle student requests for assignment changes.

The team drafts a process map of the new student enrollment process, in detail, and drafts an implementation plan. The plans are submitted to the appropriate officials, modifications are made as needed, and approval is obtained. The major breakthrough results in reduced processing time, greater accuracy, and substantial reduction in student complaints.

Certain generic steps are usually involved in initiating breakthrough improvements:

1. Ensure that there is a strong, committed leader supporting the initiative

2. Form a high-level, cross-functional steering committee

3. Create a macro-level process map for the entire organization

4. Select one of the major processes to be reengineered

5. Form a cross-functional reengineering team

6. Examine customers' requirements and wants in detail

7. Look at and understand the current process from the customer's perspective (its function, its performance, and critical concerns), but not in finite detail

8. Brainstorm ways to respond to customers' needs. Think outside the box

9. Create breakthrough process redesign (assuming that the process is still needed!):

   a. Design to include as few people as possible in the performance of the process

   b. Identify and question all assumptions and eliminate as many as possible

   c. Eliminate non-value-added steps

   d. Integrate steps and simplify everything possible

   e. Incorporate the advantages of information technology wherever feasible

   f. Prepare a new vision statement

   g. Plan how to communicate the new vision and news of the process redesign

   h. Determine how to achieve performers' "buy-in" of new process design

   i. Determine how to get management to see the wisdom of dismantling the old process design

   j. Determine how the inevitable displacement of people (new work procedures, job elimination, transfers, and downsizing) will be addressed

10. Test-drive the new process design with a portion of the business and with one or two customers who can be counted on for collaboration and feedback

11. Collect feedback from the selected customers, the involved employees, management, and other affected stakeholders (such as the union, suppliers, and stockholders)

12. Modify the process redesign as needed and communicate the changes

13. Plan a controlled rollout of the process redesign

14. Implement the rollout plan

15. Evaluate the effectiveness of the redesigned process continuously at every stage

    a. Assess assimilation of the changes by workforce and management

      • Individual acceptance of changes (technical and social)

      • Understanding of need for displacement of people (reassignments and terminations)

      • Changes to managerial and supervisory roles and status (redistribution of responsibilities and authority)

      • Changes to compensation, training, development, and other human support systems

b. Assess the impact of the changes on customers (for example, did the redesign accomplish what the customers needed and wanted?)

c. Assess the impact of the changes on other stakeholders (for example, did the redesign achieve its intended purpose with minimum negative consequences?)

A principal reason for improving processes is the removal of waste. Waste occurs in clearly visible form as well as hidden from sight. Following are examples of visible and invisible waste.[3]

EXAMPLES OF VISIBLE WASTE

- Out-of-spec incoming material: for example, invoice from supplier has incorrect pricing; aluminum sheets are wrong size

- Scrap: for example, holes drilled in wrong place; shoe soles improperly attached

- Downtime: for example, school bus not operating; process 4 cannot begin because of backlog at process 3

- Product rework: for example, failed electrical continuity test; customer number not coded on invoice

EXAMPLES OF INVISIBLE WASTE

- Inefficient setups: for example, jig requires frequent retightening; incoming orders not sorted correctly for data entry

- Queue times of work-in-process: for example, assembly line not balanced to eliminate bottlenecks (constraints); inefficient loading-zone protocol slows school bus unloading, causing late classes

- Unnecessary motion: for example, materials for assembly located out of easy reach; need to bring each completed order to dispatch desk

- Wait time of people and machines: for example, utility crew (three workers and truck) waiting until parked auto can be removed from work area; planes late in arriving due to inadequate scheduling of available terminal gates

- Inventory: for example, obsolete material returned from distributor's annual clean-out is placed in inventory anticipating possibility of a future sale; to take advantage of quantity discounts, a yearly supply of paper bags is ordered and stored

- Movement of material (work-in-process and finished goods): for example, in a function-oriented plant layout, work-in-process has to be moved from 15 to 950 feet to next operation; stacks of files are constantly being moved about to gain access to filing cabinets and machines

- Overproduction: for example, because customers usually order the same item again, overrun is produced to place in inventory "just in case";

"extras" are made at earlier operations in case they are needed in subsequent operations

- Engineering changes: for example, problems in production necessitate engineering changes; failure to clearly review customer requirements causes changes

- Unneeded reports: for example, a report initiated five years ago is still produced each week even though the need was eliminated four years ago; a hard-copy report duplicates information available on a computer screen

- Meetings that add no value: for example, morning "production meeting" is held each day whether or not there is a need (coffee and Danish are served); 15 people attend a staff meeting each week at which one of the two hours is used to solve a problem usually involving less than one-fifth of the attendees

- Management processes that take too long or have no value: for example, all requisitions (even for paper clips) must be signed by a manager; a "memo to file" must be prepared for every decision made between one department and another

For example:

Years ago, a division of a well-recognized conglomerate reengineered its manufacturing processes. The division built a new plant and installed all new processes. Integral to the new process design was an elaborate system for handling material to and from each workstation. In theory, the material conveyor system would allow a vast reduction in workspace heretofore taken up with buffer inventories in the old plant. Improved cycle time, inventory cost reduction, and smaller plant space were the touted advantages. Most of the responsibility for designing the handling system was delegated to the equipment supplier's engineers.

Unfortunately, the system was not well planned before the expensive handling equipment was ordered and installed. Within less than two months of operation, the plant was hopelessly mired in piles of work-in-process and buffer stocks stacked under and between machines—so much so that trailer trucks were rented to store overflowing materials in the parking lot. After six months of operation, the plant closed for a major overhaul with serious loss of business and financial impacts. Management was replaced.

The lessons learned were the need to better understand the processes, especially the constraints involved; to avoid becoming enamored with fancy new machinery and promises from suppliers; and to involve the people who will have to operate the system in the process redesign.

Notes

1. Imai, M. *Kaizen: The key to Japan's competitive success.* (New York: McGraw-Hill, 1986).
2. Popularized by M. Hammer and J. Champy in *Reengineering the corporation: A manifesto for business revolution.* (New York: HarperBusiness, 1993).
3. Adapted from *The certified manager of quality/organizational excellence handbook* (3rd ed.). (Milwaukee, WI: ASQ Quality Press, 2006).

Chapter 7

B. Improvement Cycles

> Define various improvement cycle phases
> (e.g., PDCA, PDSA) and use them
> appropriately. (Analyze)
>
> **CQIA BoK 2006**

WHAT IS AN IMPROVEMENT CYCLE?

An improvement cycle is an action or series of actions, taken as the result of an organized and planned effort, that makes a process better.[1]

WHAT IS PROCESS IMPROVEMENT?

Process improvement means making things better, not just fighting fires or managing crises. It means setting aside the customary practice of blaming people for problems or failures. It is a way of looking at how we can do our work better.

When we take a problem-solving approach or simply try to fix what's broken, we may never discover or understand the root cause of the difficulty. Trying to fix the problem frequently does not fix the process that created the problem, and efforts to "fix" things may actually make them worse.

However, when we engage in true process improvement, we seek to learn what causes things to happen in a process and to use this knowledge to reduce variation, remove activities that contribute no value to the product or service produced, and improve customer satisfaction. A team examines all of the factors affecting the process: the materials used in the process, the methods and machines used to transform the materials into a product or service, and the people who perform the work.

HOW DOES PROCESS IMPROVEMENT BENEFIT THE ORGANIZATION?

A standardized process improvement methodology allows us to look at how we perform work. When all of the major participants are involved in process improvement, they can collectively focus on eliminating waste—of money, people, materials, time, and opportunities. The ideal outcome is that jobs can be done more cheaply, more quickly, more easily, and, most important, more safely. Using total quality tools and methods reinforces teamwork. Using team members' collective knowledge, experience, and effort is a powerful approach to improving processes. Through teamwork, the whole becomes greater than the sum of its parts.

HOW DOES AN ORGANIZATION GET STARTED ON PROCESS IMPROVEMENT?

An essential first step in getting started on process improvement is having senior management make it an organizational priority. The importance of process improvement must be communicated from the top. Leaders need to foster an organizational environment in which a process improvement mentality can thrive and people are using quality-related tools and techniques on a regular basis. This information has been developed to provide teams with a step-by-step approach for their process improvement efforts. The focus is on improving a process over the long term, not just patching up procedures and work routines as problems occur. Managers need to start thinking in these terms:

- What process should we select for improvement?
- What resources are required for the improvement effort?
- Who are the right people to improve the selected process?
- What's the best way to learn about the process?
- How do we go about improving the process?
- How can we institutionalize the improved process?

WHAT IS INVOLVED IN THE BASIC PROCESS IMPROVEMENT MODEL?

The basic process improvement model is shown in Figure 7.1. The basic process improvement model has two parts:

- Steps 1 through 7 represent the process simplification part, in which the team begins process improvement activities
- Depending on the stability and capability of the process, the team may continue on to step 8 or go directly to step 14

The Plan—Do—Check—Act (PDCA) cycle, also known as the Plan—Do—Study—Act (PDSA) cycle (Figure 7.2), which consists of steps 8 through 14, flows from the process simplification segment. Using all 14 steps of the model will increase an

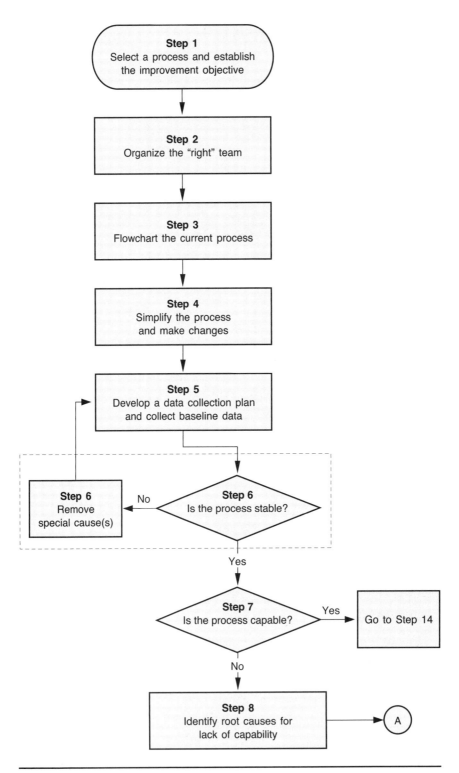

Figure 7.1 Basic process improvement model.   *Continued*

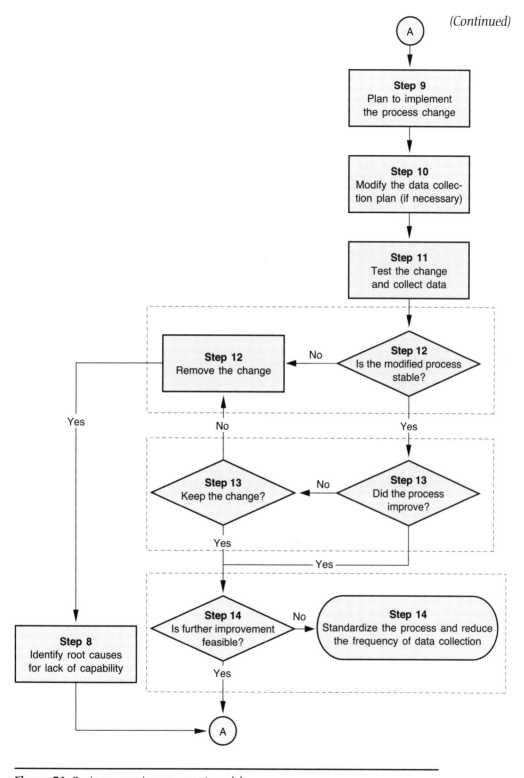

Figure 7.1 Basic process improvement model.

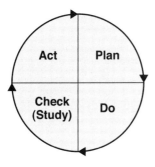

Figure 7.2 Plan–Do–Check/Study–Act cycle.

organization's process knowledge, broaden decision-making options, and enhance the likelihood of satisfactory long-term results.

PLAN

- Select project
- Define problem and aim
- Clarify/understand
- Set targets/schedules
- Inform and register the project
- Solve/come up with most suitable recommendation

DO

- Record/observe/collect data
- Examine/prioritize/analyze
- Justify/evaluate cost
- Investigate/determine most likely solutions
- Test and verify/determine cost and benefits
- Develop/test most likely causes

CHECK (STUDY)

- Consolidate ideas
- Select next project
- Seek approval from management

ACT

- Plan installation/implementation plan
- Install/implement approved project/training
- Maintain/standardize

Let's take a quick look at what's involved in each of the steps in the model.

Step 1: Select the process to be improved and establish a well-defined process improvement objective. The objective may be established by the team or may come from other interested parties, such as customers or management.

Step 2: Organize a team to improve the process. This involves selecting the "right" people to serve on the team; identifying the resources available for the improvement effort, such as people, time, money, and materials; setting reporting requirements; and determining the team's level of authority. These elements may be formalized in a written charter.

Step 3: Define the current process using a flowchart. This tool is used to generate a step-by-step map of the activities, actions, and decisions that occur between the starting and stopping points of the process.

Step 4: Simplify the process by removing redundant or unnecessary activities. People may have seen the process on paper in its entirety for the first time in step 3. This can be a real eye-opener that prepares them to take these first steps in improving the process.

Step 5: Develop a plan for collecting data and then collect baseline data. These data will be used as the yardstick for comparison later in the model. This begins the evaluation of the process against the process improvement objective established in step 1. The flowchart from step 3 helps the team determine who should collect data and where in the process data should be collected.

Step 6: Assess whether the process is stable. The team creates a control chart or run chart out of the data collected in step 5 to gain a better understanding of what is happening in the process. The follow-up actions of the team are dictated by whether special cause variation is found in the process.

Step 7: Assess whether the process is capable. The team plots a histogram to compare the data collected in step 5 against the process improvement objective established in step 1. Usually the process simplification actions in step 4 are not enough to make the process capable of meeting the objective, and the team will have to continue on to step 8 in search of root causes. Even if the data indicate that the process is meeting the objective, the team should consider whether it is feasible to improve the process further before going on to step 14.

Step 8: Identify the root causes that prevent the process from meeting the objective. The team begins the PDCA cycle here, using the cause-and-effect diagram or brainstorming tools to generate possible reasons that the process fails to meet the desired objective.

Step 9: Develop a plan for implementing a change based on the possible reasons for the process's inability to meet the objective set for it. These root causes were identified in step 8. The planned improvement involves revising the steps in the simplified flowchart created after changes were made in step 4.

Step 10: Modify the data collection plan developed in step 5, if necessary.

Step 11: Test the changed process and collect data.

Step 12: Assess whether the changed process is stable. As in step 6, the team uses a control chart or run chart to determine process stability. If the process is stable, the team can move on to step 13; if not, the team must return the process to its former state and plan another change.

Step 13: Assess whether the change improved the process. Using the data collected in step 11 and a histogram, the team determines whether the process is closer to meeting the process improvement objective established in step 1. If the objective is met, the team can progress to step 14; if not, the team must decide whether to keep or discard the change.

Step 14: Determine whether additional process improvements are feasible. The team is faced with this decision following process simplification in step 7 and again after initiating an improvement in steps 8 through 13. In step 14, the team has the choice of embarking on continuous process improvement by reentering the model at step 9 or simply monitoring the performance of the process until further improvement is indicated.

STEP 1: SELECT A PROCESS AND ESTABLISH THE PROCESS IMPROVEMENT OBJECTIVE

Selecting the Process

When an organization initially undertakes process improvement efforts, senior management may identify problem areas and nominate the first processes to be investigated. Later, processes with potential for improvement may be identified at any organizational level by any employee, with the approval of their immediate supervisor.

The following considerations are important in selecting processes for improvement:

- Total quality is predicated on understanding what is important to the customer. Every work unit, whether large or small, has both internal and external customers. Hence, the starting point in selecting a process for improvement is to obtain information from customers about their satisfaction or dissatisfaction with the products or services produced by the organization.

- It's best to start on a small scale. Once people can handle improving a simple process, they can work on more complicated ones.

- The selected process should occur often enough to be observed and documented. The team should be able to complete at least one improvement cycle within 30 to 90 days; otherwise its members may lose interest.

- The process boundaries have to be determined. These are the starting and stopping points of the process that provide the framework within which the team will conduct its process improvement efforts. As an example, the process by which an organization responds to a customer complaint call would have these boundaries:

  Starting point: The call is answered promptly and courteously.

  Stopping point: The complaint is resolved to the customer's complete satisfaction.

  It is crucial to make sure that the steps involved in meeting the process improvement objective are located inside the boundaries.

- A Pareto analysis can help the team identify one or more factors or problems that occur frequently and can be investigated by the team. This analysis would be based on some preliminary data collected by the team. After the organization members have some experience working with the basic process improvement model, processes can be selected that have been performing poorly or that offer a potentially high payback in improving organizational performance. The former category might include processes that are routinely accomplished in a less-than-satisfactory manner. The latter category includes critical processes, such as internal auditing, corrective and preventive action, and cost reductions. In each case, it's best to move from the simple to the complicated and from the better-performing to the worst-performing processes.

- A process that is primarily controlled or significantly constrained by outside factors is probably not a good candidate for improvement by the organization's personnel. Processes selected must be controlled entirely within the authority of the organization's personnel.

- Only one team should be assigned to work on each process improvement.

Establishing the Process Improvement Objective

Once a process is selected, a well-defined process improvement objective needs to be established. The definition of the objective should answer this question:

What improvement do we want to accomplish by using a process improvement methodology?

The process improvement objective is frequently discovered by listening to internal and external customers. The team can use interviews or written surveys to identify target values to use as objectives for improving the product or service produced by the process.

Identifying a problem associated with the process helps define the process improvement objective. The people working in the process can identify activities that take too long, involve too many man-hours, include redundant or unnecessary steps, or are subject to frequent breakdowns or other delays. But this is not just a problem-solving exercise; this is process improvement. Problems are symptoms of

Table 7.1 Setting objectives the S.M.A.R.T. W.A.Y.	

S	Focus on *specific* needs and opportunities
M	Establish a *measurement* for each objective
A	Be sure objectives are *achievable* as well as challenging
R	Set stretch objectives that are also *realistic*
T	Indicate a *time* frame for each objective
W	Ensure that every objective is *worth* doing
A	*Assign* responsibility for each objective
Y	Ensure that all objectives stated will *yield* desired return

Source: Reprinted with permission of R. T. Westcott & Associates.

process failure, and it is the deficiencies in the process that must be identified and corrected.

For an improvement effort to be successful, the team must start with a clear definition of what the problem is and what is expected from the process improvement. Let's look at an example:

> *The organization's internal audit activity has found only three deviations from process requirements in the last six audits. The team knows from experience that there are many day-to-day problems that should be detected by the internal audit process. The team defines the problem as "an internal audit process that is not functioning to its full potential." In beginning to formulate a process improvement objective, the initial words could be "Improve the internal audit process so it will routinely find day-to-day process deviations." A time frame, measures, and so forth, will then be added.*

A team formulating a process improvement objective may find it helpful to proceed in this way:

- Write a description of the process that starts, "The process by which we . . ."

- Specify the objective of the process improvement effort

- Follow the guidelines for setting objectives the S.M.A.R.T. W.A.Y. (see Table 7.1)

A final note: Without a stated improvement objective, the team may conduct meetings but achieve little improvement in the effectiveness, efficiency, or safety of its process. A clearly stated process improvement objective keeps the team's efforts focused on results.

STEP 2: ORGANIZE THE "RIGHT" TEAM

Team Composition

Once the process has been selected and the boundaries established, the next critical step is selecting the "right" team to work on improving it. The right team consists of a good representation of people who work inside the boundaries of the process and have an intimate knowledge of the way it works.

Team Size

Teams consisting of 5 to 7 members seem to function most effectively much of the time. Though larger teams are not uncommon, studies have shown that teams with more than 8 to 10 members may have trouble reaching consensus and achieving objectives.

Team Leader

The team leader may be chosen in any of several ways. The department head or process owner may appoint a knowledgeable individual to lead the team, or the process owner may opt to fill the position personally. Alternatively, the team members may elect the team leader from their own ranks during the first meeting. Any of these methods of selecting a leader is acceptable.

The team leader has the following responsibilities:

- Schedule and run the team's meetings.

  - Come to an understanding with the supervisor or whoever formed or chartered the team on the following:

  - The team's decision-making authority. The team may only be able to make recommendations based on its data collection and analysis efforts, or it may be able to implement and test changes without prior approval.

  - The time limit for the team to complete the improvement actions, if any.

- Determine how the team's results and recommendations will be communicated up through the organization.

- Arrange for the resources—money, material, training, additional people— that the team needs to do the job.

- Decide how much time the team will devote to process improvement. Sometimes, improving a process is important enough to require a full-time effort by team members for a short period. At other times, the improvement effort is best conducted at intervals in one- or two-hour segments.

Team Members

Team members are selected by the team leader or the individual who formed the team. Members may have various skills, pay rates, or supervisory status. Depending on the nature of the process, they may come from different departments, divisions, work centers, or offices. The key factor is that the people selected for the team should be closely involved in the process that is being improved.

Being a team member carries certain obligations. Members are responsible for carrying out all team-related work assignments, such as data collection, data analysis, presentation development, sharing of knowledge, and participation in team discussions and decisions. Ideally, when actual process workers are on a team, they approach these responsibilities as an opportunity to improve the way their jobs are done rather than as extra work. (Many of the points made in this section about teams have been further amplified in Chapters 3, 4, and 5.)

Team Charter

A *charter* is a document that describes the boundaries, expected results, and resources to be used by a process improvement team. A charter is usually provided by the individual or group who formed the team. Sometimes the process owner or the team members develop a charter. A charter is always required for a team working on a process that crosses departmental lines. A charter may not be necessary for a team that is improving a process found solely within a single work unit.

A charter should identify the following:

- The process to be improved
- Time constraints, if applicable
- The process improvement objective
- The team's decision-making authority
- The team leader
- The resources to be provided
- The team members
- Reporting requirements

Other information pertinent to the improvement effort may also be included, such as the name of the process owner, the recommended frequency of meetings, or any other elements deemed necessary by those chartering the team.

STEP 3: FLOWCHART THE CURRENT PROCESS

Before a team can improve a process, the members must understand how it works. The most useful tool for studying the current process is a flowchart. To develop an accurate flowchart, the team assigns one or more members to observe the flow of work through the process. It may be necessary for the observers to follow the flow of activity through the process several times before they can see and chart what actually occurs. This record of where actions are taken, decisions are made, inspections are performed, and approvals are required becomes the "as-is" flowchart. It may be the first accurate and complete picture of the process from beginning to end.

As the team participants start work on this first flowchart, they need to be careful to depict what is really happening in the process. They don't want to fall into the trap of flowcharting how people think the process is working, how they would like it to work, or how an instruction or manual says it should work. Only an as-is flowchart that displays the process as it is actually working today can reveal the improvements that may be needed. When teams work on processes that cross departmental lines, they will have to talk to people at all levels across the organization who are involved in or affected by the process they are working on. It is even more important to get an accurate picture of these cross-functional processes than of those whose boundaries are inside a work unit or office. The goal of this step is for the team to fully understand the process before making any attempt to change it. Changing a process before it is fully understood can cause more problems than already exist.

The team can define the current situation by answering these questions:

- Does the flowchart show exactly how things are done now?

- If not, what needs to be added or modified to make it an as-is picture of the process?

- Have the workers involved in the process contributed their knowledge of the process steps and their sequence?

- Are other members of the organization involved in the process, perhaps as customers? What do they have to say about how it really works?

- After gathering this information, is it necessary to rewrite the process improvement objective (step 1)?

STEP 4: SIMPLIFY THE PROCESS AND MAKE CHANGES

The team described the current process by developing a flowchart in step 3. Reviewing this depiction of how the process really works helps team members spot problems in the process flow. They may locate steps or decision points that are redundant. They may find that the process contains unnecessary inspections. They may discover procedures that were installed in the past in an attempt to mistake-proof the process after errors or failures were experienced. All of these consume scarce resources. Besides identifying areas where resources are being wasted, the team may find a weak link in the process that it can strengthen by adding one or more steps.

But before stepping in to make changes in the process based on this preliminary review of the as-is flowchart, the team should answer the following questions for each step of the process:

- Can this step be done in parallel with other steps, rather than in sequence?

- Does this step have to be completed before another can be started, or can two or more steps be performed at the same time?

- What would happen if this step were eliminated? Would the output of the process remain the same?

- Would the output be unacceptable because it is incomplete or has too many defects?

- Would eliminating this step achieve the process improvement objective?

- Is the step being performed by the appropriate person?

- Is the step a work-around because of poor training or a safety net inserted to prevent recurrence of a failure?

- Is the step a single repeated action, or is it part of a rework loop that can be eliminated?

- Does the step add value to the product or service produced by the process?

If the answers to these questions indicate waste, the team should consider doing away with the step. If a step or decision block can be removed without degrading the process, the team may be recovering resources that can be used elsewhere in the organization.

Eliminating redundant or unnecessary steps decreases cycle time. Only part of the time it takes to complete most processes is productive time; the rest is delay. Delay consists of waiting for someone to take action, waiting for a part to be received, and similar unproductive activities. Consequently, removing a step that causes delay reduces cycle time by decreasing the total time it takes to complete the process.

After making preliminary changes in the process, the team should create a flowchart of the simplified process. Now the team does a sanity check:

> *Can the simplified process produce products or services acceptable to customers and in compliance with applicable existing standards and regulations?*

If the answer is yes, and the team has the authority to make changes, it should institute the simplified flowchart as the new standard process. Should the team require permission to make the recommended changes, a comparison of the simplified flowchart with the original flowchart can become the centerpiece of a briefing to those in a position to grant approval.

At this point, the people working in the process must be trained using the new flowchart of the simplified process. It is vital to ensure that they understand and adhere to the new way of doing business. Otherwise, the process will rapidly revert to the way it was before the improvement team started work.

STEP 5: DEVELOP A DATA COLLECTION PLAN AND COLLECT BASELINE DATA

Steps 1 through 4 have taken the team through a process simplification phase of process improvement. In this phase, all decisions were based on experience, qualitative knowledge of the process, and perceptions of the best way to operate.

For the remaining steps in the basic process improvement model, the team will be using a more scientific approach. Steps 5 through 14 of the model rely on statistical data that, when collected and analyzed, are used to make decisions about the process. In step 5, the team develops a data collection plan.

The process improvement objective established in step 1 is based on customers' expectations and needs regarding the product or service produced by the process. When the team develops a data collection plan, it must first identify the characteristic of the product or service that has to be changed in order to meet the objective. Let's look at an example:

> *The local coffeehouse prepares coffee and sells it to patrons. The coffee is brewed in a separate urn in the kitchen, then transferred to an urn in the front of the store. Lately, customers have been complaining that the coffee is too cold when it's received.*
>
> *A team interested in improving this situation developed a process improvement objective that the coffee would be delivered to customers at a*

temperature between 109°F and 111°F. The team members then looked at their simplified flowchart to identify individual steps where measurements should be taken.

Some members of the team thought that the water temperature should be measured as it boiled prior to the actual brewing of the coffee. Others thought that such a measurement might be easy to obtain, and even interesting, but would not help them understand why cold coffee was given to customers.

The key to this segment of the model is to use process knowledge and common sense in determining where to take measurements. The team should ask: Will the data collected at this point help us decide what to do to improve the process?

The team in the example investigated the process further and opted to take temperature measurements of the coffee just after it was poured into the urn at the front of the store.

Once the team determines what data to collect—and why, how, where, and when to collect it—it has the rudiments of a data collection plan. To implement the data collection plan, the team develops a data collection sheet. This data collection sheet must include explicit directions on how and when to use it. The team should try to make it as user-friendly as possible.

The team can collect baseline data when, and only when, the data collection plan is in place, the data collection sheet has been developed, and the data collectors have been trained in the procedures to use.

STEP 6: IS THE PROCESS STABLE?

In this step, the team analyzes the baseline data collected in step 5. Two tools that are useful in this analysis are a control chart and a run chart. Both of these tools organize the data and allow the team to make sense of a mass of confusing information. They are explained in Chapter 9, Improvement Tools.

Control charts are better at revealing whether a process is stable and its future performance predictable. However, even if a team begins with the simpler run chart, it can convert the run chart to a control chart with a little extra work. These two tools are important because they help teams identify special cause variation in the process.

Whenever an individual or a team repeats a sequence of actions, there will be some variation in the process. Let's look at an example:

Think about the amount of time it took you to get up in the morning, get dressed, and leave your house for work during the past four weeks. Although the average time may have been 28 minutes, no two days were exactly the same. On one occasion it may have taken 48 minutes for you to get out of the house.

This is where a control chart or a run chart can help you analyze the data. Control charts, and to a lesser extent run charts, display variation and unusual patterns such as runs, trends, and cycles. Data that are outside the computed control limits, or unusual patterns in the graphic display of data, may be signals of the presence of special cause variation that should be investigated. In our example:

Investigation revealed that you were delayed by an early morning phone call from one of your children who is at college. The data provided a signal of special cause variation in your getting-off-to-work process.

But what if, over a period of 10 days, a series of times is recorded that averages 48 minutes? It seems that your getting-off-to-work process now includes making breakfast for your son and daughter. This is not just a variation—the data indicate that your process has changed.

Though this example portrays an obvious change in the process, subtle changes often occur without the knowledge of workers. These minor changes produce enough variation to be evident when the data are analyzed. If special cause variation is found in the process, the team is obligated to find the cause before moving on to the next step in the model. Depending on the nature of the special cause, the team may act to remove it, take note of it but take no action, or incorporate it in the process:

- When special cause variation reduces the effectiveness and efficiency of the process, the team must investigate the root cause and take action to remove it.

- If it is determined that the special cause was temporary in nature, no action may be required beyond understanding the reason for it. In the current example, the early phone call caused a variation in the data that was easily explained and required no further action.

- Occasionally, special cause variation actually signals a need for improvement in the process to bring it closer to the process improvement objective. When that happens, the team may want to incorporate the change permanently.

If the team fails to investigate a signal of special cause variation and continues with its improvement activities, the process may be neither stable nor predictable when fully implemented, thus preventing the team from achieving the process improvement objective.

STEP 7: IS THE PROCESS CAPABLE?

Once the process has been stabilized, the data collected in step 5 is used again. This time the team plots the individual data points to produce a type of bar graph called a histogram. This tool is explained in Chapter 9, Improvement Tools.

To prepare the histogram, the team superimposes the target value for the process on the bar graph. The target value was established in step 1 as the process improvement objective.

If there are upper and/or lower specification limits for the process, the team should plot them as well. (Note: Specification limits are not the same as the upper and lower control limits used in control charts.)

Once the data, the target value, and the specification limits (if applicable) are plotted, the team can determine whether the process is capable. The following questions can be used to guide the team's thinking:

- Are there any unusual patterns in the plotted data? Does the histogram have multiple tall peaks and steep valleys? This may be an indication that other processes are influencing the process the team is investigating.

- Do all of the data points fall inside the upper and lower specification limits (if applicable)? If not, the process is not capable.

- If all of the data points fall within the specification limits, are the points grouped closely enough to the target value? This is a judgment call by the team. Even when the process is capable, the team may not be satisfied with the results it produces. If that's the case, the team may elect to continue trying to improve the process by entering step 8 of the basic process improvement model.

- If there are no specification limits for the process, does the shape of the histogram approximate a bell curve? After examining the shape created by plotting the data on the histogram, the team has to decide whether the shape is satisfactory and whether the data points are close enough to the target value. These are subjective decisions. If the team is satisfied with both the shape and the clustering of data points, it can choose to standardize the simplified process or to continue through the steps of the basic process improvement model.

From here to the end of the basic process improvement model, the team will use the scientific methodology of the PDCA cycle for conducting process improvement. The team will plan a change, conduct a test and collect data, evaluate the test results to find out whether the process improved, and decide whether to standardize or continue to improve the process. The PDCA cycle is just that—a cycle. There are no limitations on how many times the team can attempt to improve the process incrementally.

STEP 8: IDENTIFY ROOT CAUSES FOR LACK OF CAPABILITY

Steps 1 through 7 of the model were concerned with gaining an understanding of the process and documenting it. In step 8, the team begins the PDCA cycle by identifying the root causes for the lack of process capability.

The data the team has looked at so far measure the output of the process. To improve the process, the team must find what causes the product or service to be unsatisfactory. The team uses a cause-and-effect diagram to identify root causes. This tool is explained in Chapter 9, Improvement Tools.

Once the team identifies possible root causes, it is important to collect data to determine how much these causes actually affect the results. People are often surprised to find that the data do not substantiate their predictions or perceptions as to root causes.

The team can use a Pareto chart to show the relative importance of the causes it has identified. This tool is explained in Chapter 9, Improvement Tools.

STEP 9: PLAN TO IMPLEMENT THE PROCESS CHANGE

Step 9 begins the "plan" phase of the PDCA cycle. Step 10 completes this phase.

After considering the possible root causes identified in step 8, the team picks one to work on. The team then develops a plan to implement a change in the process to reduce or eliminate the root cause.

The major features of the plan include changing the simplified flowchart created in step 4 and making all of the preparations required to implement the change.

The team can use the following list of questions as a guide in developing the plan:

- What steps in the process will be changed?
- Are there any risks associated with the proposed change?
- What will the change cost? (The cost includes not only money but time, number of people, materials used, customer perceptions, and other factors.)
- Which workers or customers will be affected by the change?
- Who is responsible for implementing the change?
- What has to be done to implement the change?
- Where and when will the change be implemented?
- How will the implementation be controlled?
- At what steps in the process will measurements be taken?
- How will data be collected?
- Is a small-scale test necessary prior to full implementation of the change?
- How long will the test last?
- What is the probability of success?
- Is there a downside to the proposed change?

Once the improvement plan is formulated, the team makes the planned changes in the process, if empowered by the team charter to do so. Otherwise, the team presents the improvement plan to the process owner, or other individual who formed the team, to obtain approval to proceed.

STEP 10: MODIFY THE DATA COLLECTION PLAN, IF NECESSARY

Step 10 concludes the "plan" phase of the PDCA cycle.

Reviewing and Modifying the Data Collection Plan

The data collection plan was originally developed in step 5. Because the process is going to change when the planned improvement is instituted, the team must now review the original plan to ensure that it is still capable of providing the data the team needs to assess process performance. If the determination is made that the data collection plan should be modified, the team considers the same things and applies the same methodologies as in step 5.

STEP 11: TEST THE CHANGE AND COLLECT DATA

Step 11 is the "do" phase of the PDCA cycle. If feasible, the change should be implemented on a limited basis before it is applied to the entire organization. For example, the changed process could be instituted in a single office or work center while the rest of the organization continues to use the old process. If the organization is working on a shift basis, the changed process could be tried on one shift while the other shifts continue as before. Whatever method the team applies, the goals are to prove the effectiveness of the change, avoid widespread failure, and maintain organization-wide support.

In some situations, a small-scale test is not feasible. If that is the case, the team will have to inform everyone involved of the nature and expected effects of the change and conduct training adequate to support a full-scale test.

The information that the team developed in step 9 provides the outline for the test plan. During the test, it is important to collect appropriate data so that the results of the change can be evaluated. The team will have to take the following actions in conducting the test to determine whether the change actually results in process improvement:

- Finalize the test plan

- Prepare the data collection sheets

- Train everyone involved in the test

- Distribute the data collection sheets

- Change the process and run it to test the improvement

- Collect and collate the data

STEP 12: IS THE MODIFIED PROCESS STABLE?

Steps 12 and 13 together constitute the "check" phase of the PDCA cycle.

The team has modified the process based on the improvement plan and conducted a test. During the test of the new procedure, data was collected. Now the team determines whether the expected results were achieved.

The procedures in this step are identical to those in step 6. The team uses the data it has collected to check the process for stability by preparing a control chart or run chart. Because the process has changed, it is appropriate to recompute the control limits for the control chart using the new data.

If the data collected in step 11 show that process performance is worse, the team must return to step 8 and try to improve the process again. The process must be stable before the team goes on to the next step.

STEP 13: DID THE PROCESS IMPROVE?

Step 13 completes the "check" phase of the PDCA cycle. The procedures are similar to those in step 7.

This is a good place for the team members to identify any differences between the way they planned the process improvement and the way it was executed.

The following questions will guide the team in checking the test results:

- Did the change in the process eliminate the root cause of the problem? Whether the answer is yes or no, describe what occurred.

- Are the data taken in step 11 closer to the process improvement objective than the baseline data collected in step 5? The answer indicates how much or how little the process has improved.

- Were the expected results achieved? If not, the team should analyze the data further to find out why process performance improved less than expected or even became worse.

- Were there any problems with the plan? The team needs to review the planned improvement as well as the execution of the data collection effort.

STEP 14: STANDARDIZE THE PROCESS AND REDUCE THE FREQUENCY OF DATA COLLECTION

Step 14 is the "act" phase of the PDCA cycle. In this step, the team makes some important decisions. First, the members of the team must decide whether or not to implement the change on a full-scale basis. In making this decision, they should answer the following:

- Is the process stable?

- Is the process capable?

- Do the results satisfy customers?

- Are the necessary resources available?

- Does the team have authorization?

If the answers are affirmative, the changed process can be installed as the new standard process.

Second, they must decide what to do next. Even when everything is in place for implementing and standardizing the process, the team still has to choose between two courses of action:

- *Identifying possibilities for making further process changes.* Assuming that resources are available and approval given, the team may choose to continue trying to improve the process by reentering the PDCA cycle at step 9.

- *Standardizing the changed process without further efforts to improve it.* If this decision is made, the team is still involved—documenting the changes, monitoring process performance, and institutionalizing the process improvement.

To standardize the changed process, the team initiates changes in documentation involving procedures, instructions, manuals, and other related issues. Training will have to be developed and provided to make sure everyone is using the new standard process correctly.

The team continues to use the data collection plan developed in step 11 but significantly reduces the frequency of data collection by process workers. There are no hard-and-fast rules on how often to collect data at this stage, but, as a rule of thumb, the team can try reducing collection to a quarter of what is called for in the data collection plan. The team can then adjust the frequency of measurement as necessary. The point is that enough data must be collected to enable the team to monitor the performance of the process.

The team must periodically assess whether the process remains stable and capable. To do this, the data collected in step 14 should be entered into the control chart or run chart and histogram developed in steps 12 and 13, respectively.

Whichever course of action the team pursues, it should complete one last task: documenting the lessons learned during the process improvement effort and making the information available to others.

Note

1. Much of the information in this section is adapted from the *U.S. Navy Handbook for Basic Process Improvement*. Department of the Navy, Total Quality Leadership Office, Arlington, VA 22202-4016. (1996).

Chapter 8

C. Problem-Solving Process

Apply the basic problem solving steps:
understand the problem, determine the
root cause, develop/implement solutions
and verify effectiveness. (Apply)

CQIA BoK

WHY?

There is a difference between "fixing" a problem and "solving" a problem. Fixing the problem, though it may be necessary to provide immediate relief, does not guarantee the problem will not recur. Injecting a medicine to relieve a symptom does not imply that the underlying cause has been cured. Of course, many everyday problems can be easily fixed without taking elaborate steps; for example, squirting oil on a squeaky door-hinge will fix that problem. In time, of course, the hinge may dry out and squeak again.

More complex problems fall into two broad categories: a problem related to a deficiency or failure of some kind (a sensor failed to signal an error) and a problem of discovering something new (seeking a drug that will cure a rare disease). This chapter will deal with the former type of problem—instances where a nonconformance has occurred and the true or root cause is not immediately obvious.

If you always do what you have always done, you will always get what you always got.

PROBLEM-SOLVING MODEL

In addition to the simple model suggested by the chapter-opening BoK, numerous models exist for problem solving, each with a series of steps; some are very simple and others are more complex. A seven-step model is shown in Figure 8.1 and described as follows:

1. Understand and define the problem

2. Collect, analyze, and prioritize data about the problem symptoms; determine the root cause(s) of the most significant symptoms

3. Identify possible solutions

4. Select the best solution

5. Develop an action plan

6. Implement the solution

7. Evaluate the effectiveness of the solution in solving the problem

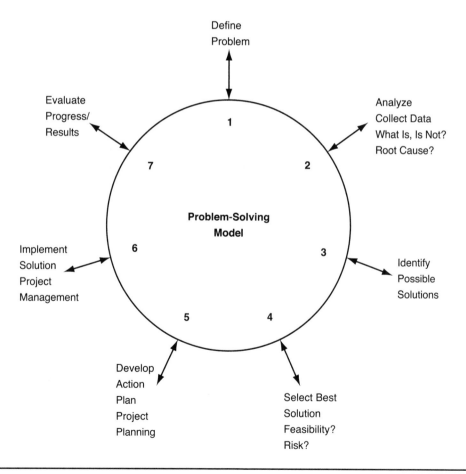

Figure 8.1   Problem–solving model.

1. Define the Problem

It is usually relatively simple to list the symptoms of a problem. Unfortunately, identifying the symptoms is often where problem analysis stops and selecting a solution takes over. The result can be missing the real cause, the *root cause*, and applying an inappropriate solution. The outcome can be that the problem was never solved and thus resurfaces again later, or in a worst-case scenario, the patient dies as a result of the problem.

> *For there are few things as useless if not as dangerous—As the right answer to the wrong question.*
>
> Peter E. Ducker, *The Practice of Management*

Realize that not all problems require a multistep process to resolve. If your morning newspaper is not lying in your driveway, as it usually is, you call the newspaper distribution office and they rush the paper to you. No need for you to analyze why the carrier missed the delivery. It's missing, you call, and it's delivered. Annoying, yes, but not a complex problem.

Useful questions to ask in explaining the problem are:

- What "it" is—what are we trying to explain?
- Where was "it" observed?
- Is "it" a real or assumed problem?
- How did "it" become a problem?
- When did "it" occur?
- Has "it" been a problem before, how long ago, and what was done at the time?
- Is "it" a technical or nontechnical problem?
- What is unsatisfactory about the present situation?
- What are the observed symptoms? How often do these symptoms occur?
- What could have occurred, but didn't?
- Who or what is impacted/affected by the present situation?
- How widely spread is the problem?
- How serious is the problem according to those affected?
- What previous actions have already been taken to solve this occurrence of "it"?
- Is the cause of the problem truly known or merely suspect?

Additional ways to redefine the problem may be assisted by:

- Reversing the problem (turn it around, look at "it" from upside down, back to front) to get a different perspective
- Breaking a set (does "it" occur in the whole product line, or just in certain products?)

Using information from these questions, develop a written problem statement and the desired results. State why the problem is important to solve.

2. Analyze and Find the Root Cause

> *I keep six honest serving men*
> *(They taught me all I know);*
> *Their names are What and Why and When*
> *And How and Where and Who.*

> **Rudyard Kipling**

A symptom is an observable phenomenon arising from and accompanying a defect.

A cause is an identified reason for the presence of a defect or problem.

Collect data to help identify potential causes. Some of the techniques and tools that are useful include:

- Brainstorming (Chapter 9)
- Cause-and-effect diagram (Chapter 9)
- Force-field diagram (Chapter 9)
- Flowchart (Chapter 9)
- "What is, what is not" chart [1]

Identify the most likely causes. Useful tools include:

- "Five Whys" (don't stop at five if more will be better) (Chapter 9)
- Pareto chart (prioritizing the potential causes) (Chapter 9)
- Reality check (Is the problem statement still valid?)

3. Identify Possible Solutions

Create a list of possible solutions. Creativity tools that may be useful include:

- Brainstorming (Chapter 9)
- Mind mapping [2]
- Analogies[3]

4. Select the Best Solution

Reduce the number of alternatives from which to choose in three substeps:

- Use a paired-choice decision matrix to identify a small number of best solutions.
- Subject each of the two to five selections made in the previous substep to:
  - Feasibility analysis (Do we have the resources to pursue this solution? Does this solution fit the organization's strategy? etc.)

- Risk analysis (What is the organization's exposure to risk if this solution is chosen?)

- Develop final selection criteria (up to six) and assign weights to criteria ("1"—low, "5"—highest). Apply weights to each criterion within each solution alternative. The solution having the highest total weight is the choice.

5. Develop the Action Plan

In all but very simple solutions, a project to implement the solution must be planned and managed. Figures 8.2a and 8.2b provide a sample form for action planning. A more complex problem solution may require more sophisticated project management methodology and tools.

6. Implement Solution

Follow the plan.

7. Track and Measure Progress, Evaluate Results

Track the progress of the solution implementation against the action plan implementation schedule. Make necessary adjustments to achieve the solution objectives.

Evaluate accomplishment of outputs at completion of implementation. Evaluate outcomes of the solution after an appropriate period of time has elapsed. Ask:

- Has the problem been successfully eliminated?

- Is the process in which the problem occurred now stable?

- Has the solution produced a positive payback?

- Have all the steps been taken to ensure the problem will not recur?

- Have other processes where a similar problem might occur been examined and has preventive action been taken?

- Have the lessons learned from experience with this problem been documented and made accessible for future training and problem-solving use?

ADDITIONAL CONSIDERATIONS IN DEALING WITH PEOPLE PERFORMANCE PROBLEMS

- Does the performer have time to do the job well? (The job may need to be redesigned or the work better organized so the worker is not overburdened. Fix the job, not the worker.)

- Does the performer know what is supposed to be done? (Provide instruction and performance feedback.)

- Has the performer ever done the job correctly? (Refresh instruction and provide performance feedback.)

ACTION PLAN

Problem addressed:	Plan No.:	
	Date Initiated:	
	Date Needed:	
	Approval:	
	Team (L):	
Solution description:	Team:	

Major Outcomes/Objectives Desired/Required:

Scope (Where will the solution/implementation be applied? What limitations?):

By what criteria/measures will completion and success of project be measured?

Assumptions made, which may impact project (resources, circumstances outside this project):

Describe the overall approach to be taken:

When should the project be started to meet the date needed/wanted?

Estimate the resources required (Time and Money):

Outline the tentative major steps to be taken, a projected start and complete date for each step, and the person to be responsible for each step. (Use the back to sketch your timeline.)

Figure 8.2 a   Action Plan Form. (front)

ACTION PLAN IMPLEMENTATION SCHEDULE

Step No.	Activity/Task/Event Description	Responsi-bility	Start Date	End Date	Est. Hours	Est. Cost
					Totals →	

Figure 8.2 b   Action Plan Form. (back)

Table 8.1   Distinguishing between performance and skill/knowledge issues.

Relative to Target Population (TP)	J	T	F	C
Does TP have time to do job well?	X	X		
Does TP have proper facilities in which to work?	X			
Does TP have the proper tools to do the work?	X			
Does TP have proper procedures, instructions, job aids?	X			
Does TP know what they are supposed to do?		X	X	
Has TP ever done the job correctly?		X	X	
Could TP do the job properly if their lives depended on it?		X		X
If TP could do the job in an exemplary way, would they?				X
Are there more negative than positive consequences in doing the job?				X
Does TP know when they are not performing as supervisor expects?			X	
Do supervisors of TP have requisite knowledge/skills		X	X	X

Source: Reprinted with permission of R. T. Westcott & Associates.
J = Job Satisfaction   T = Training Solution   F = Feedback Solution   C = Consequences Solution

- Can the performer do the job if his/her life depended on it? (Change the consequences for performing the job to increase correct performance. Provide positive performance feedback.)

- Does the worker's supervisor have the requisite skills to fix the task, provide appropriate feedback and positive consequences? (If not, train the supervisor.)

Table 8.1 summarizes actions to consider. An "X" in a column indicates the focus of potential action to be taken.

A situation might involve both a knowledge/skill deficiency and a problem with the task. The task problem should be resolved first so that any training efforts are not wasted.

BENEFITS OF APPLYING A GOOD PROBLEM-SOLVING PROCESS

Some of the benefits of a well-constructed problem-solving process are:

- The right problem gets solved

- Future waste is saved because the problem does not recur

- Successful use of the problem-solving method fosters further use of the method

- It provides a basis for not only evaluating the effectiveness of the problem solution but also the effectiveness of the methodology used

DECISION MAKING

Problem solving and *decision making* are often combined in the same phrase. Though there are decisions to be made in the problem-solving process, such as how to define the problem and which solution is best, the decision-making process is generally considered distinct from problem solving. One differentiation is that decision making may be applied at three levels and time frames:

- Long-term, strategic-type decisions (3 to 5-year or longer period)
- Tactical decisions made to translate strategic decisions into functional requirements (within a year)
- Operational decisions concerning the day-to-day running of the business[4]

CONCLUSION

The inherent tendency of many managers and professionals is often to leap from an inadequate definition of a problem to selection of an inappropriate or wrong solution. Because of this there is increased emphasis needed on *root-cause analysis—the core of problem solving.*

Notes

1. Kepner, Charles H., and Benjamin B. Tregoe. *New rational manager: An updated edition for a new world.* (Princeton, NJ: Kepner-Tregoe, Inc., 1997).
2. Westcott, Russell T., ed. *The certified manager of quality/organizational excellence handbook* (3rd ed.). (Milwaukee, WI: ASQ Quality Press, 2006).
3. Ibid.
4. Beecroft, G. Dennis, Grace L. Duffy, and John W. Moran. *The Executive Guide to Improvement and Change.* (Milwaukee, WI: ASQ Quality Press, 2003).

Additional Resources

Ammerman, Max. *The root cause analysis handbook: A simplified approach to identifying, correcting, and reporting workplace errors.* (New York: Quality Resources, 1998).

Andersen, Bjørn, and Tom Fagerhaug. *Root cause analysis: Simplified tools and techniques* (2nd ed.). (Milwaukee, WI: ASQ Quality Press, 2006).

Chang, Richard Y., and P. Keith Kelly. *Step-by-step problem solving: A practical guide to ensure problems get (and stay) solved.* (Irvine, CA: Richard Chang Associates, Inc., 1993).

GOAL/QSP. *The problem solving memory jogger: Seven steps to improved processes.* (Salem, NH: GOAL/QSP, 2000).

Kempner, Charles H., and Benjamin B. Tregoe. *New rational manager: An updated edition for a new world.* (Princeton, NJ: Kepner-Tregoe, Inc., 1997).

Ritter, Diane, and Michael Brassard. *The creativity tools memory jogger: A pocket guide for creative thinking.* (Salem, NH: GOAL/QSP, 1998).

Westcott, Russell T., ed. *The certified manager of quality/organizational excellence handbook* (3rd ed.). (Milwaukee, WI: ASQ Quality Press, 2006).

Wilson, Paul F., Larry D. Dell, and Gaylord F. Anderson. *Root cause analysis: A tool for total quality management.* (Milwaukee, WI: ASQ Quality Press, 1993).

Chapter 9

D. Improvement Tools

Use, interpret, and explain flowcharts, histograms, Pareto charts, scatter diagrams, run charts, cause and effect diagrams, checklists (check sheets), affinity diagrams, cost of quality, benchmarking, brainstorming, and audits as improvement tools. Understand control chart concepts (e.g., centerlines, control limits, out-of-control conditions), and recognize when control charts should be used. (Apply)

CQIA BoK 2006

A *tool* is defined as a device used to help accomplish the purpose of a technique. Quality improvement tools are numeric and graphic devices used to help individuals and teams work with, understand, and improve processes.[1]

Walter Shewhart and W. Edwards Deming began developing the initial quality improvement tools in the 1930s and 1940s. This development resulted in better understanding of processes and led to the expansion of the use of these tools. In the 1950s, the Japanese began to learn and apply the statistical quality control tools and thinking taught by Kaoru Ishikawa, head of the Japanese Union of Scientists and Engineers (JUSE). These tools were further expanded by the Japanese in the 1960s with the introduction of the following seven (old) basic quality control tools:[2]

1. Cause-and-effect diagram (also called *fishbone diagram* and *Ishikawa diagram*)

2. Run chart

3. Scatter diagram

4. Flowchart

5. Pareto chart

6. Histogram

7. Control chart

In 1976, the Japanese Society for Quality Control Technique Development proposed the following seven new tools for quality improvement:

1. Relations diagram (interrelationship digraph)

2. Affinity diagram

3. Systematic diagram (tree diagram)

4. Matrix diagram

5. Matrix data analysis

6. Process decision program chart (PDPC)

7. Arrow diagram

At the beginning of a process improvement project, it's important to understand the current state or condition of the process. Check sheets, flowcharts, and histograms are useful for acquiring and displaying basic data for this purpose. Control charts can be used to determine whether the process is in control or not. If there is a possibility of interrelated factors, then scatter diagrams may be used to test for correlations between two sets of variables.

Once a problem has been defined using the methods described, various approaches can be used to find solutions. Of the seven basic tools, the fishbone diagram works very well for teams wishing to seek the most likely root cause for a problem. Once the causes are identified, they can be prioritized and displayed in a Pareto diagram to help in making the decision about which problem should be addressed first.

The following information describes many of the basic quality improvement tools and how they are used. The tools are discussed in alphabetical order, not in any order of preference.

AFFINITY DIAGRAM

An *affinity diagram* is a tool to facilitate consideration and organization of a group of ideas about an issue by a team through a consensus decision. The team members take turns writing each of their ideas on separate slips of paper. The team then gathers all the ideas into natural (affinity) groups; in other words, it groups the ideas in a manner that allows those with a natural relationship or relevance to be placed together in the same group or category.

An affinity diagram is used to organize verbal information into a visual pattern. An affinity diagram starts with specific ideas and helps work toward broad categories.

Affinity diagrams can help:

• Organize and give structure to a list of factors that contribute to a problem

• Identify key areas where improvement is most needed

The steps to generate an affinity diagram are as follows:

1. Identify the problem. Write the problem or issue on a blackboard or flip chart.

2. Generate ideas. Use an idea-generation technique, such as brainstorming, to identify all facets of the problem. Use index cards or sticky-back notes to record the ideas.

3. Cluster ideas, on cards or paper, into related groups. Ask, "Which other ideas are similar?" and "Is this idea somehow connected to any others?" to help group the ideas together.

4. Create an affinity card (header card) for each group with a short statement describing the entire group of ideas.

5. Attempt to group the initial affinity cards into even broader groups (clusters). Continue until the definition of an affinity cluster becomes too broad to have any meaning.

6. Complete the affinity diagram. Lay out all of the ideas and affinity cards on a single piece of paper or a blackboard. Draw borders around each of the affinity clusters. The resulting structure will provide valuable insights about the problem.

Figure 9.1 shows a completed affinity diagram after the team has completed step 6.

ARROW DIAGRAM

The *arrow diagramming* method establishes a sequenced plan and a tool for monitoring progress. It may be represented graphically by either a horizontal or vertical structure connecting the planned activities or events.

The arrow diagram method can be used to:

- Implement plans for new product development and its follow-up

- Develop product improvement plans and follow-up activities

- Establish daily plans for experimental trials and follow-up activities

- Establish daily plans for increases in production and their follow-up activities

- Synchronize the preceding plans for quality control (QC) activities

- Develop plans for a facility move and for monitoring follow-up

- Implement a periodic facility maintenance plan and its follow-up

- Analyze a manufacturing process and draw up plans for improved efficiency

- Plan and follow-up QC inspections and diagnostic tests

- Plan and follow-up QC conferences and QC circle conferences

- Plan an office move or furniture rearrangement for improved personnel communication

Causes of Typographical Errors

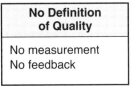

Figure 9.1 Affinity diagram.

- Establish a better process for moving a supplies request form through the office for signatures

Figure 9.2 shows the interdependencies of steps for a systems project.

AUDIT

A quality *audit* is defined as "a systematic and independent examination to determine whether quality activities and related results comply with planned arrangements and whether these arrangements are implemented effectively and are suitable to achieve objectives" (ANSI/ASQC Q10011-1-94). An audit of a quality management system is carried out to ensure that actual practices conform to the documented procedures.

There should be a schedule for carrying out audits, with different activities requiring different frequencies based on their importance to the organization. An audit should not be conducted just with the aim of revealing defects or irregularities—audits are for establishing the facts rather than finding faults. Au-

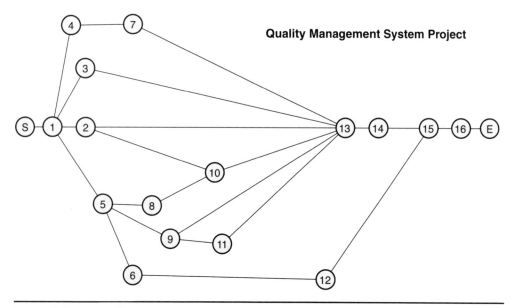

Figure 9.2 Arrow diagram.

dits do indicate necessary improvement and corrective actions, but they must also determine whether processes are effective and whether responsibilities have been correctly assigned.

The basic steps involved in conducting an audit are as follows:

1. Initiation and preparation, which includes defining the audit scope and objectives, assigning the resources (lead and support auditors), and developing an audit plan and checklists

2. Performance of the audit, which includes briefing concerned personnel and conducting the collection, evaluation, verification, and recording of information

3. Reporting, which includes developing an audit report and briefing concerned personnel on the audit results

4. Completion, which includes evaluating any corrective action taken as a result of the audit and closing out the audit process

The assessment of a quality system against a standard or set of requirements by the organization's own employees is known as a *first-party assessment* or *internal audit*.[3] If an external customer makes an assessment of a supplier, against either its own or a national or international standard, a *second-party audit* has been conducted.

An assessment by an independent organization that is not connected with any contract between the customer and supplier but is acceptable to them both is an in-dependent *third-party assessment*. The latter can result in some form of certification or registration, such as ISO 9001 certification, provided by the assessing organization.

When an organization places emphasis on process improvement and enhanc-ing customer satisfaction, the audit process becomes one of the most important process improvement tools.

BAR CHART

A *bar chart* is a graphic display of data in the form of a "bar" showing the number of units (for example, frequency) in each category. Different types of bar charts (histograms, Pareto charts, and so forth) are described in this chapter.

BENCHMARKING

Benchmarking is an evaluation technique in which an organization compares its own performance for a specific process with the "best practice" performance of a recognized leader in a comparable process. The evaluation helps the initiating organization identify shortcomings and establishes a baseline or standard against which to measure its progress in the development and maintenance of a quality assurance program.

Several different approaches to benchmarking have been described, including the following:

- Competitive—comparing with direct competitors, locally, nationally, or worldwide

- Functional—comparing with companies that have similar processes in the same function outside one's industry

- Performance—comparing pricing, technical quality, features, and other quality or performance characteristics

- Process—comparing work processes such as billing, order entry, or employee training

- Strategic—comparing how companies compete and examining winning strategies that have led to competitive advantage and market success

The basic steps involved in benchmarking are as follows:

1. Identify what is to be benchmarked. Be specific in deciding what the team wants to benchmark.

2. Decide which organizations/functions to benchmark. The comparison should be conducted not only against peers but also against recognized leading organizations with similar functions.

3. Determine the data collection method and collect data. Keep the data collection process simple. There is no one right way to benchmark. It is important to look outward, be innovative, and search for new and different ways to improve the process under study.

4. Contact a peer in the benchmark organization. Explain the purpose of the benchmarking study and what information is desired. Give assurance that confidential information will not be asked for. Proceed to inquire about the peer's organization: what they do, why they do it, how they measure and/or evaluate it and what their performance measures are, what has worked well, and what has not been successful.

5. Determine whether what the team has learned from benchmarking can be applied to improve the organization's process. Are there new and

different ways to solve the problem or improve the process? Are there other solutions to the problem that the team has overlooked? It's important to keep an open mind about new and perhaps radically different ways of doing things.

BRAINSTORMING

Brainstorming is a group process used to generate ideas in a nonjudgmental environment. Group members are presented with the issue and are asked, first, to be wide-ranging in their own thinking about the issue and, second, not to criticize the thinking of others. The purpose of the tool is to generate a large number of ideas about the issue. Team members interact to generate many ideas in a short time period.

As the goal of brainstorming is to generate ideas, make sure everyone in the group understands the importance of postponing judgment until after the brainstorming session is completed.

The basic steps involved in brainstorming are as follows:

1. Write the problem or topic on a blackboard or flip chart where all participants can see it

2. Write all ideas on the board and do as little editing as possible

3. Number each idea for future reference

4. There are several brainstorming techniques: structured brainstorming, unstructured (or free-form) brainstorming, and silent brainstorming

In *structured* brainstorming (the one-at-a-time or "round-robin" method):

- One idea is solicited from each person in sequence

- Participants who don't have an idea at the moment may say, "pass"

- A complete round of passes ends the brainstorming session

The advantage of structured brainstorming is that each person has an equal chance to participate, regardless of rank or personality. The disadvantage of structured brainstorming is that it lacks spontaneity and can sometimes feel rigid and restrictive. Encourage participation and building on the ideas of others.

In *unstructured* (or free-form) brainstorming, participants simply contribute ideas as they come to mind. The advantage of free-form brainstorming is that participants can build off each other's ideas. The atmosphere is very informal but hectic. The disadvantage of free-form brainstorming is that less assertive or lower-ranking participants may not contribute. An ideal approach is to combine these two methods. Begin the session with a few rounds of structured brainstorming and finish up with a period of unstructured brainstorming.

In *silent* (or "write-it-down") brainstorming:

- The participants write their ideas individually on sticky-back notes or small slips of paper

- The papers are collected and posted for all to see

The advantage of silent brainstorming is that it prevents individuals from making disruptive "analysis" comments during the brainstorming session and provides

confidentiality. It can help prevent a group from being unduly influenced by a single participant or common flow of ideas. The disadvantage of silent brainstorming is that the group loses the synergy that comes from an open session. Silent brainstorming is best used in combination with other brainstorming techniques.
After brainstorming:

- Reduce your list to the most important items

- Combine items that are similar

- Discuss each item in turn—on its own merits

- Eliminate items that may not apply to the original issue or topic

- Give each person one final chance to add items

There are several points to remember about brainstorming:

- Never judge ideas as they are generated. The goal of brainstorming is to generate a lot of ideas in a short time. Analysis of these ideas is a separate process, to be done later.

- Don't quit at the first lull. All brainstorming sessions reach lulls, which are uncomfortable for the participants. Research indicates that most of the best ideas occur during the last part of a session. Try to encourage the group to push through at least two or three lulls.

- Try to write down all of the ideas exactly as they are presented. When you condense an idea to one or two words for ease of recording, you are doing analysis. Analysis should be done later.

- Encourage outrageous ideas. Although these ideas may not be practical, they may start a flow of creative ideas that can be used. This can help break through a lull.

- Try to have a diverse group. Involve process owners, customers, and suppliers to obtain a diverse set of ideas from several perspectives.

CAUSE-AND-EFFECT DIAGRAM

The cause-and-effect diagram graphically illustrates the relationship between a given outcome and all the factors that influence the outcome. It is sometimes called the *Ishikawa diagram* (after its creator, Kaoru Ishikawa) or the *fishbone diagram* (due to its shape). This type of diagram displays the factors that are thought to affect a particular output or outcome in a system. The factors are often shown as groupings of related subfactors that act in concert to form the overall effect of the group. The diagram helps show the relationship of the parts (and subparts) to the whole by:

- Determining the factors that cause a positive or negative outcome (or effect)

- Focusing on a specific issue without resorting to complaints and irrelevant discussion

- Determining the root causes of a given effect

- Identifying areas where there is a lack of data

Although both individuals and teams can use the cause-and-effect diagram, it is probably most effectively used with a group of people. A typical approach is one in which the team leader draws the fishbone diagram on a blackboard, states the main problem, and asks for assistance from the group to determine the main causes, which are subsequently drawn on the board as the "main bones." The team assists by making suggestions, and eventually the entire cause-and-effect diagram is filled out. Then team discussion takes place to decide which are the most likely root causes of the problem. Figure 9.3 shows the completed diagram resulting from a team's initial effort to identify potential causes for poor photocopy quality.

The cause-and-effect diagram is used for identifying potential causes of a problem or issue in an orderly way. It can help answer questions such as "Why has membership in the organization decreased?" "Why isn't mail being answered on time?" and "Why is the shipping process suddenly producing so many defects?" It is also used for summarizing major causes into categories.

The basic steps involved in creating a cause-and-effect diagram are as follows:

1. Draw a long horizontal line with a box at the far right end of the line.

2. Indicate in the box at the far right of the diagram what effect, output, or improvement goal is being portrayed. The effect can be positive (an objective) or negative (a problem). When possible use a positive effect instead of a negative one as the effect to be discussed. Focusing on problems can produce "finger-pointing," whereas focusing on desired outcomes fosters pride and ownership over productive areas. The resulting positive atmosphere will enhance the group's creativity.

3. Draw four diagonal lines emanating from the horizontal line. Terminate each diagonal line with a box.

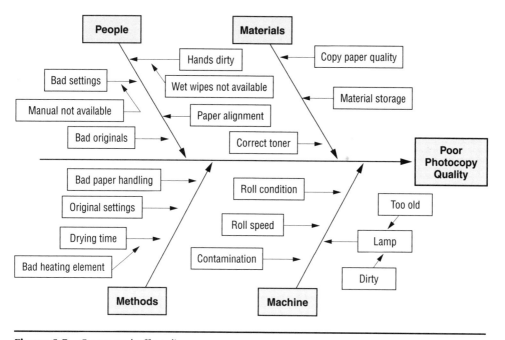

Figure 9.3   Cause-and-effect diagram.

4. Label the boxes on the diagonal lines to show the four categories of potential major causes (Men/Women, Machines, Methods, and Materials or, alternatively, Policies, Procedures, People, and Plant). The team can substitute other category names if desired.

5. On each of the four diagonal lines, draw smaller horizontal lines (smaller "bones") to represent subcategories and indicate on these lines information that is thought to be related to the cause. Draw as many lines as are needed, making sure that the information is legible. Use an idea-generating technique to identify the factors and subfactors within each major category.

6. Use the diagram as a discussion tool to better understand how to proceed with process improvement efforts. The diagram can also be used to communicate the many potential causes of quality that impact the effect/output/improvement goal. Look for factors that appear repeatedly and list them. Also, list those factors that have a significant effect, based on the data available. Keep in mind that the location of a cause in your diagram is not an indicator of its importance. A subfactor may be the root cause of all of the problems. You may also decide to collect more data on a factor that has not been previously identified.

Cause-and-effect diagrams can be used at varying levels of specificity and can be applied at a number of different times in process improvement efforts. They are very effective in summarizing and describing a process and the factors impacting the output of that process. Use this tool when it fits with a particular process improvement effort. It is possible to have a number of cause-and-effect diagrams depicting various aspects of the team's process improvement efforts.

CHECK SHEET

A *check sheet* is a form used to record the frequency of specific events during a data collection period. It is a simple form that you can use to collect data in an organized manner and easily convert it into readily useful information. The most straightforward way to use a check sheet is simply to make a list of items that you expect will appear in a process and to make a checkmark beside each item when it does appear. This type of data collection can be used for almost anything, from checking off the occurrence of particular types of defects to counting expected items (for example, the number of times the telephone rings before it is answered). Check sheets can be directly coupled to histograms to provide a direct visualization of the information collected. Figure 9.4 was used to capture the frequency of reasons for misplaced letters over a one-week period.

Various innovations in check sheets are possible. Consider, for example, using a map of the United States as a check sheet. The idea in this check sheet is for the user to simply mark on the map the location of each sale that is made. The map becomes a very effective graphic presentation of where sales are the strongest. Another name for this type of check sheet is a *measles chart*.

A check sheet may be used to:

• Collect data with minimal effort

• Convert raw data into useful information

Reasons for Misplaced Letters

Type of Defect	April 23	April 24	April 25	April 26	April 27	Total Defects
Illegible address	IIIII IIIII IIIII IIIII I	IIIII II	IIIII IIIII IIIII III	IIIII IIIII IIII	IIIII IIIII I	71
Wrong state	IIIII I	II	IIII	IIIII	IIIII	22
Wrong zip code	IIIII IIIII IIIII IIIII	IIIII	IIIII IIIII II	IIIII IIIII II	IIIII IIII	59
Bad office symbol	III	IIIII	I	III	IIII	16
Total Defects	50	19	36	34	29	168

Figure 9.4   Check sheet.

- Translate perceptions of what is happening into what is actually happening

The basic steps involved in creating a check sheet are as follows:

1. Clarify the measurement objectives. Ask questions such as "What is the problem?" "Why should data be collected?" "Who will use the information being collected?" and "Who will collect the data?"

2. Create a form for collecting data. Determine the specific things that will be measured and write them down the left side of the check sheet. Determine the time or place being measured and write this across the top of the columns.

3. Label the measure for which data will be collected.

4. Collect the data by recording each occurrence directly on the check sheet as it happens.

5. Tally the data by totaling the number of occurrences for each category being measured.

6. The data from the check sheet can be summarized in a number of ways, such as with a Pareto chart or a histogram.

CONSENSUS

Consensus is a form of group decision making in which everyone agrees with—or can at least live with—the decision. If even one person says, "I'm sorry, but I can't support this decision," then the team needs to keep working toward consensus.

Consensus can be more time consuming than deciding by simple majority, but organizations around the world have learned that the decisions that come from building consensus are generally better and, in the long run, much more effective. The most important rule in coming to consensus is honesty. A consensus decision is one that everyone on the team agrees to support. This means that no one can say later, "I never really liked that decision, so I'm not going to support it." When a consensus vote is taken, everyone votes with a show of thumbs:

- Thumbs-up means, "I like this option and I fully support it."

- Thumbs-sideways means, "I'm not thrilled with this option, but I can live with it and will support it fully."

- Thumbs-down means, "I cannot live with this option and cannot support it."

If there are a lot of thumbs-sideways votes, you may want to spend the time to find a more appealing option. If someone does not vote, take it as an automatic thumbs-down, because it is important that the entire team agrees to support the decision fully. Generally, teams should talk about consensus as a decision-making process, and people should agree that they would use it and abide by it.

CONTINUOUS QUALITY IMPROVEMENT

Continuous quality improvement (CQI) is a management approach to improving and maintaining quality that emphasizes internally driven and relatively constant (as contrasted with intermittent) assessments of potential causes of quality defects, followed by action aimed either at avoiding a decrease in quality or else correcting it in an early stage. CQI uses most if not all of the tools discussed in this chapter at some point or another.

CONTROL CHART

A *control chart* is used to measure sequential or time-related process performance and variability. The control chart is probably the best known, most useful, and most difficult-to-understand quality tool. It is a sophisticated tool of quality improvement.

A control chart is a line chart (run chart) with control limits. It is based on the work of Drs. Shewhart and Deming. Control charts are statistically based. The underlying concept is that processes have statistical variation. One must assess this variation to determine whether a process is operating between the expected boundaries or whether something has happened that has caused the process to go "out of control." Control limits are mathematically constructed at three standard deviations above and below the average. Extensive research by Dr. Shewhart indicated that 99.73 percent of common cause variation would fall within upper and lower limits established at three times the standard deviation of the process (plus and minus, respectively).

Data are collected by repeated samples and are charted. Based on the graphic presentation of the data on the control chart, one can observe variation and investigate to determine whether it is due to normal, inherent (common causes) or is produced by unique events (special causes).

A typical control chart contains a centerline that represents the average value (mean) of the quality characteristic corresponding to the in-control state. Two other horizontal lines, called the *upper control limit* (UCL) and the *lower control limit* (LCL), are also drawn. These control limits are chosen so that when the process is in control, nearly all of the sample points will fall between them. As long as the points plot within the control limits, the process is assumed to be in control, and no action is necessary. A point that plots outside of the control limits is interpreted as evidence that the process may be out of control and investigation and corrective action could be required to find and eliminate the causes responsible for this behavior. The control points are connected with straight lines for easy visualization. Even if all the points plot inside the control limits, if over several consecutive time intervals they behave in a repetitive or other nonrandom manner, then this is an indication that the process is out of control. Figure 9.5 shows points representing the variable measurement taken for each of 10 items.

Note that upper and lower control limits are not specification limits. They have a mathematical relationship to the process outputs. Specification limits are based on product or customer requirements.

There are several types of control charts, but all have the same basic structure. The two main categories of control charts are those that display attribute data and those that display variables data.

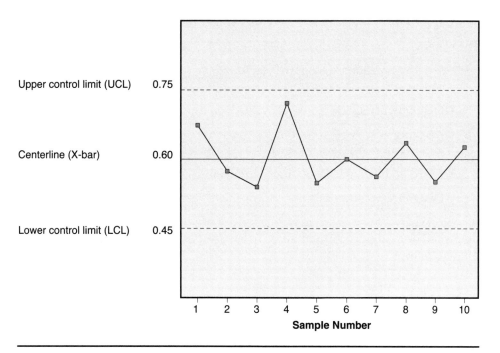

Figure 9.5 Control chart (process in control).

Attribute Data

This category of control chart displays data that result from counting the number of occurrences or items in a single category of similar items or occurrences. These "count" data may be expressed as pass/fail, yes/no, or presence/absence of a defect. Charting the proportion of failed items results in the ability to observe whether failures are in control or out of control.

Variables Data

This category of control chart displays values resulting from the measurement of a continuous variable. Examples of variables data are elapsed time, temperature, and radiation dose. Explanation of these chart types and their characteristics requires more space than is available in this publication.

Control charts may be used to:

- Display and understand variation in a process

- Help the investigator determine when actual events fall outside of specified limits of tolerance (control limits) and become "outliers" that are out of control

- Determine whether quality improvement efforts have made a statistically significant difference to a key quality indicator

- Monitor a process output (such as cost or a quality characteristic) to determine whether special causes of variation have occurred in the process

- Determine how capable the current process is of meeting specifications, if specification limits exist, and of allowing for improvements in the process

The benefits of control charts are that they:

- Help organizations recognize and understand variation and how to control it

- Help identify special causes of variation and changes in performance

- Keep organizations from trying to fix a process that is varying randomly within control limits (that is, no special causes are present)

- Assist in the diagnosis of process problems

- Determine whether process improvements are having the desired effects

A control chart may indicate an out-of-control condition either when one or more points fall beyond the control limits or when the plotted points exhibit some non-random pattern of behavior.

COST OF QUALITY

Cost of quality is a methodology that allows an organization to determine the extent to which organizational resources are used for activities that prevent poor quality, that appraise the quality of the organization's products or services, and that result from internal and external failures. Having such information allows an organization to determine the potential savings to be gained by implementing process improvements.

Quality-related activities that incur costs may be divided into prevention costs, appraisal costs, and internal and external failure costs.

Prevention costs are incurred to prevent or avoid quality problems. These costs are associated with the design, implementation, and maintenance of the quality management system. They are planned and incurred before actual operation, and they could include:

- Product or service requirements—establishment of specifications for incoming materials, processes, finished products, and services

- Quality planning—creation of plans for quality, reliability, operations, production, and inspection

- Quality assurance—creation and maintenance of the quality system

- Training—development, preparation, and maintenance of programs

Appraisal costs are associated with measuring and monitoring activities related to quality. These costs are associated with the suppliers' and customers' evaluation of purchased materials, processes, products, and services to ensure that they conform to specifications. They could include:

- Verification—checking of incoming material, process setup, and products against agreed specifications

- Quality audits—confirmation that the quality system is functioning correctly

- Supplier rating—assessment and approval of suppliers of products and services

Internal failure costs are incurred to remedy defects discovered before the product or service is delivered to the customer. These costs occur when the results of work fail to reach design quality standards and are detected before they are transferred to the customer. They could include:

- Waste—performance of unnecessary work or holding of stock as a result of errors, poor organization, or communication

- Scrap—defective product or material that cannot be repaired, used, or sold

- Rework or rectification—correction of defective material or errors

- Failure analysis—activity required to establish the causes of internal product or service failure

External failure costs are incurred to remedy defects discovered by customers. These costs occur when the products or services fail to reach design quality standards but are not detected until after transfer to the customer. They could include:

- Repairs and servicing—both of returned products and of those in the field

- Warranty claims—failed products that are replaced or services that are reperformed under a guarantee

- Complaints—all work and costs associated with handling and servicing customers' complaints

- Returns—handling and investigation of rejected or recalled products, including transport costs

The costs of doing a quality job, conducting quality improvements, and achieving goals must be carefully managed so that the long-term effect of quality on the organization is a desirable one. These costs must be a true measure of the quality effort, and they are best determined from an analysis of the costs of quality. Such an analysis provides:

- A method of assessing the effectiveness of the management of quality

- A means of determining problem areas, opportunities, savings, and action priorities

Cost of quality is also an important communication tool. Crosby demonstrated what a powerful tool it could be to raise awareness of the importance of quality. He referred to the measure as the "price of nonconformance" and argued that organizations choose to pay for poor quality. Many organizations will have true quality-related costs as high as 15 to 20 percent of their sales revenue, and effective quality improvement programs can reduce this substantially, thus making a direct contribution to profits.

To identify, understand, and reap the cost benefits of quality improvement activities, an organization should include the following fundamental steps in its approach:

- Management commitment to finding the true costs of quality

- A quality costing system to identify, report, and analyze quality-related cost

- A quality-related cost management team responsible for direction and coordination of the quality costing system

- The inclusion of quality-costing training to enable everyone to understand the financial implications of quality improvement

- The presentation of significant costs of quality to all personnel to promote the approach and identify areas for improvement

- The introduction of schemes to achieve the maximum participation of all employees

The quality cost system, once established, should become dynamic and have a positive impact on the achievement of the organization's mission, goals, and objectives.

DESIGN OF EXPERIMENTS (DOE)

Design of experiments (DOE) provides a structured way to characterize processes. A multifunctional team analyzes a process and identifies key characteristics, or factors, that most impact the quality of the end item. Using DOE, the team runs a limited number of tests, and data is collected and analyzed. The results will indicate which factors contribute the most to final quality and will also define the parameter settings for those factors. Now, rather than tweaking or tampering with the system, managers have the profound knowledge of their factory floor processes that allows them to build quality in, starting at the earliest stages of design. This allows management to determine that equitable requirement trade-offs are made between the design and manufacturing processes during development.

FIVE WHYS

The "five whys" is a simple technique for getting at the root causes of a problem by asking why after each successive response, up to five times. Asking why is a favorite technique of the Japanese for discovering the root cause (or causes) of a problem. By asking the question "Why?" a number of times (five is only an arbitrary figure), you peel away layer after layer of "symptoms" to get to the real heart of an issue. You may never know ahead of time exactly how many times you'll have to ask why.

This technique helps to:

- Identify the root cause(s) of a problem

- See how the different causes of a problem might be related

The basic steps involved in using the "five whys" technique are as follows:

1. Describe the problem in very specific terms.

2. Ask why it happens.

3. If the answer doesn't identify a root cause, ask why again. You know you've identified the root cause when asking why doesn't yield any more useful information.

4. Continue asking why until the root causes are identified. This may take more or fewer than five whys.

5. Always focus on the process aspects of a problem rather than the personalities involved. Finding scapegoats does not solve problems!

FLOWCHART

A *flowchart* is a graphic representation of the flow of a process. It is a useful way to examine how the various steps in a process relate to each other, to define the boundaries of the process, to verify and identify customer–supplier relationships in a process, to create common understanding of the process flow, to determine the current "best method" of performing the process, and to identify redundancy and unnecessary complexity.

A flowchart displays the order of activities. The rounded-rectangle symbol indicates the beginning or end of the process. Boxes indicate action items, and diamonds indicate decision points.

Flowcharts can be used to:

- Identify and communicate the steps in a work process

- Identify areas that may be the source of a problem or determine improvement opportunities

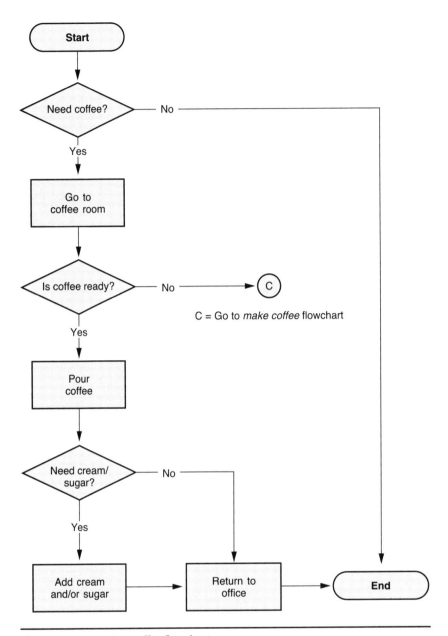

Figure 9.6   Morning coffee flowchart.

A flowchart provides the visualization of a process by the use of symbols that represent different types of actions, activities, or situations. Figure 9.6 displays a typical process flowchart that describes the simple process of getting a cup of coffee. The symbols used are connected with arrows that show the flow of information between the symbols used to represent the steps in the process.

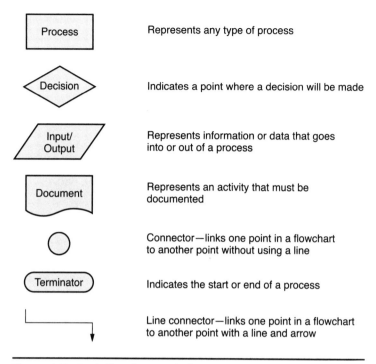

Process	Represents any type of process
Decision	Indicates a point where a decision will be made
Input/ Output	Represents information or data that goes into or out of a process
Document	Represents an activity that must be documented
	Connector—links one point in a flowchart to another point without using a line
Terminator	Indicates the start or end of a process
	Line connector—links one point in a flowchart to another point with a line and arrow

Figure 9.7   Basic flowchart symbols.

The basic steps involved in creating a flowchart are as follows:

1. Select the process to chart.

2. Determine whether to develop a high-level or detailed flowchart.

3. Define the boundaries of the selected process.

4. Identify the "start block" and place it on the top left corner of the page.

5. Identify the "finish block," or the end point, and place it on the bottom right corner of the page.

6. Try to identify the easiest and most efficient way to go from the "start block" to the "finish block." Though this step isn't absolutely necessary, it does make it easier to do the next step.

7. Document each step in sequence, starting with the first (or last) step.

8. Use the appropriate symbol for each step (see Figure 9.7).

9. Be sure to chart how the work is actually done, not how it is supposed to be done.

10. At each decision point, choose one branch and continue flowcharting that section of the process.

11. If a segment of the process is unfamiliar to everyone, make a note and continue flowcharting.

12. Repeat steps 6, 7, and 8 until that section of the process is complete. Go back and flowchart the other branches from the decision symbols.

13. Identify all the areas that hinder your process or add little or no value.

14. After the flowchart is accurate and complete, analyze it.

15. Build a new flowchart that corrects the problems you identified in the previous step.

Note: You can put the steps of your process on index cards or sticky-back notes. This lets you rearrange the diagram without erasing and redrawing and prevents ideas from being discarded simply because it's too much work to redraw the diagram.

A completed flowchart shows several useful pieces of information:

- How the process *actually* occurs

  - Encourages communication between customers and suppliers

  - Illustrates the relationship of various steps in a process

  - Educates team members about all the steps within the process

  - Can be used to train new employees involved in the process

- Who is involved in the process

  - Helps set the boundaries of the process

  - Identifies team members needed

- Where the process can be improved

  - Is useful for data collection

  - May identify immediate improvement opportunities

Failure to document the actual process is an important pitfall that should be avoided. The failure to reflect reality may result from a variety of causes:

- The process is drawn as it was designed and not as it actually happens

- Team members are reluctant to draw parts of the process that might expose weaknesses in their areas

- Rework loops are seen as small and unimportant and are overlooked

- Team members truly do not know how the process operates

Two types of flowcharts are:

- *Process flowcharts,* which use symbols to represent the input from suppliers, the sequential work activities, the decisions to be made, and the output to the stakeholder

- *Deployment flowcharts,* which show the people responsible for tasks as well as the flow of tasks in a process

Flowcharting has been around for a very long time and is used to gain vital process information by many organizations. The reason for this is obvious. A flowchart can be customized to fit any need or purpose. For this reason, flowcharts are recognized as a very valuable quality improvement method.

FOCUS GROUP

The *focus group* is a customer-oriented approach for collecting information wherein a group of participants (10–12), unfamiliar to each other, meet to discuss and share ideas about a certain issue. Focus groups are a useful qualitative analysis tool for helping to understand the beliefs and perceptions of the population represented by the group.

FORCE-FIELD ANALYSIS

Force-field analysis (FFA) is a tool that uses a creative process for encouraging agreement about all facets of a desired change. It is used for clarifying and strengthening the "driving forces" for change (for example, what things are "driving" us toward school improvement?). It can also be used to identify obstacles, or "restraining forces," to change (for example, what is "restraining" us from achieving increased test scores?). Finally, it can be used for encouraging agreement on the relative priority of factors on each side of the balance sheet.

The basic steps involved in force-field analysis are:

1. Discuss and come to agreement with a group (usually five to seven people) on the current situation and the goal

2. Write this situation on a flip chart

3. Brainstorm the "driving" and "restraining" forces

4. Driving forces are things (actions, skills, equipment, procedures, culture, people, and so forth) that help move toward the goal

5. Restraining forces are things that can inhibit reaching the goal

6. Prioritize the driving and restraining forces

7. Discuss action strategies to eliminate the restraining forces and to capitalize on the driving forces

To create an FFA diagram, start by drawing a large letter T on a piece of paper. Write the issue at hand at the top of the paper (see Figure 9.8). As a group, describe the ideal situation, and write the resolution in the upper right-hand corner of the paper.

Have a facilitator work with the group to brainstorm forces leading to or preventing the ideal situation. These forces may be internal or external. List positive forces on the left side of the T and, on the right side, forces restraining movement toward the ideal state.

As in any planning activity, the team should identify potential obstacles that could affect the successful completion of a task. It should identify both positive and negative forces affecting the task.

Once all positive and negative forces are listed, prioritize the forces that need to be strengthened or identify the restraining forces that need to be minimized to accomplish the goal—for instance, increased test scores. This provides a positive

Issue: School improvement

**Ideal state: An effective
learning environment**

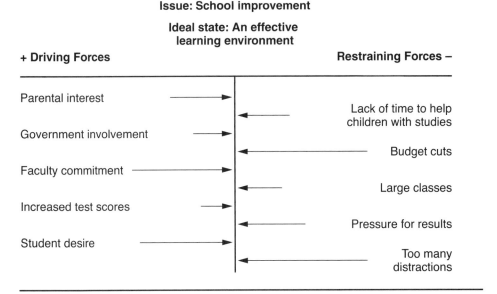

+ Driving Forces

Parental interest

Government involvement

Faculty commitment

Increased test scores

Student desire

Restraining Forces −

Lack of time to help
children with studies

Budget cuts

Large classes

Pressure for results

Too many
distractions

Figure 9.8   Force-field analysis diagram.

structure and removes the negative force of increased pressure on students to perform. The facilitator keeps discussion going among the participants until consensus is reached on each impediment to increasing student test scores. Arrow lines are used to indicate the relative priority of restraining and driving forces. Users of FFA often vary the length of the horizontal arrow lines to indicate the relative strength of each of the forces.

Force-field analysis encourages team members to raise questions and concerns throughout the process. These concerns and questions shouldn't be considered obstacles to successful planning that need to be rejected, but should instead be valued. The process of openly considering individual ideas encourages diversity in the planning process.

Force-field analysis is a powerful tool that encourages communication at all levels of management.[4] By creating a structured environment for problem solving, it minimizes feelings of defensiveness. There is a feeling of openness about problem solving because all members of the group are focused on the issue rather than personal agendas. FFA inhibits hierarchical or traditional power structures that are likely to restrict the flow of creative ideas.

GANTT CHART

The *Gantt chart* is a type of bar chart used by project managers and others in planning and control to display planned work and targets as well as work that has been completed. A Gantt chart/action plan is a graphic representation of a project's schedule, showing the sequence of critical tasks in relation to time. The chart indicates which tasks can be performed simultaneously. The chart/plan can be used for an entire project or for a key phase of a project. It allows a team to avoid unrealistic timetables and schedule expectations, to help identify and shorten tasks that act as bottlenecks, and to focus attention on the most critical tasks. By adding mile-

18-Month ISO 9001 Quality Management System Implementation Project

Task	Weeks 1–13	Weeks 14–26	Weeks 27–39	Weeks 40–52	Weeks 53–65	Weeks 66–78
Select consultant	▽					
Conduct briefing	▽					
Gap analysis	▽					
Form steering comm.	▽					
Q. system procedures	▬▬▬▬▬▬					
Q. policy, objectives		▽				
Work instructions		▬▬▬▬▬				
Employee kickoff		▽				
Evaluate registrars			▽			
Train internal auditors			▽		▽	
Implement QSPs				▬▬▬▬		
Select registrar			▽			
Conduct internal audits				▬▬▬▬▬		
Q. system manual				▬▬▬		
Audit prep meeting					▽	
Preassessment					▽	
Corrective actions					▬▬▬	
Final assessment						▽
Pass and celebrate						▽

Figure 9.9   Gantt chart.

stones (interim checkpoints) and completion indicators, the Gantt chart becomes a tool for ongoing monitoring of progress.

Because they are primarily project management tools, Gantt charts/action plans are most useful for planning and tracking entire projects or for scheduling and tracking the implementation phase of a planning or improvement effort.

A Gantt chart is used to:

- Identify critical tasks or project components

- Identify the first task that must be completed

- Identify any other tasks that can be started simultaneously with task 1

- Identify the next task that must be completed

- Identify any other tasks that can be started simultaneously with task 2

- Continue this process until all component tasks are sequenced

- Identify task durations

- Monitor progress

Readers should refer to a project management text for further information. Most commercially available project management software will routinely generate a Gantt chart/action plan, similar to the example shown in Figure 9.9.

HISTOGRAM

A *histogram* is a graphic representation (bar chart) used to plot the frequency with which different values of a given variable occur. Histograms are used to examine existing patterns, identify the range of variables, and suggest a central tendency in variables.

An example would be to line up, by height, a group of people in a class. Normally, one would be the tallest, one would be the shortest, and there would be a cluster of people around an average height. Hence the phrase *normal distribution.* This tool helps identify the cause of problems in a process by the shape of the distribution as well as the width of the distribution.

The histogram evolved to meet the need to evaluate data that occurs at a certain frequency. This is possible because it allows for a concise portrayal of information in a bar-graph format. This tool clearly portrays information on location, spread, and shape, which enables the user to perceive subtleties regarding the functioning of the physical process that is generating the data. It can also help suggest both the nature of and possible improvements for the physical mechanisms at work in the process. When combined with the concept of the normal curve and knowledge of a particular process, the histogram becomes an effective, practical working tool to use in the early stages of data analysis. A histogram may be interpreted by asking three questions:

- Is the process performing within specification limits?

- Does the process seem to exhibit wide variation?

- If action needs to be taken on the process, what action is appropriate?

The answers to these three questions lie in analyzing three characteristics of the histogram. How well is the histogram centered? The centering of the data provides information on the process aim about some mean or nominal value. How wide is the histogram? Looking at histogram width defines the variability of the process about the target value. What is the shape of the histogram? Remember that the data is expected to form a normal or bell-shaped curve. Any significant change or anomaly usually indicates that there is something going on in the process causing the quality problem.

Figure 9.10 shows a histogram with an abnormal distribution. Histograms are built to examine characteristics of variation and provide an excellent visualization tool for varying data. The utility of histograms is in gaining a rapid look at how the data collected from a process are distributed.

The basic steps involved in developing a histogram are as follows:

1. Determine the type of data you want to collect.

2. Be sure that the data are measurable (for example, time, length, and speed).

3. Collect as many measurable data points as possible.

4. Collect data on one parameter at a time.

5. Count the total number of points you have collected.

6. Determine the number of intervals required.

7. Determine the range. To do this, subtract the smallest value in the dataset from the largest. This value is the range of your dataset.

8. Determine the interval width. To do this, divide the range by the number of intervals.

Figure 9.10   Histogram.

9. Determine the starting point of each interval.

10. Draw horizontal (x) and vertical (y) axis lines.

11. Label the horizontal axis to indicate what is being displayed and mark the unit of measure (smallest to largest values).

12. Label the vertical axis to indicate what is being measured and mark the unit of measure (smallest to largest values).

13. Plot the data. Construct vertical bars for each of the values, with the height corresponding to the frequency of occurrence of each value.

MATRIX ANALYSIS

The *matrix analysis* method quantifies and arranges matrix diagram data so that the information is easy to visualize and comprehend. The relationships between the elements shown in a matrix diagram are quantified by obtaining numerical data for intersecting cells.

The matrix data analysis method can be used to:

• Analyze production processes in which factors are complexly intertwined

• Analyze causes of nonconformities that involve a large volume of data

• Grasp the desired quality level indicated by the results of a market survey

• Classify sensory characteristics systematically

- Accomplish complex quality evaluations
- Analyze curvilinear data

MATRIX DIAGRAM

The *matrix diagram* method clarifies problematic spots through multidimensional thinking. This method identifies corresponding elements involved in a problem situation or event. These elements are arranged in rows and columns on a chart that shows the presence or absence of relationships among collected pairs of elements.

Matrix diagrams can be used to:

- Establish ideas and concepts for the development and improvement of system products

- Achieve quality deployment in product materials

- Establish and strengthen the quality assurance system by linking certified levels of quality with various control functions

- Reinforce and improve the efficiency of the quality evaluation system

- Pursue the causes of nonconformities in the manufacturing process

- Establish strategies for the mix of products to send to market by evaluating the relationships between the products and market conditions

- Plan the allocation of resources (see the Resource Allocation Matrix subsection on page 140)

MULTIVOTING

Multivoting is a quick and easy way for a group to identify the items of the highest priority in a list. This technique helps a team to:

- Prioritize a large list without creating a win-lose situation in the group that generated the list

- Separate the "vital few" items from the "useful many" on a large list

The basic steps involved in multivoting are as follows:

1. Give each team member a number of votes equal to approximately half the number of items on the list (for example, 10 votes for a 20-item list).

2. Have the members vote individually for the items they believe have high priority. Voters can "spend" their votes as they wish, even giving all to one item.

3. Compile the votes given to each item and record the quantity of votes beside each item.

4. Select the four to six items receiving the highest number of votes.

5. Discuss and prioritize the selected items relative to each other. If there is difficulty in reaching agreement, remove the items that received the fewest votes from the list and then conduct another vote.

Multivoting is best suited for use with large groups and long lists. Its simplicity makes it very quick and easy to use.

NOMINAL GROUP TECHNIQUE

The *nominal group technique* (NGT) is a structured process that identifies and ranks major problems or issues that need addressing. It can be used to identify the major strengths of a department/unit/institution or to make decisions by consensus when selecting problem solutions in a business. This technique provides each participant with an equal voice.

The basic steps involved in using NGT are:

1. Request that all participants (usually 5 to 10 persons) write or say which problem or issue they feel is most important.

2. Record all the problems or issues.

3. Develop a master list of the problems or issues.

4. Generate and distribute to each participant a form that numbers the problems or issues in no particular order.

5. Request that each participant rank the top five problems or issues by assigning five points to their most important perceived problem and one point to the least important of their top five.

6. Tally the results by adding the points for each problem or issue.

7. The problem or issue with the highest number is the most important one for the team as a whole.

8. Discuss the results and generate a final ranked list for process improvement action planning.

PARETO CHART

A *Pareto chart* is a graphic representation of the frequency with which certain events occur. It is a rank-order chart that displays the relative importance of variables in a dataset and may be used to set priorities regarding opportunities for improvement. Pareto charts are bar charts, prioritized in descending order from left to right, used to identify the vital few opportunities for improvement. It shows where to put your initial effort to get the most gain. The tool is named after Vilfredo Pareto, an Italian sociologist and economist, who invented this method of information presentation toward the end of the 19th century.

Figure 9.11 is an example of a Pareto chart. The chart appears much the same as a histogram or bar chart. The bars are arranged in decreasing order of magnitude from left to right along the x-axis, excepting an "other" category. The fundamental use of the Pareto chart in quality improvement is the ordering of factors that contribute to a quality deficiency. The purpose of the chart is to identify which of the problems should be worked on first and how much of the total problem correcting one or more of the identified problems will solve. The Pareto chart is useful in summarizing information and in predicting how much of a problem can be corrected by attacking any specific part of the problem.

Figure 9.11 Pareto chart.

The Pareto chart was derived from Vilfredo Pareto's 80/20 rule. Pareto noticed that 80 percent of the wealth in Italy was held by 20 percent of the people. Later, Joseph Juran, a leading quality expert, noticed that this rule could also be applied to the causes of defects: 80 percent of defects are due to only 20 percent of causes. Therefore, by minimizing 20 percent of the causes, we can eliminate 80 percent of the problems. The 20 percent of the problems are the "vital few," and the remaining problems are the "useful many." A Pareto chart can help organizations to:

- Separate the few major problems from the many possible problems in order to focus improvement efforts

- Arrange data according to priority or importance

- Determine which problems are the most important using data, not perception

The basic steps involved in constructing a Pareto chart are as follows:

1. Define the measurement scale for the potential causes. (This is usually the frequency of occurrence or cost.)

2. Define the time period during which to collect data about the potential causes (days, weeks, or as much time as is required to observe a significant number of occurrences).

3. Collect and tally data for each potential cause.

4. Label the horizontal (x) axis with all the possible root causes in descending order of value.

5. Label the measurement scale on the vertical (y) axis.

6. Draw one bar for each possible cause to represent the value of the measurement.

7. If desired, add a vertical (y) axis on the right side of the chart to represent cumulative percentage values.

8. Draw a line to show the cumulative percentage from left to right as each cause is added to the chart.

Pareto charts are used to:

- Identify the most important problems using different measurement scales
- Point out that most frequent may not always mean most costly
- Analyze different groups of data
- Measure the impact of changes made in the process before and after
- Break down broad causes into more specific parts

PLAN—DO—CHECK—ACT (PDCA) OR PLAN—DO—STUDY—ACT (PDSA)

The key steps involved in the implementation and evaluation of quality improvement efforts are symbolized by the PDCA/PDSA cycle (see Chapter 7, Figure 7.2). The goal is to engage in a continuous endeavor to learn about all aspects of a process and then use this knowledge to change the process to reduce variation and complexity and to improve the level of process performance. Process improvement begins by understanding how customers define quality, how processes work, and how understanding the variation in those processes can lead to wise management action. The major process improvement techniques and tools are discussed throughout this chapter.

POKA-YOKE

The term *poka-yoke* is a hybrid word created by Japanese manufacturing engineer Shigeo Shingo. It comes from the words *yokeru* ("to avoid") and *poka* ("inadvertent error"). Hence, the combination word means *avoiding inadvertent errors.* The term can be further anglicized as mistake proofing, or making it impossible to do a task incorrectly. It involves creating processes that prevent the making of mistakes. As an example, if a part must fit into an assembly in only one orientation, the part is designed so that it is physically impossible to place the part in any other orientation.

PROCESS DECISION PROGRAM CHART (PDPC)

The *process decision program chart* (PDPC) method helps determine which processes to use to obtain the desired results by evaluating the progress of events and the variety of conceivable outcomes. Implementation plans do not always progress as anticipated. When problems, technical or otherwise, arise, solutions are frequently not apparent. The PDPC method, in response to these kinds of problems, anticipates possible outcomes and prepares countermeasures that will lead to the best

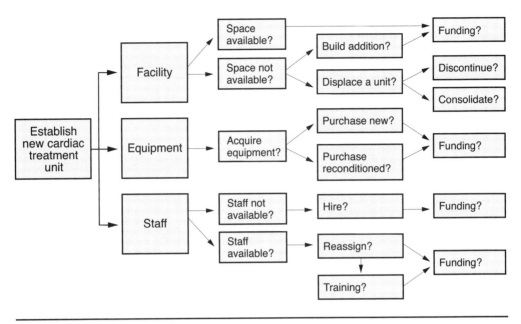

Figure 9.12 Process decision program chart (PDPC).

possible solutions. Figure 9.12 charts the decisions needed to establish a cardiac treatment unit in a small, underfunded hospital.

The PDPC method can be used to:

- Establish an implementation plan for management by objectives

- Establish an implementation plan for technology-development themes

- Establish a policy of forecasting and responding in advance to major events predicted in the system

- Implement countermeasures to minimize nonconformities in the manufacturing process

- Set up and select measures for process improvements

The PDPC diagram is a simple graphic tool that can be used to mitigate risk in virtually any undertaking.

QUALITY FUNCTION DEPLOYMENT (QFD)

Quality function deployment (QFD) is a planning process that uses multifunctional teams to transform the voice of the customer into design specifications. User requirements and preferences are defined and categorized as user attributes, which are then weighted based on their importance to the user. Users are then asked to compare how their requirements are being met now by a current product design versus a new design. QFD provides the design team with an understanding of customer desires (in clear-text language), forces the customer to prioritize those desires, and compares/benchmarks one design approach against another. Each customer attribute is then satisfied by at least one technical solution. Values for

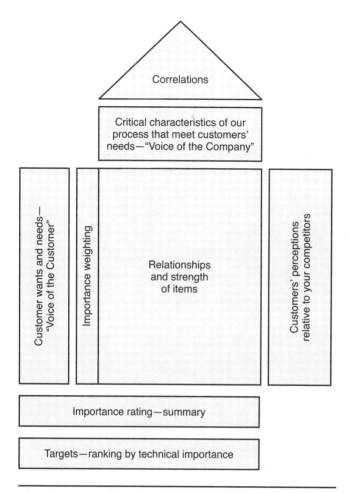

Figure 9.13   Quality function deployment (QFD) matrix "house of quality."

those technical solutions are determined and again rated among competing designs. Finally, the technical solutions are evaluated against each other to identify conflicts. A convenient form for viewing the ultimate product is the "house of quality" graphic, which should help the design team translate customer attribute information into firm operating or engineering goals as well as identify key manufacturing characteristics. Figure 9.13 shows the basic framework of the QFD matrix. QFD is also called the "house of quality" because of its resemblance to a house.

RELATIONS DIAGRAM (INTERRELATIONSHIP DIGRAPH)

The *relations diagramming* method is a technique developed to clarify intertwined causal relationships in a complex situation in order to find an appropriate solution.
Relations diagrams can be used to:

- Determine and develop quality assurance policies

- Establish promotional plans for total quality control introduction

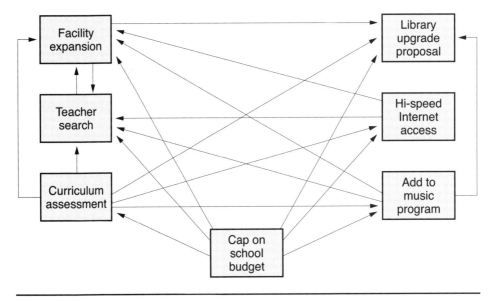

Figure 9.14 Interrelationship digraph.

- Design steps to counter market complaints
- Improve quality in the manufacturing process (especially in planning to eliminate latent defects)
- Promote quality control in purchased or ordered items
- Provide measures against troubles related to payment and process control
- Promote small group activities effectively
- Reform administrative and business departments

The digraph in Figure 9.14 shows some of the interrelating factors pertaining to on-going and proposed projects.

RESOURCE ALLOCATION MATRIX

A matrix chart is useful in planning the allocation of resources (such as personnel, equipment, facilities, and funds). It is frequently used in planning larger projects. The matrix enables planners to see where potential conflicts may arise in utilizing resources for a project that are already committed to ongoing operations. Figure 9.15 shows a matrix for allocation of five types of personnel required for a project.

RUN CHART

A *run chart* is a line graph that shows data points plotted in the order in which they occur. This type of chart is used to reveal trends and shifts in a process over time, to show variation over time, or to identify decline or improvement in a process over time. It can be used to examine both variables and attribute data.

Project Delta Team—Personnel Requirements—October through May
(Days)

Task	Data Entry Operator	Design Engineer	Systems Analyst	Computer Operator	Production Planner	Total
Build test data file	Nov. 15.0	Oct.–Nov. 5.5	Oct. 3.5	Oct. 6.25		30.25
Run desk check of data		Nov. 3.0	Nov. 2.0	Nov. 1.25		6.25
Modify test data	Dec. 1.5	Dec. 1.0	Dec. 1.0	Dec. 2.0		5.50
Run computer test				Dec. 8.0		8.00
Analyze test results		Dec.–Jan. 15.0	Dec.–Jan. 15.0	Dec.–Jan. 5.0		35.00
Make modifications		Jan.–Feb. 25.0	Jan.–Feb. 12.0	Jan.–Feb. 3.0		40.00
Prepare first month data	Mar. 6.0		Mar. 1.0	Mar. 3.0		10.00
Prepare second month data	Apr. 5.0		Apr. .5	Apr. 1.0		6.50
Prepare third month data	May 5.0		May .5	May .5		6.00
Run full-scale production				May 1.5	May .75	2.25
Analyze results		May 3.0				3.00
	32.5	52.5	35.5	31.5	.75	152.75

Figure 9.15 Resource allocation matrix.

Figure 9.16 Run Chart.

The data must be collected in a chronological or sequential form starting from and ending at any point. For best results, 25 or more samples must be taken in order to get an accurate run chart.

The chart in Figure 9.16 plots the average rod diameter of each of 10 lots of rods. A lot is one day's total run.

Run charts can help an organization to:

- Recognize patterns of performance in a process

- Document changes over time

A run chart shows the history and pattern of variation. It is helpful to indicate on the chart whether up is good or down is good.

Run charts can be used to:

- Summarize occurrences of a particular situation

- Display measurement results over time

- Identify trends, fluctuations, or unusual events

- Determine common cause versus special cause variation

The basic steps involved in constructing a run chart are as follows:

1. Construct a horizontal (x) axis line and a vertical (y) axis line.

2. The horizontal axis represents time.

3. The vertical axis represents the values of measurement or the frequency at which an event occurs.

4. Collect data for an appropriate number of time periods, in accordance with your data collection strategy.

5. Plot a point for each time a measurement is taken.

6. Connect the points with a line.

7. Identify questions that the data should answer about the process. Record any questions or observations that can be made as a result of the data.

8. Compute the average for subsequent blocks of time, or after a significant change has occurred.

Keeping in mind the process, interpret the chart. Possible signals that the process has significantly changed are:

- Six points in a row that steadily increase or decrease

- Nine points in a row that are on the same side of the average

- Other patterns such as significant shifts in levels, cyclical patterns, and bunching of data points

Run charts provide information that helps to:

- Identify trends in which more points are above or below the average. We should find an equal number of points above and below the average. When a larger number of points lie either above or below the average, this indicates that there has been an unusual event and that the average has changed. Such changes should be investigated.

- Identify trends in which several points steadily increase or decrease with no reversals. Neither pattern would be expected to happen based on random chance. This would likely indicate an important change and the need to investigate.

- Identify common and special cause variation within a process.

SCATTER DIAGRAM

A *scatter diagram* is a chart in which one variable is plotted against another to determine whether there is a correlation between the two variables. These diagrams are used to plot the distribution of information in two dimensions. Scatter diagrams are useful in rapidly screening for a relationship between two variables.

A scatter diagram shows the pattern of relationship between two variables that are thought to be related. For example, is there a relationship between outside temperature and cases of the common cold? As temperatures drop, do colds increase? The more closely the points hug a diagonal line, the more closely there is a one-to-one relationship.

The purpose of the scatter diagram is to display what happens to one variable when another variable is changed. The diagram is used to test a theory that the two variables are related. The slope of the diagram indicates the type of relationship that exists.

Figure 9.17 shows a plot of two variables—in this example, predicted values versus observed values. As the predicted value increases, so does the actual measured value. These variables are said to be positively correlated; that is, if one increases, so does the other. The line plotted is a "regression" line, which shows the average linear relationship between the variables. If the line in a scatter diagram

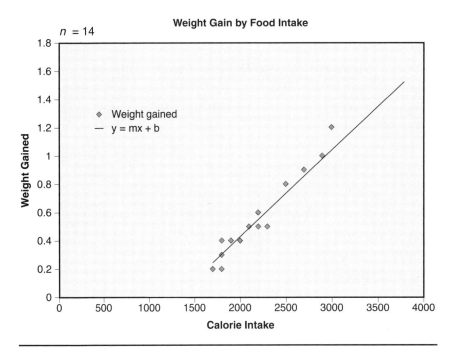

Figure 9.17   Scatter diagram.

has a negative slope, the variables are negatively correlated; that is, when one increases, the other decreases, and vice versa. When no regression line can be plotted and the scatter diagram appears to simply be a ball of diffuse points, then the variables are said to be uncorrelated.

The utility of the scatter diagram for quality assessment lies in its measurement of variables in a process to see whether any two or more variables are correlated or uncorrelated. The specific utility of finding correlations is to infer causal relationships among variables and ultimately to find the root causes of problems.

The basic steps involved in constructing a scatter diagram are as follows:

1. Define the x variable on a graph paper scatter diagram form. This variable is often thought of as the cause variable and is typically plotted on the horizontal axis.

2. Define the y variable on the diagram. This variable is often thought of as the effect variable and is typically plotted on the vertical axis.

3. Number the pairs of x and y variable measurements consecutively. Record each pair of measures for x and y in the appropriate columns. Make sure that the x measures and the corresponding y measures remain paired so that the data are accurate.

. Plot the x and y data pairs on the diagram. Locate the x value on the horizontal axis, and then locate the y value on the vertical axis. Place a point on the graph where these two intersect.

5. Study the shape that is formed by the series of data points plotted. In general, conclusions can be made about the association between two

variables (referred to as x and y) based on the shape of the scatter diagram. Scatter diagrams that display associations between two variables tend to look like elliptical spheres or even straight lines.

6. Scatter diagrams on which the plotted points appear in a circular fashion show little or no correlation between x and y.

7. Scatter diagrams on which the points form a pattern of increasing values for both variables show a positive correlation; as values of x increase, so do values of y. The more tightly the points are clustered in a linear fashion, the stronger the positive correlation, or the association between the two variables.

8. Scatter diagrams on which one variable increases in value while the second variable decreases in value show a negative correlation between x and y. Again, the more tightly the points are clustered in a linear fashion, the stronger the association between the two variables.

If there appears to be a relationship between two variables, they are said to be correlated. Both negative and positive correlations are useful for continuous process improvement.

Scatter diagrams show only that a relationship exists, not that one variable causes the other. Further analysis using advanced statistical techniques can quantify how strong the relationship is between two variables.

STRATIFICATION

A technique called *stratification* is often very useful in analyzing data in order to find improvement opportunities. Stratification helps analyze cases in which data actually mask the real facts. This often happens when the recorded data are from many sources but are treated as one number.

The basic idea in stratification is that data that are examined may be secured from sources with different statistical characteristics. For example, consider that two different machines, such as a cutting machine and a polishing machine, may influence the measurement of the width of a particular part in a manufacturing assembly. Each machine will contribute to variations in the width of the final product, but with potentially different statistical variations.

Data on complaints may be recorded as a single figure (either rising or falling). However, that number is actually the sum total of complaints (including those, for example, about office staff, field nurses, home health aides, and so forth). Stratification breaks down single numbers into meaningful categories or classifications in order to focus corrective action.

TOTAL QUALITY MANAGEMENT (TQM)

Total quality management is an approach to quality management that emphasizes a thorough understanding by all members of an organization of the needs and desires of the ultimate product/service recipient, a viewpoint of wishing to provide world-class products/services to internal and external customers, and a knowledge of how to use specific data-related techniques and process improvement tools to assess and improve the quality of all organizational outputs.

Vision Tree Diagram

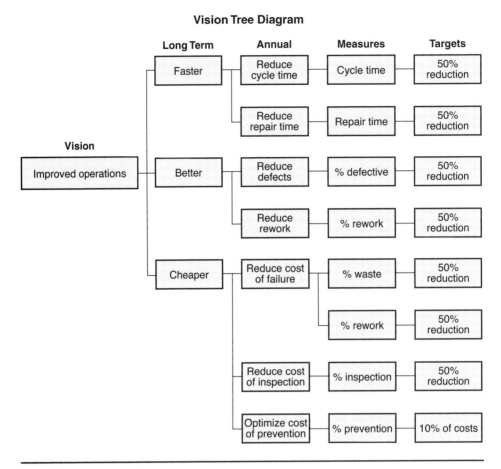

Figure 9.18   Tree diagram.

TREE DIAGRAM

A *tree diagram* is a graphic representation of the separation of broad, general information into increasing levels of detail. The tool ensures that action plans remain visibly linked to overall goals, that actions flow logically from identified goals, and that the true level of a project's complexity will be fully understood. The goal to establish objectives for improving operations is diagrammed in Figure 9.18.

Tree diagrams are used in the quality planning process. The diagram begins with a generalized goal (the tree trunk) and then identifies progressively finer levels of actions (the branches) needed to accomplish the goal. As part of process improvement, it can be used to help identify root causes of trouble. The tool is especially useful in designing new products or services and in creating an implementation plan to remedy identified process problems. In order for the diagram to accurately reflect the project, it is essential that the team using it have a detailed understanding of the tasks required.

The steps involved in generating a tree diagram are as follows:

1. *Identify the goal statement or primary objective.* This should be a clear, action-oriented statement to which the entire team agrees. Such statements may come from the root cause/driver identified in an interrelationship digraph or from the headings of an affinity diagram. Write this goal on the extreme left of the chart.

2. *Subdivide the goal statement into major secondary categories.* These branches should represent goals, activities, or events that directly lead to the primary objective or that are directly required to achieve the overall goal. The team should continually ask, "What is required to meet this condition?" "What happens next?" and "What needs to be addressed?" Write the secondary categories to the right of the goal statement. Using sticky-back notes at this stage makes later changes easier to accomplish.

3. *Break each major heading into greater detail.* As you move from left to right in the tree, the tasks and activities should become more and more specific. Stop the breakdown of each level once there are assignable tasks. If the team does not have enough knowledge to continue at some point, identify the individuals who can supply the information and continue the breakdown later with those individuals present.

4. *Review the diagram for logic and completeness.* Make sure that each subheading and path has a direct cause-and-effect relationship with the one before. Examine the paths to ensure that no obvious steps have been left out. Also ensure that the completion of listed actions will indeed lead to the anticipated results.

SUMMARY OF QUALITY IMPROVEMENT TOOLS AND TECHNIQUES

The quality improvement tools and techniques described in this chapter provide a simple yet powerful set of methodologies for collecting, analyzing, and visualizing information from different perspectives. The problem with the methodologies is the lack of their use by organizations. An organization cannot solve its own problems without understanding the way these methodologies operate and how they can assist the organization in understanding and improving its processes.

Many of the tools and techniques mentioned in this chapter are discussed in greater depth in the reference materials cited in Appendix D. *The Memory Jogger II* is suggested as an essential "toolbox."[5] For the more adventurous, *Improving Performance through Statistical Thinking* is a good read for gaining useful insight into the value of statistics in quality improvement.[6] For more on Quality Function Deployment (QFD), see Beecroft et al.[7] Cost of quality is discussed in greater detail in *Principles of Quality Costs*.[8]

Notes

1. Much of the information in this section is adapted from the *U.S. Navy Handbook for Basic Process Improvement* and the *U.S. Air Force Quality Institute Process Improvement Guide,* 2nd ed. (1994).

2. In more recent times, the run chart has been dropped from the list and the check sheet has been added, maintaining the basic count of seven tools.

3. The term *audit* is gradually being replaced by the term *assessment* in relation to management systems, where the emphasis is less on strict conformance to specifications than on the effectiveness of the management process. Accredited ISO 9000 registrars "assess" quality management systems prior to granting a certificate. The Baldrige National Quality Program uses volunteer "assessors" to conduct "assessments" of organizations applying for the award.

4. Bauer, J. E., G. L. Duffy, and J. W. Moran. Solve problems with open communication. *Quality Progress* (July 2001): 160.

5. Brassard, M., and D. Ritter. *The memory jogger II: A pocket guide of tools for continuous improvement and effective planning.* (Methuen, MA: GOAL/QPC, 1994).

6. ASQ Statistics Division. *Improving performance through statistical thinking.* (Milwaukee, WI: ASQ Quality Press, 2000).

7. Beecroft, G. Dennis, Grace L. Duffy, and John W. Moran, eds. *The executive guide to improvement and change.* (Milwaukee, WI: ASQ Quality Press, 2003).

8. Campanella, Jack, ed. *Principles of quality costs* (3rd ed.). (Milwaukee, WI: ASQ Quality Press, 1999).

Chapter 10

E. Customer–Supplier Relationships

I do not consider a sale complete until the goods are worn out and the customer is still satisfied.

Leon Leonwood Bean, founder of L. L. Bean

There is only one boss—the customer. And he can fire everybody in the company from the chairman on down simply by spending his money somewhere else.

Sam Walton, founder of Wal-Mart

Anyone who thinks customers aren't important should try doing without them for 90 days.

Anonymous

1. INTERNAL AND EXTERNAL CUSTOMERS

> Know how customers are defined. Understand the importance of working with customers to improve processes and services, and how customers influence organizational processes. Know how to distinguish between different external customer types (consumers and end-users). (Understand)
>
> **CQIA BoK 2006**

Internal Customers

Internal customers are those within the organization. The term *next operation as customer* is often used to describe the relationship of internal provider to internal receiver.[1] Every function and work group in an organization is both a receiver of services and/or products from internal and/or external sources and a provider of services and/or products to internal and/or external customers. These interfaces between provider and receiver may be one to one, one to many, many to one, or many to many. Each receiver has needs and requirements. Whether the delivered service or product meets the needs and requirements of the receiver it impacts the effectiveness and quality of services and/or products to their customers, and so on. Following are some examples of internal customer situations:

- If A delivers part X to B one hour late, B may have to apply extra effort and cost to make up the time or else perpetuate the delay by delivering late to the next customer.

- Engineering designs a product based on a salesperson's understanding of the external customer's need. Production produces the product, expending resources. The external customer rejects the product because it fails to meet the customer's needs. The provider reengineers the product and production makes a new one, which the customer accepts beyond the original required delivery date. The result is waste and possibly no further orders from this customer.

- Information technology (IT) delivers copies of a production cost report (which averages 50 pages of fine print per week) to six internal customers. IT has established elaborate quality control of the accuracy, timeliness, and physical quality of the report. However, of the six report receivers, only two still need information of this type. Neither of these finds the report directly usable for their current needs. Each has assigned clerical people to manually extract pertinent data for their specific use. All six admit that they diligently store the reports for the prescribed retention period.

- Production tickets, computer-printed on light card stock, are attached by removable tape to modules. When each module reaches the paint shop, it is given an acid bath, a rinse, high-temperature drying, painting, and high-temperature baking. Very few tickets survive intact and readable. The operation following the paint shop requires attaching other parts to the painted modules, based on information contained on the tickets. Operators depend on their experience to guess which goes with what. About 95 percent of the modules emerge from this process correctly, except when a product variation is ordered or when an experienced operator is absent.

The steps to improve process and services are as follows:

1. Identify internal customer interfaces (providers of services/products and receivers of their services/products).

2. Establish internal customers' service/product needs and requirements.

3. Ensure that the internal customer requirements are consistent with and supportive of external customer requirements.

4. Document service-level agreements between providers and receivers.[2]

5. Establish improvement goals and measurements.

6. Implement systems for tracking and reporting performance and for supporting the continuous improvement of the process.

Effect of Treatment of Internal Customers on That of External Customers

Care-less behavior of management (and management's systems) toward internal customers (poor tools and equipment, defective or late material from a previous operation, incorrect/incomplete instructions, ineligible work orders or prints, circumvention of worker safety procedures and practices, unhealthy work environment, lack of interest in internal complaints, disregard for external customer feedback, and so forth) may engender care-less or indifferent treatment of external customers. Continued, this indifference may generate a downward spiral that could adversely affect an organization's business. Ignoring the needs of internal customers makes it very difficult to instill a desire to care for the needs of external customers.

So many organizations fail to learn, or ignore, the internal customers' needs and wonder why their management's exhortations fail to stimulate internal customers to care about what they do for external customers and how they do it. The surly and uncooperative sales representative, waitperson, housekeeping employee, health-care provider, delivery person, and customer service representative often reflect a lack of caring for internal customers.

Organizations must work constantly to address the internal customers' lament: "How do you expect me to care about the next operator, or external customer, when no one cares whether I get what I need to do my job right?"

External Customers

External customers are those who are served by or who receive products from the supplier organization. There are many types of external customers:

1. Consumers/end users

   - *Retail buyer of products.* The retail buyer influences the design and usability of product features and accessories based on the volume purchased. Consumer product "watch" organizations warn purchasers of potential problems. For example:

     In the late 1990s, a fake fat substance was introduced in a number of food products as a boon to weight-conscious people. These products didn't taste good and were found to have harmful side effects. Many consumers stopped buying the products.

     The factors important to this type of buyer, depending on the type of product, are: reasonable price, ease of use, performance, safety, aesthetics, and durability. Other influences on product offerings include: easy purchase process, installation, instructions for use, postpurchase service, warranty period, packaging, friendliness of seller's personnel, and brand name.

- *Discount buyer.* The discount buyer shops primarily for price, is more willing to accept less-well-known brands, and is willing to buy quantities in excess of immediate needs. These buyers have relatively little influence on the products, except for, perhaps, creating a market for off-brands, production surpluses, and discontinued items.

- *Employee buyer.* The employee buyer purchases the employer's products, usually at a deep discount. Often being familiar with or even a contributor to the products bought, this buyer can provide valuable feedback to the employer (both directly, through surveys, and indirectly, through volume and items purchased).

- *Service buyer.* The buyer of services (such as TV repair, dental work, and tax preparation) often buys by word-of-mouth. Word of good or poor service spreads rapidly and influences the continuance of the service provider's business.

- *Service user.* The captive service user (such as the user of electricity, gas, water, municipal services, and schools) generally has little choice as to from which supplier they receive services. Until competition is introduced, there is little incentive for providers to vary their services. Recent deregulation has resulted in a more competitive marketplace for some utilities.

- *Organization buyer.* Buyers for organizations that use a product or service in the course of their business or activity can have a significant influence on the types of products offered them as well as on the organization from which they buy. Raw materials or devices that become part of a manufactured product are especially critical in sustaining quality and competitiveness for the buyer's organization (including performance, serviceability, price, ease of use, durability, simplicity of design, safety, and ease of disposal). Other factors include: flexibility in delivery, discounts, allowances for returned material, extraordinary guarantees, and so forth.

  Factors that particularly pertain to purchased services are the reputation and credibility of the provider, range of services offered, degree of customization offered, timeliness, fee structure, and so forth.

2. Intermediate customers

- *Wholesale buyer.* Wholesalers buy what they expect they can sell. They typically buy in large quantities. They may have little direct influence on product design and manufacture, but they do influence the providers' production schedules, pricing policies, warehousing and delivery arrangements, return policies for unsold merchandise, and so forth.

- *Distributor.* Distributors are similar to wholesalers in some ways but differ in the fact that they may stock a wider variety of products from a wide range of producers. What they stock is directly influenced by their customers' demands and needs. Their customers' orders are often small and may consist of a mix of products. The distributors' forte is stocking thousands of catalog items that can be "picked" and shipped on short notice, at an attractive price. Customers seeking an industry level of quality, at a good price, and immediately available mainly influence distributors stocking commodity-type items, such as sheet metal, construction materials, mineral products, and stationary items. "Blanket-orders" for a yearly quantity delivered at specified intervals are prevalent for some materials.

- *Retail chain buyer.* Buyers for large retail chains, because of the size of their orders, place major demands on their providers, such as pricing concessions, very flexible deliveries, requirements that the providers assume warehousing costs for already-purchased products, special packaging requirements, no-cost return policy, and requirements that the providers be able to accept electronically sent orders.

- *Other volume buyers.* Government entities, educational institutions, health-care organizations, transportation companies, public utilities, cruise lines, hotel chains, and restaurant chains all represent large-volume buyers that provide services to customers. Such organizations have regulations governing their services. Each requires a wide range of products, materials, and external services in delivering its services, much of which is transparent to the consumer. Each requires high quality and each has tight limitations on what it can pay (for example, based on appropriations, cost-control mandates, tariffs, or heavy competition). Each such buyer demands much for its money but may offer long-term contracts for fixed quantities. The buying organizations' internal customers frequently generate the influences on the products required.

- *Service providers.* The diversity of service providers buying products and services from other providers is mind-boggling. These buyers include plumbers, public accountants, dentists, doctors, building contractors, cleaning services, computer programmers, Web site designers, consultants, manufacturer's reps, actors, and taxi drivers, among many others. This type of buyer, often self-employed, buys very small quantities, shops for value, buys only when the product or service is needed (when the buyer has a job, patient, or client), and relies on high quality of purchases to maintain customers' satisfaction. Influences on products or services for this type of buyer range from having the provider be able to furnish service and/or replacement parts for old or obsolete equipment, be able to supply extremely small quantities of an extremely large number of products (such as those supplied by a hardware store, construction materials depot, or medical products supply house), and have product knowledge that extends to knowing how the product is to be used.

A simplified hypothetical product/service flow through several types of customers for a consumer product sold via an Internet Web page would be as follows:

a. A consumer (external customer) accesses the Web through an external Internet service provider (ISP).

b. The consumer searches for a particular book at the lowest price available, accessing various product sellers (the ISP is an external service provider to the various sellers).

c. The consumer selects a seller and places an order via the seller's Web page.

d. The seller forwards the order to a selected publisher's order service (the seller is an external customer of the publisher).

e. The order service department of the publisher notifies the seller, who notifies the consumer that the book order has been placed.

f. The publisher's order service department forwards a "pick" order to the warehouse, which picks the book from inventory and sends the book to shipping (the warehouse is an internal customer of the order service department, and shipping is an internal customer of the warehouse).

g. Shipping packages and sends the book via Package Delivery Service (PDS) directly to the consumer, notifying the publisher's order service and billing departments and the seller that shipment has taken place (PDS is a service provider to the publisher, and the billing department is an internal customer of shipping).

h. The publisher's billing department adds the shipment to the amount to be billed to the seller at month end.

i. PDS delivers the book to the consumer.

j. The seller bills the consumer (the consumer is an external customer of the seller's billing department).

With some exceptions (such as very small organizations), most organizations segment their customer base in order to better serve the needs of different types of customers. Providing one product or service to every type of customer is no longer feasible.

> Henry Ford is reported to have said, "People can have the Model T in any color—so long as it's black." (Black was the only color of paint available that dried fast enough to allow Ford's assembly-line approach to work.)

Customers sharing particular wants or needs may be segmented by:

- Purchase volume

- Profitability (to the selling organization)

- Industry classification

- Geographic factors (such as municipalities, regions, states, countries, and continents)

- Demographic factors (such as age, income, marital status, education, and gender)

- Psychographic factors (such as values, beliefs, and attitudes)

An organization must decide whether it is interested in simply pursuing more customers (or contributors, in the case of a not-for-profit fund-raiser) or in targeting the right customers. It is not unusual for an organization, after segmenting its customer base, to find that it is not economically feasible to continue to serve a particular segment. Conversely, an organization may find that it is uniquely capable of further penetrating a particular market segment or may even discover a niche not presently served by other organizations.

Deploying the Voice of the Customer

In becoming a customer-focused organization it is important that the requirements and expectations of the customer permeate every function within the organization. One tool for deploying (cascading) the voice of the customer downward throughout the organization is *quality function deployment (QFD)*. QFD consists of a series of interlocking matrices, outlined in Figure 10.1. In this example, customer requirements are aligned with internal design requirements, design requirements are aligned with parts requirements, parts requirements with process requirements, and process requirements with production requirements—to produce a product that meets the customer's requirements and expectations.

A *focus group* is both a means for capturing insightful information about customers' expectations before a product or service is designed and launched as well as a means for gathering customers' satisfaction with products or services purchased.

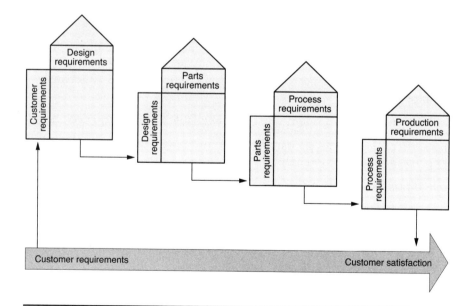

Figure 10.1 Voice of the customer deployed.

2. CUSTOMER FEEDBACK

> Know the different types of customer
> feedback (e.g., surveys, complaints) and
> understand the value in using the data to
> drive continuous improvement activities.
> (Understand)
>
> **CQIA BoK 2006**

Customer relationship management (CRM), also referred to as *relationship marketing* or *one-to-one marketing* (serving the unique needs of each customer), is receiving emphasis in the fast-paced, ever-changing environment in which organizations must survive and prosper. CRM relates less to the product or service provided and more to the way business is conducted. In a customer-focused organization, the thrust is usually more toward nurturing the existing customers than a drive to attract new customers. A key principle of good customer relations is determining and ensuring customer satisfaction.

Perceptions of customer satisfaction need to be corroborated or rejected through sound means for collecting, analyzing, and acting upon customer feedback. Effective systems for utilizing customer feedback involve several elements:

- There are formal processes for collecting, measuring, and analyzing customer data and for communicating results to the appropriate business functions for action.

- Feedback mechanisms are in place to determine how well an organization is meeting customers' requirements.

- Most organizations choose a combination of methods to get a more complete picture. Once customer satisfaction data have been gathered, sophisticated techniques can be used to analyze the data and target areas for improvement.

- Data are stored appropriately and made available to those who need it.

Some examples of the origins of customer data that can be useful in determining customer needs and satisfaction are:

Data from within the organization

- Customer complaints, when logged and tracked

- Past records of claim resolutions

- Product warranty registration cards and guarantee usage

- Service records—product failure, product maintenance

- Input from customer contact personnel

- Customer satisfaction surveys

- Transaction data
- Data from established "listening posts"
- Lost-customer analysis
- Market research

Data from outside the organization

- Data about competitors' customers
- Research: magazine and newspaper articles, trade journal information
- Public information, for example, customers' and competitors' annual reports
- Advertising media: brochures, TV, radio, Web sites
- Industry market research

Product Warranty Registration Cards

Often these are found in the packages of new products. These cards provide some basic customer data that can help the seller better understand buyers' needs when the consumer completes the card and sends it in. The real value, however, lies in analyzing the customer's purchasing decision (by the types of questions asked on the cards) and determining whether and, later, when the consumer files a claim within the warranty period.

Complaints

Complaint data, when appropriately captured and analyzed, provides a wealth of information about customers' satisfaction. However, it must be realized that the data do not constitute a valid statistical sample: Many customers find it a burden to complain unless there is a very serious problem, and the majority of customers have no discernable complaint to register.

Many organizations openly solicit complaints—think of the restaurant waitperson who inquires about your satisfaction with your food, the organization that serves mail-order customers and includes a self-addressed, stamped reply card, and the hotel that seeks feedback on your satisfaction with your stay at its facility. It has been proven that a buyer's satisfaction is often greatly improved when a complaint is quickly resolved. Research by the U.S. Office of Consumer Affairs/Technical Assistance Research Programs (TARP) shows that the speed of complaint resolution also affects repurchase intent, which is significantly higher when resolution is achieved quickly.

Customer Surveys

Many organizations solicit customer feedback with formal customer surveys. The aims of a survey are to get as high a response rate as possible so as to obtain the most representative sampling of the customer population surveyed and as much useful data as possible. Designing surveys and analyzing the data received are processes involving much expertise and knowledge. Administering the survey process is expensive. Misinterpretation and inappropriate use of the data can be even more expensive.

Methods of administering surveys include:

- Mail

- Electronic (e-mail or through a Web site)

- Telephone

- In person, one-to-one

- In person, group

- In person, panel

Each method has its advantages and disadvantages. The relative effectiveness of one over another also depends on the purpose of the survey, the population to be surveyed, and the benefit-to-cost ratio of conducting the survey. For example, one-to-one interviews can generally only reach a small number of persons and are expensive to conduct, but the personal contact involved often yields great insights. The mailed survey has its costs but can reach unlimited numbers of potential respondents. The response rate can be low and the types of customers responding may not represent a reasonable sample, but this method is far less expensive than one-to-one surveys. Electronic surveys are relatively inexpensive when integrated with other Web site material, but they can yield very low response rates and may produce responses from only the wildly delighted, the highly dissatisfied customers, and the "loyal" customers willing to help.

Some of the mistakes to avoid in using surveys are:

- Using an annoying methodology, poor survey design, an overall unappealing presentation, or questions that seem silly, without reason, or not pertinent gives the customer a reason to decline to respond.

- The organization should not formulate its questions based solely on what it thinks the customer would want to answer. Good survey design calls for the customers to be asked what is most important to them and what they want to have included on the survey.

- Another common error is selecting customers that are neither random nor representative, resulting in responses that are not statistically valid. This can also happen when a low quantity of responses is analyzed. The analysis ignores the fact that customers at the extremes of satisfaction and dissatisfaction tend to respond to surveys more frequently than those who are neutral.

- Results from inept or misdirected questions can cause the organization to focus on the wrong or least-important improvement effort.

- Designing questions that force an answer where none of the choices are applicable to the customer is unacceptable.

- Another question design flaw is failure to write at a level that the customer can understand. Survey validity may be compromised.

- Some organizations conduct surveys and then fail to use the results in their strategic planning and continuous improvement efforts.

Transaction Data

Many organizations collect a wealth of data about their customers through direct transactions with them. Examples include data collected on consumer buying habits through the use of store-issued identification cards (the use of the cards is supported by discount incentives) and through the analysis of "hits" and "buys" from users of Web sites.

EDI: Electronic data interchange (EDI) is the paperless electronic transmission of a customer's order data (requirements) to the supplier's internal order fulfillment system. In some fully automated systems, the EDI data transmitted may trigger the order entry, production of the product, shipping, delivery, and billing—with minimum human intervention. EDI is becoming a contractual requirement from many customers.

Another way to gather transaction data is to engage external "mystery shoppers" to make purchases of your product and provide feedback to your organization about the experience. (The same approach is also used to "shop" the competitors and check out their approaches.)

Data from Established "Listening Posts"

Organizations have many people within them who periodically or occasionally interact with customers: engineer to engineer, salesperson to salesperson, CEO to CEO, and delivery person to customer's receiving person, among others. In a majority of these interactions (face-to-face, telephone, fax, e-mail, and so forth), the customers' people express opinions, suggestions, complaints, or compliments about the supplier's organization, the quality of its products/services, delivery, price—even about the personal attention they receive (or don't receive). Excepting severe negative expressions, these comments, casually and informally made, are seldom captured. By not having a formal process for collecting and analyzing these data (for example, trending), an organization is unable to spot the early stages of an eventual customer problem. It also misses compliments that should get back to the responsible people as positive feedback.[3]

> Jan Carlzon, president of Scandinavian Airlines, in his book Moments of Truth, *discusses the often-unrecognized opportunities all employees have for gathering customer data. A "moment of truth" is any contact a customer has with an organization.*

Lost-Customer Analysis

This method involves creating a rating scale for the reasons an organization loses its customers, applying the rating to customers lost, developing a Pareto chart for quantity lost in each rating category, and creating a trend chart showing the losses by category over time. Preventive action is initiated to decrease losses. Customer satisfaction data are analyzed to improve customer satisfaction and retain customers. Retaining customers costs money but is still much less expensive than seeking new customers. Table 10.1 presents another way to view your customers.

	Table 10.1	Levels of customer satisfaction.	

Level	Is Your Customer:	Then Your Customer:
1	dissatisfied?	has probably departed forever.
2	marginally satisfied?	is casual (any supplier will do).
3	basically satisfied?	is borderline, uncommitted.
4	delighted?	is a return customer (retained).
5	a committed advocate?	is loyal, appreciates what you do, and tells others.

Reprinted with permission of R. T. Westcott & Associates

Tracking, Measuring, and Reporting Customer Satisfaction

Producing tabulations of customer satisfaction data, trend charts, and so forth is of minimal value unless there is an established objective against which to compare. To make sense of the time and energy involved in collecting the data, there must be a target. To justify the preventive action that may be indicated by the analyzed data, there needs to be a basis for estimating the anticipated gain to be achieved by the action, a means for tracking progress toward achieving the objective, and a basis for evaluating the effectiveness of the action taken.

Tracking, measuring, and reporting on a real-dollar basis is usually more meaningful than doing so on the basis of percentages or quantities alone. Knowing what it now costs to lose a customer is a good place to start. Improvement in customer retention has the potential for a substantive dollar payoff. The figures have a direct impact on the profit or cost-containment goals of the organization.

Simplified steps for determining what it is worth to retain customers are as follows:

1. Segment the customer base by types of products or services sold to each segment.

2. Select an appropriate time period: for example, for customers buying consumer products, perhaps 2 years, for homeowner insurance buyers, maybe 30 years.

3. Compute the average annual profit each segment of customers produces.

   As an example, for the home computer buyer segment, the average initial purchase price (including a three-year service contract) plus the average price of add-ons purchased within the three years, divided by three, times the number of customers in this segment equals the annual value of this segment.

4. Compute the worth to retain the customer:

   To the value of an individual customer in this segment, add the dollar value of upgrading the customer to a new computer at the end of the three-year period. Determine how many customers' upgrades represent a challenging but possible goal. Multiply the individual customer's figure by this number of upgrades. This is what it is worth to retain your customers through their first upgrade.

5. Determine what actions are needed, based on your customer satisfaction data, to retain your present customers and estimate the cost of these actions.

6. Compute the estimated net gain from customer retention efforts: worth of customers minus cost to retain the customers.[4]

7. Do this for each segment. Note: Not all segments may be worth added retention effort. You may also discover a segment of customers for which even initial efforts to sell to them may not be economically wise.

   A supermarket, the only large chain present in a small town, estimates that its customers spend an average of $70 a week at the store ($3,640 a year) and that the average customer stays with the store for seven years (total average customer worth equals $25,480). Data analysis shows that customer satisfaction, in addition to the number of retained buyers, is at or above the industry norm for this type of location and store. Great! But the store does lose customers. At an average value of $25,480, it's worth exploring why the losses are occurring and what it would be worth to add efforts to retain more of these lost customers. And, as the town grows, the area is attracting other interested store chains. Action now to improve and sustain retention may be wise.

Kano Model

In an organization's efforts to increase customer satisfaction, it is critical to understand what satisfies customers, what does not, and what new or improved products and services could excite customers. Japanese professor Noriaki Kano devised a model that describes the interrelationship among three product qualities: those qualities that must be present, those that are "delighters" or "exciters," and those that are "one-dimensional." A "must be" quality is a dissatisfier when absent and is acceptable (and often not consciously noticed) when present. A "delighter" is unexpected and is a satisfier. However, over time, a "delighter" becomes a "must be," as in the case of the remote TV controller. A "one-dimensional" quality affects satisfaction in direct relationship to its presence; for example, as the price of gasoline goes down, satisfaction increases. Customer research is often used to determine dissatisfiers, satisfiers, and potential delighters. Problems do arise when an organization "thinks" it knows what its customers need and want without having done adequate testing within the various market segments it purports to serve. See Figure 10.2.

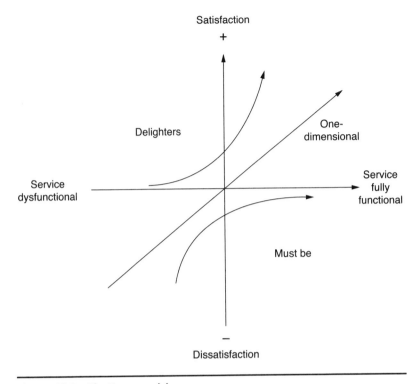

Figure 10.2   The Kano model.

3. INTERNAL AND EXTERNAL SUPPLIERS

> Understand the value in communicating
> expectations and the impact of supplier
> performance. Understand the value of
> working with suppliers to improve
> products, processes, or services.
> (Understand)
>
> **CQIA BoK 2006**

Internal Suppliers

These are the "providers" discussed in the earlier section on internal customers. *Internal suppliers* include not only those providers directly involved in producing the products/services, but also support functions, such as tariff checkers in a trucking company, materials management and cost accounting functions in manufacturing, facility maintenance in a school, the pharmacy in a hospital, the motor pool in a government agency, and market research.

In many organizations, internal suppliers establish *service-level agreements* (SLAs) with their customers. These agreements, usually for primary processes or subprocesses, provide the requirements that must be met by the supplier and allow for quantitative measurement of results. Internal data processing and information technology groups have used SLAs for many years to mutually establish customer requirements and measure performance to requirements.[5]

External Suppliers

Communicating stated expectations and requirements between customer and supplier is frequently a problem. Because of the pressures to get and keep business, suppliers often accept poorly communicated requirements. Consider the ramifications of the following incoming phone call:

> *"This is Acme. Joe, send me 150 more of those things you sold me last week. Goodbye."*
>
> *Exaggerated? Maybe, but it frequently happens like this. Look at the potential for error. The supplier may have more than one customer called "Acme." The caller's company received two shipments over the last seven working days. These last two shipments were for different products. Each shipment required different delivery methods: one went UPS, and the customer picked the other up. One order was for parts costing Joe's company $5 each to make. The other order was for parts costing $50 each to make. Though the parts looked similar, the more expensive part was made to a more stringent government specification. Does Joe's company take a guess as to what to make and ship for this telephone order? Unfortunately, the guess prevails all too often. Joe's past experience with the customer causes him to guess that the customer needs the more expensive part (which turns out not to be so). The consequences can be that the customer is satisfied to get what was expected or that the customer is frantic about having received the wrong parts and having to wait for the correct parts to be made and shipped. Joe's company has lost $7,500 in material and manufacturing costs for the wrong parts, the cost of shipping, and the cost of upsetting scheduling in order to get the replacement parts produced and shipped on an emergency basis. Who's to blame? Joe's company assumes the burden of clarifying the customer's requirements, up front, and the consequences of not doing so.*

Often, a smaller organization fears losing business by antagonizing a large customer, and perhaps major customer, with more extensive probing as to what the customer really needs. In some situations, this may mean asking the customer more about how and where the supplier's product will be used (usually imperative in medical device manufacturing). A commonly used international standard for quality management systems requires reviewing contracts and clarifying customers' requirements before accepting an order.

Given the ambiguous call Joe received, Joe's company should have had a policy of confirming the order in writing (by fax or e-mail) to request customer approval before accepting the order. Short of that, Joe should have called back with what he understood to be the requirement and to get an oral confirmation.

Many organizations are changing their approach to their external suppliers from the traditional adversarial relationship to a collaborative relationship. In past times, a supplier (more often called a "vendor") was considered an entity beneath the status of the buying organization. The "purchasing agent" of old would seek to pressure vendors until the lowest price was obtained. Often the buying organization was significantly larger than the vendor's organization and wielded the power of offering potentially large orders. Price and delivery were the primary drivers in the vendor selection process. If quality became a problem, an order was canceled and another vendor selected.

Increasingly, buying and selling organizations are forming quasi-partnerships and alliances to collaborate on improving the buyer–seller relationship as well as the quality of the products or services being purchased. Buying organizations have been able to substantially reduce the number of suppliers for any given product or service and cut costs through improved quality. It is not uncommon now for the buying organization to assist a supplier with training to use quality tools, material handling and stocking practices, and so forth. In this collaboration, the buying organization expects that the established quality and service levels will be consistent with its needs, that the supplier's practices will be continuously improved, and that lower prices will result. The supplier often receives assurance of longer-term contracts, assistance in making improvements, and sometimes certification as a preferred supplier.

4. SUPPLIER FEEDBACK

> Know the different types of supplier feedback (e.g., surveys, complaints, ratings) and understand the value in using the data to drive continuous improvement activities. (Understand)
>
> **CQIA BoK 2006**

Suppliers need to know how they are performing. This means that for suppliers providing products or services vital to quality, the customer must have a formal process for collecting, analyzing, and reporting supplier performance. Some common assessment and measurement tools for supplier performance are described next.

Questionnaires/Assessments

Suppliers may be asked to complete a survey about how their quality systems are designed and what plans for improvement have been developed. The customer may also conduct on-site assessments.

Survey questionnaires are usually mailed. They may be used to assess prospective or new suppliers or to reassess existing suppliers on a periodic basis. Use of questionnaires is one of the ways suppliers are "qualified" for the customer's qualified supplier list. The same design comments and cautions that apply to customer surveys pertain here as well. The difference between supplier questionnaires and customer questionnaires is that the customer expects a 100 percent response from suppliers. Many suppliers begrudgingly fill out the questionnaires because not to do so would mean loss of business. Large customers sometimes require lengthy questionnaires of even their smallest suppliers, without considering the burden placed on the suppliers.

Product Data

Suppliers may be requested to provide product quality data from the pertinent production run with each delivery, which is used in place of formal verification by the customer. The customer may then analyze the data for compliance to specification as well as process stability and capability.

Delivery Performance

Supplier performance against delivery requirements (for example, total number of days early and total late) is typically tracked and compared against order requirements.

Complaints

Tracking and reporting complaints about supplier performance is necessary in order to maintain suppliers' status on the qualified supplier list. An unacceptable number of complaints may result in a supplier's being suspended from the list, placed on probation, or totally removed. Usually a hierarchy of categories (types of reasons) is devised for use in coding complaints. The acceptance tolerance for numbers of complaints may vary depending upon the category.

Corrective Actions

When a problem is reported to a supplier with a formal request for corrective action, this requires a tracking process for ensuring that the supplier responds. These records should be analyzed to determine whether the supplier has been timely in its responses as well as effective with its corrective actions. Without good follow-up by the customer, some suppliers will tend to ignore corrective action requests. Making supplier action mandatory through contracts is a way to resolve this situation.

Product Price and Total Cost

Organizations continually try to reduce the cost of raw materials and services, or at least to minimize increases. The ability of suppliers to continually show progress in this arena is encouraged and tracked.

Reporting of Supplier Performance

This is usually done on a regular basis (such as quarterly). Typical indices used in tracking supplier performance are:

- Past performance index (PPI)
- Supplier performance index (SPI)
- Commodity performance index (CPI)

- Quality performance index (QPI)
- Delivery performance index (DPI)

Certification and Supplier Rating

Some customers have programs for "certifying" qualified suppliers. Typically, certified suppliers have demonstrated their ability to consistently meet the customer's requirements over a period of time. Suppliers are rated on a predetermined scale that may include most of the measurements already noted, as well as others. As the supplier fulfills the time and rating requirements, the supplier moves up through a two- or three-phase plan to full recognition as a certified supplier. The customer usually provides concessions to the certified supplier, such as no incoming inspection requirement, arrangements to ship directly to stock, a long-term purchasing contract, and "preferred supplier" status.

Value in Using Supplier Performance Data in Driving Continuous Improvement

Material and services from suppliers, when they are direct inputs to the product realization process, can substantially impact the quality of the product, customers' satisfaction, and profitability. Efforts to improve incoming material and services from suppliers (including their correctness, completeness, accuracy, timeliness, and appearance) are often given less attention by the customer than the customer's own internal processes. It should be noted, though, that defective material and inadequate services just received have not yet incurred the added costs of the production process. When a product is rejected at any stage up to and including its use by an end user, *costs have been added at each stage in the cycle.* At any stage, including the failure of a product under warranty, the quality of the incoming material or services could be the real root cause of failure. The tendency of some customers to "work around" supplier deficiencies is no longer acceptable.

Initiatives to continually improve suppliers' performance are critical to build and sustain customers' confidence. As mentioned earlier, the emerging trend of greater collaboration between customers and their suppliers is opening new opportunities for improvement, often developing into partnerships and alliances.

Cycle for Improving Customer–Supplier Relationships

Plan   A strategic plan addressing customer focus, a customer satisfaction feedback process design, and customer satisfaction improvement objectives constitute the "plan."

Do   Administration of the plan and collection of the data are the "do."

Check   Analysis of customer satisfaction data and supplier data, measurement against objectives, and identification of areas for improvement constitute the "check."

Act   Development of improvement action plans, implementation of the improvements, and assimilation of the improvements into daily operations is the "act."

When a customer complains, consider getting down on your knees to offer profuse gratitude because that person has just provided you with priceless advice—free of charge.

Owen Harari, *Management Review*

Notes

1. Concept initiated by Dr. Kaoru Ishikawa.
2. Westcott, R. T. Quality level agreements for clarity of expectations. *Stepping up to ISO 9004:2000*. (Chico, CA: Paton Press, 2003), appendix C.
3. Westcott, R. T. Tapping the customer's many voices. *Stepping up to ISO 9004:2000*. (Chico, CA: Paton Press, 2003), appendix B. Article describes the "LCALI" (listen, capture, analyze, learn, and improve) process for establishing listening posts and using the data collected.
4. F. Reicheld, and C. Fornell present a more sophisticated approach to determining the worth of retaining customers in "What's a Loyal Customer Worth?" *Fortune* (December 1995).
5. Westcott, R. T. Quality-Level Agreements.

Additional Resources

Allen, D., and T. R. Rao. *Analysis of customer satisfaction data*. (Milwaukee: ASQ Quality Press, 2000).

Barlow, J., and C. Moller. *A complaint is a gift*. (San Francisco: Berrett-Koehler Publishers, 1996).

Beecroft, G. Dennis, Grace L. Duffy, and John W. Moran, eds. *The executive guide to improvement and change*. (Milwaukee, WI: ASQ Quality Press, 2003).

Bell, C. R. *Customers as partners*. (San Francisco: Berrett-Koehler Publishers, 1994).

Berry, L. L. *On great service*. (New York: The Free Press, 1995).

Bossert, J. L., ed. *The supplier management handbook* (6th ed.). (Milwaukee: ASQ Quality Press, 2004).

Juran, J. M., and A. B. Godfrey, eds. *Juran's quality handbook* (5th ed.). (New York: McGraw-Hill, 1999).

Poirier, C. C., and W. F. Houser. *Business partnering for continuous improvement: How to forge enduring alliances among employees, suppliers, and customers*. (San Francisco: Berrett-Koehler Publishers, 1993).

Vavra, T. G. *Improving your measurement of customer satisfaction: A guide to creating, conducting, analyzing, and reporting customer satisfaction measurement programs*. (Milwaukee: ASQ Quality Press, 1997).

Westcott, Russell T., ed. *The certified manager of quality/organizational excellence handbook* (3rd ed.). (Milwaukee, WI: ASQ Quality Press, 2006), chapters 16–18.

Woodruff, R. B., and S. F. Gardial. *Know your customer: New approaches to understanding customer value and satisfaction*. (Cambridge, MA: Blackwell Publishers, 1996).

Appendix A

BODY OF KNOWLEDGE: ASQ Certified Quality Improvement Associate

(100 Questions—3 Hour Test)

The topics in this Body of Knowledge include subtext explanations and the cognitive level at which the questions will be written. This information will provide useful guidance for both the Exam Development Committee and the candidate preparing to take the exam. The subtext is not intended to limit the subject matter or be all-inclusive of that material that will be covered in the exam. It is meant to clarify the type of content that will be included on the exam. The descriptor in parentheses at the end of each entry refers to the maximum cognitive level at which the topic will be tested. A complete description of cognitive levels is provided at the end of this document.

I. Quality Basics (25 Questions)

   A. Terms, Concepts, and Principles

      1. **Quality**
Define and know how to use this term correctly. (Apply)

      2. **Quality planning**
Understand a quality plan and its purpose for the organization as a whole and who in the organization contributes to its development. (Understand)

      3. **The importance of employees**
Understand employee involvement and employee empowerment, and understand the benefits of both concepts; distinguish between involvement and empowerment. (Understand)

      4. **Systems and processes**
Define a system and a process; distinguish between a system and a process; understand the interrelationship between process and system; and know how the components of a system (supplier,

input, process, output, customer, and feedback) impact the system as a whole. (Analyze)

5. **Variation**
Understand the concept of variation and common and special cause variation. (Understand)

B. Benefits of Quality
Understand how improved process, product, and/or service quality will benefit any function, area of an organization, or industry. Understand how each stakeholder (e.g., employees, organization, customers, suppliers, community) benefits from quality and how the benefits may differ for each type of stakeholder. (Understand)

C. Quality Philosophies
Understand each of these philosophies and how they differ from one another. (Remember)

1. Deming (14 points)

2. Juran (Trilogy)

3. Crosby (Zero defects)

II. Teams (25 Questions)

A. Understanding Teams

1. **Purpose**
Understand the definition of a team, when to use a team, and for how long. (Apply)

2. **Characteristics and types**
Recognize characteristics and types of teams and how they are structured; know how teams differ and how they are similar; know which type of team to use in a given situation. (Apply)

3. **Value**
Understand how a team's work relates to the organization's key strategies and the value of using different types of teams. (Understand)

B. Roles and Responsibilities
Identify major team roles and the attributes of good role performance for champions, sponsors, leaders, facilitators, timekeepers, and members. (Understand)

C. Team Formation and Group Dynamics

1. **Initiating teams**
Apply the elements of launching a team: clear purpose, goals, commitment, ground rules, schedules, support from management, and team empowerment. (Apply)

2. **Selecting team members**
Know how to select team members who have appropriate skill sets and knowledge (e.g., number of members, expertise, and representation). (Apply)

3. **Team stages**
Describe the classic stages of team evolution (forming, storming, norming, and performing). (Understand)

4. **Team barriers**
   Understand the value of conflict, know how to resolve team conflict, define and recognize groupthink and how to overcome it, understand how poor logistics and agendas as well as lack of training become barriers to a team. (Analyze)
5. **Decision making**
   Understand and apply different decision models (voting, consensus, etc.). (Apply)

III. Continuous Improvement (50 Questions)
  A. Incremental and Breakthrough Improvement
     Understand how process improvement can identify waste and non-value-added activities. Understand how both incremental and breakthrough improvement processes achieve results. Know the steps required for both types of improvement. Recognize which type of improvement approach is being used in specific situations. Know the similarities and differences between the two approaches. (Understand)
  B. Improvement Cycles
     Define various improvement cycle phases (e.g., PDCA, PDSA) and use them appropriately. (Analyze)
  C. Problem-Solving Process
     Apply the basic problem-solving steps: understand the problem, determine the root cause, develop/implement solutions, and verify effectiveness. (Apply)
  D. Improvement Tools
     Use, interpret, and explain flowcharts, histograms, Pareto charts, scatter diagrams, run charts, cause-and-effect diagrams, checklists (check sheets), affinity diagrams, cost of quality, benchmarking, brainstorming, and audits as improvement tools. Understand control chart concepts (e.g., centerlines, control limits, out-of-control conditions), and recognize when control charts should be used. (Apply)
  E. Customer-Supplier Relationships
    1. **Internal and external customers**
       Know how customers are defined. Understand the importance of working with customers to improve processes and services, and how customers influence organizational processes. Know how to distinguish between different external customer types (consumers and end-users). (Understand)
    2. **Customer feedback**
       Know the different types of customer feedback (e.g., surveys, complaints) and understand the value in using the data to drive continuous improvement activities. (Understand)
    3. **Internal and external suppliers**
       Understand the value in communicating expectations and the impact of supplier performance. Understand the value of

working with suppliers to improve products, processes, or services. (Understand)

4. **Supplier feedback**
   Know the different types of supplier feedback (e.g., surveys, complaints, ratings) and understand the value in using the data to drive continuous improvement activities (Understand)

Levels of Cognition based on Bloom's Taxonomy—Revised (2001)

In addition to **content** specifics, the subtext for each topic in this BOK also indicates the intended **complexity level** of the test questions for that topic. These levels are based on "Levels of Cognition" (from Bloom's Taxonomy—Revised, 2001) and are presented below in rank order, from least complex to most complex.

Remember (Knowledge Level). Recall or recognize terms, definitions, facts, ideas, materials, patterns, sequences, methods, principles, and so on.

Understand (Comprehension Level). Read and understand descriptions, communications, reports, tables, diagrams, directions, regulations, and so on.

Apply (Application Level). Know when and how to use ideas, procedures, methods, formulas, principles, theories, and so on.

Analyze (Analysis Level). Break down information into its constituent parts and recognize their relationship to one another and how they are organized; identify sublevel factors or salient data from a complex scenario.

Evaluate (Evaluation Level). Make judgments about the value of proposed ideas, solutions, and so on, by comparing the proposal to specific criteria or standards.

Create (Synthesis Level). Put parts or elements together in such a way as to reveal a pattern or structure not clearly there before; identify which data or information from a complex set is appropriate to examine further or from which supported conclusions can be drawn.

Appendix B
ASQ Code of Ethics

Fundamental Principles

ASQ requires its members and certification holders to conduct themselves ethically by:

    I. Being honest and impartial in serving the public, their employers, customers, and clients.

    II. Striving to increase the competence and prestige of the quality profession, and

    III. Using their knowledge and skill for the enhancement of human welfare.

Members and certification holders are required to observe the tenets set forth below:

Relations With the Public

    Article 1—Hold paramount the safety, health, and welfare of the public in the performance of their professional duties.

Relations With Employers and Clients

    Article 2—Perform services only in their areas of competence.

    Article 3—Continue their professional development throughout their careers and provide opportunities for the professional and ethical development of others.

    Article 4—Act in a professional manner in dealings with ASQ staff and each employer, customer, or client.

    Article 5—Act as faithful agents or trustees and avoid conflict of interest and the appearance of conflicts of interest.

Relations With Peers

Article 6—Build their professional reputation on the merit of their services and not compete unfairly with others.

Article 7—Assure that credit for the work of others is given to those to whom it is due.

Appendix C
Quality Glossary

A

acceptable quality level (AQL)—When a continuing series of lots is considered, a quality level that, for the purposes of sampling inspection, is the limit of a satisfactory process average.

acceptance sampling—Inspection of a sample from a lot to decide whether to accept or not accept that lot. There are two types: attributes sampling and variables sampling. In attributes sampling, the presence or absence of a characteristic is noted in each of the units inspected. In variables sampling, the numerical magnitude of a characteristic is measured and recorded for each inspected unit; this involves reference to a continuous scale of some kind.

accuracy—A characteristic of measurement that addresses how close an observed value is to the true value. It answers the question, "Is it right?"

ACSI—The American Customer Satisfaction Index, released for the first time in October 1994, is a new economic indicator, a cross-industry measure of the satisfaction of U.S. household customers with the quality of the goods and services available to them—both those goods and services produced within the United States and those provided as imports from foreign firms that have substantial market shares or dollar sales. The ACSI is cosponsored by the University of Michigan Business School and the American Society for Quality (ASQ).

action plan—The detailed plan to implement the actions needed to achieve strategic goals and objectives (similar to, but not as comprehensive as, a project plan).

activity network diagram (AND)—*See* arrow diagram.

ad hoc team—*See* temporary team.

affinity diagram—A management and planning tool used to organize ideas into natural groupings in a way that stimulates new, creative ideas. Also known as the "KJ" method.

alignment—The actions taken to ensure that a process or activity supports the organization's strategy, goals, and objectives.

alliance—*See* partnership/alliance.

alpha risk—*See* producer's risk.

analysis of variance (ANOVA)—A basic statistical technique for analyzing experimental data. It subdivides the total variation of a data set into meaningful component parts associated with specific sources of variation in order to test a hypothesis on the parameters of the model or to estimate variance components. There are three models: fixed, random, and mixed.

ANSI—American National Standards Institute.

AOQ—Average outgoing quality.

appraisal costs—The costs associated with measuring, evaluating, or auditing products or services to assure conformance to quality standards and performance requirements.

AQL—Acceptable quality level.

arrow diagram—A management and planning tool used to develop the best possible schedule and appropriate controls to accomplish the schedule; the critical path method (CPM) and the program evaluation review technique (PERT) expand the use of arrow diagrams.

assessment—An estimate or determination of the significance, importance, or value of something.

assignable cause—*See* special causes.

attribute data—Go/no-go information. The control charts based on attribute data include fraction defective chart, number of affected units chart, count chart, count-per-unit chart, quality score chart, and demerit chart.

audit—A planned, independent, and documented assessment to determine whether agreed-upon requirements are being met.

audit program—The organized structure, commitment, and documented methods used to plan and perform audits.

audit team—The group of trained individuals conducting an audit under the direction of a team leader, relevant to a particular product, process, service, contract, or project.

auditee—The individual or organization being audited.

auditor—An individual or organization carrying out an audit.

average—*See* mean.

average outgoing quality (AOQ)—The expected average quality level of outgoing product or service for a given value of incoming product or service quality.

B

balanced scorecard—Translates an organization's mission and strategy into a comprehensive set of performance measures to provide a basis for strategic measurement and management, typically using four balanced views: financial, customers, internal business processes, and learning and growth.

Baldrige National Quality Program (BNQP)—An award established by Congress in 1987 to raise awareness of quality management and to recognize U.S. companies that have implemented successful quality management systems. The accompanying *Criteria for Performance Excellence* is published each year. Three awards may be given annually in each of five categories: manufacturing businesses, service businesses, small businesses, education institutions, and health-care organizations. The award is named after the late Secretary of Commerce Malcolm Baldrige, a proponent of quality management. The U.S. Commerce Department's National Institute of Standards and Technology manages the award, and ASQ administers it. The major emphasis in determining success is achieving results.

baseline measurement—The beginning point, based on an evaluation of the output over a period of time, used to determine the process parameters prior to any improvement effort; the basis against which change is measured.

benchmarking—An improvement process in which a company measures its performance against that of best-in-class companies (or others who are good performers), determines how those companies achieved their performance levels, and uses the information to improve its own performance. The areas that can be benchmarked include strategies, operations, processes, and procedures.

benefit-cost analysis—Collection of the dollar value of benefits derived from an initiative and the associated costs incurred and computing the ratio of benefits to cost.

beta risk—*See* consumer's risk.

bias—Generally, an effect that causes a statistical result to be distorted; that is, there is a difference between the true value and the observed value.

Big Q, little q—Terms used to contrast the difference between managing for quality in all business processes and products (Big Q) and managing for quality in a limited capacity, traditionally in only factory products and processes (little q).

Bloom's Taxonomy (levels of cognition)—*See* Appendix A.

brainstorming—A problem-solving tool that teams use to generate as many ideas as possible related to a particular subject. Team members begin by offering all their ideas; the ideas are not discussed or reviewed until after the brainstorming session.

breakthrough improvement—A method of solving chronic problems that results from the effective execution of a strategy designed to reach the next level of quality. Contrasted with incremental improvement, a breakthrough improvement is a one-time major reengineering of change that may cross many interorganizational boundaries. Such change often requires a paradigm shift within the organization.

business partnering—The creation of cooperative business alliances between constituencies within an organization or between an organization and its customers or suppliers. Partnering occurs through a pooling of resources in a trusting atmosphere focused on continuous, mutual improvement (*see also* customer–supplier partnership).

business processes—Processes that focus on what the organization does as a business and how it goes about doing it. A business has functional processes (generating output within a single department) and cross-functional processes (generating output across several functions or departments).

C

c chart—Count chart.

calibration—The comparison of a measurement instrument or system of unverified accuracy to a measurement instrument or system of a known accuracy to detect any variation from the true value.

capability—The natural tolerance of a machine or process generally defined to include 99.7 percent of all population values.

capable process—A process is said to be capable if the product or output of the process always conforms to the specified specifications of the customer—that is, 100 percent conformance to the customer requirements.

cascading training—Training implemented in an organization from the top down, where each level acts as trainers to those below.

cause-and-effect diagram—A tool for analyzing process variables. It is also referred to as the Ishikawa diagram, because Kaoru Ishikawa developed it, and also the fishbone diagram, because the complete diagram resembles a fish skeleton. The diagram illustrates the main causes and subcauses leading to an effect (symptom). The cause-and-effect diagram is one of the seven tools of quality.

centerline—A line on a graph that represents the overall average (mean) operating level of the process charted.

central tendency—The propensity of data collected on a process to concentrate around a value situated somewhere midway between the lowest and highest value.

certification—The receipt of a document from an authorized source stating that a device, process, or operator has been certified to a known standard.

chain reaction—A series of interacting events described by W. Edwards Deming: improve quality → decrease costs → improve productivity → increase market share with better quality and lower price → stay in business, provide jobs, and provide more jobs.

champion—An individual who has accountability and responsibility for many processes or who is involved in making strategic-level decisions for the organization. The champion ensures ongoing dedication of project resources and monitors strategic alignment (may also be referred to as a *sponsor*).

change agent—The person, from inside or from outside the organization, who facilitates change within the organization. May not be the initiator of the change effort.

characteristic—A property that helps to identify or to differentiate between entities and that can be described or measured to determine conformance or nonconformance to requirements.

charter—A documented statement officially initiating the formation of a committee, team, project, or other effort in which a clearly stated purpose and approval is conferred.

check sheet—A simple data-recording device. The check sheet is custom-designed for the particular use, allowing ease in interpreting the results. The check sheet is one of the seven tools of quality. Check sheets should not be confused with data sheets and checklists.

checklist—A tool for organizing and ensuring that all important steps or actions in an operation have been taken. Checklists contain items that are important or relevant to an issue or situation. Checklists should not be confused with check sheets and data sheets.

coaching—A continual improvement technique by which people receive one-to-one learning through demonstration and practice and that is characterized by immediate feedback and correction.

code of conduct—The expected behavior that has been mutually developed and agreed upon by an organization or a team.

common causes of variation—Causes that are inherent in any process all the time. A process that has only common causes of variation is said to be stable, predictable, or in control. Also called *chance causes.*

competence—Refers to a person's ability to learn and perform a particular activity. Competence consists of knowledge, experience, skills, aptitude, and attitude components (KESAA factors).

complaint handling—The process and practices involved in receiving and resolving complaints from customers.

compliance—An affirmative indication or judgment that the supplier of a product or service has met the requirements of the relevant specifications, contract, or regulation; also the state of meeting the requirements.

conflict resolution—A process for resolving disagreements in a manner acceptable to all parties.

conformance—An affirmative indication or judgment that a product or service has met the requirements of a relevant specification, contract, or regulation.

consensus—Finding a proposal acceptable enough that all team members can support the decision and no member opposes it.

consumer market customers—End users of a product or service.

consumer's risk—For a sampling plan, refers to the probability of acceptance of a lot, the quality of which has a designated numerical value representing a level that is seldom desirable. Usually the designated value will be the lot tolerance percent defective (LPTD). Also called *beta risk* or *type 2 error.*

continual process improvement—Includes the actions taken throughout an organization to increase the effectiveness and efficiency of activities and processes in order to provide added benefits to the customer and organization. It is considered a subset of total quality management and operates according to the premise that organizations can always make improvements. Continual improvement can also be equated with reducing process variation.

control chart—A basic tool that consists of a chart with upper and lower control limits on which values of some statistical measure for a series of samples or subgroups are plotted. It frequently shows a central line to help detect a trend of plotted values toward either control limit. It is used to monitor and analyze variation from a process to see whether the process is in statistical control.

control limits—The natural boundaries of a process within specified confidence levels, expressed as the upper control limit (UCL) and the lower control limit (LCL).

control plan—A document, or documents, that may include the characteristics for quality of a product or service, measurements, and methods of control.

core competency—Pertains to the unique features and characteristics of an organization's overall capability.

corrective action—The implementation of solutions resulting in the reduction or elimination of an identified problem.

corrective action—Action taken to eliminate the root cause(s) and symptom(s) of an existing deviation or nonconformity to prevent recurrence.

correlation—Refers to the measure of the relationship between two sets of numbers or variables.

cost of poor quality (COPQ)—The costs associated with the production of nonconforming material.

cost-benefit analysis—*See* benefit-cost analysis.

cost of quality (COQ)—The total costs incurred relating to the quality of a product or service. There are four categories of quality costs: internal failure costs; external failure costs; appraisal costs; and prevention costs (*see* individual entries).

count chart—A control chart for evaluating the stability of a process in terms of the count of events of a given classification occurring in a sample.

Cp—A widely used process capability index. It is expressed as Cp = (upper specification limit − lower specification limit) divided by 6s.

Cpk—A widely used process capability index. It is expressed as the ratio with smallest answer:

$$\frac{\text{upper specification limit} - \text{X-bar}}{3\sigma} \quad \text{or} \quad \frac{\text{X-bar} - \text{lower specification limit}}{3\sigma}$$

criterion—A standard, rule, or test upon which a decision can be based.

critical-to-quality (CTQ)—Characteristics that, from a customer's perception of quality, are critical to the achievement of quality goals, objectives, standards, and/or specifications.

cross-functional team—A group consisting of members from more than one department or work unit that is organized to accomplish a project.

culture—*See* organization culture.

cumulative sum control chart—A control chart on which the plotted value is the cumulative sum of deviations of successive samples from a target value. The ordinate of each plotted point represents the algebraic sum of the previous ordinate and the most recent deviations from the target.

customer—Recipient of a product or service provided by a supplier (*see also* external customer and internal customer).

customer council—A group usually composed of representatives from an organization's largest customers who meet to discuss common issues.

customer delight—The result achieved when customer requirements are exceeded in unexpected ways the customer finds valuable.

customer expectations—Customers' perceptions of the value they will receive from the purchase of a product or experience with a service. Customers form expectations by analyzing available information, which may include experience, word-of-mouth, and advertising and sales promises.

customer loyalty/retention—The result of an organization's plans, processes, practices, and efforts designed to deliver its services or products in ways that create retained and committed customers.

customer-oriented organization—An organization whose mission, purpose, and actions are dedicated to serving and satisfying customers.

customer relationship management (CRM)—Refers to an organization's knowledge of its customers' unique requirements and expectations, and use of that information to develop a closer and more profitable link to business processes and strategies.

customer requirements—Specific characteristics of products and services determined by customers' needs or wants.

customer satisfaction—The result of delivering a product or service that meets customer requirements, needs, and expectations.

customer segmentation—Refers to the process of differentiating customers based on one or more dimensions for the purpose of developing a marketing strategy to address specific segments.

customer service—The activities of dealing with customer questions; also sometimes the department that takes customer orders or provides postdelivery services.

customer–supplier partnership—A long-term relationship between a buyer and supplier characterized by teamwork and mutual confidence. The supplier is considered an extension of the buyer's organization. The partnership is based on several commitments. The buyer provides long-term contracts and uses fewer suppliers. The supplier implements quality assurance processes so that incoming inspection can be minimized. The supplier also helps the buyer reduce costs and improve product and process designs.

cycle time—Refers to the time that it takes to complete a process from beginning to end.

D

d chart—Demerit chart.

data—Quantitative or qualitative facts presented in descriptive, numeric, or graphic form. There are two kinds of numerical data: measured or variable data, such as "16 ounces," "4 miles," and ".075 inches"; and counted or attribute data, such as "162 defects." Data may also be nonnumeric, expressed as words or symbols.

decision matrix—A matrix used by teams to evaluate problems or possible solutions. After a matrix is drawn to evaluate possible solutions, for example, the team lists them in the far-left vertical column. Next, the team selects criteria to rate the possible solutions, writing them across the top row. Third, each possible solution is rated on a scale of 1 to 5 for each criterion and the rating recorded in the corresponding grid. Finally, the ratings of all the criteria for each possible solution are added to determine its total score. The total score is then used to help decide which solution deserves the most attention.

defect—A product or service's nonfulfillment of an intended requirement or reasonable expectation for use, including safety considerations. They are often classified, such as:

- Class 1, Critical, leads directly to severe injury or catastrophic economic loss
- Class 2, Serious, leads directly to significant injury or significant economic loss
- Class 3, Major, is related to major problems with respect to intended normal or reasonably foreseeable use
- Class 4, Minor, is related to minor problems with respect to intended normal or reasonably foreseeable use (*see also* blemish, imperfection, and nonconformity).

defective—A product that contains one or more defects relative to the quality characteristics being measured.

deficiencies—Units of product are considered to have defects. Errors or flaws in a process are described in a hospital setting as "deficiencies." Medical procedures, job tasks, or documented processes, for example, may have deficiencies that reduce their ability to satisfy the patient, physician, or other stakeholder in the organization.

Deming cycle—*See* Plan—Do—Check—Act cycle.

dependability—The degree to which a product or service is operable and capable of performing its required function at any randomly chosen time during its specified operating time, provided that the product or service is available at the start of that period. (Nonoperation-related influences are not included.) Dependability can be expressed by the ratio: time available divided by (time available + time required).

deployment—(to spread out) Used in strategic planning to describe the process of cascading goals, objectives, and plans throughout an organization.

design of experiments (DOE)—A branch of applied statistics dealing with planning, conducting, analyzing, and interpreting controlled tests to evaluate the factors that control the value of a parameter or group of parameters.

deviation—A nonconformance or departure of a characteristic from specified product, process, or system requirements.

diagnostic journey and remedial journey—A two-phase investigation used by teams to solve chronic quality problems. In the first phase, the diagnostic journey, the team moves from the symptom of a problem to its cause. In the second phase, the remedial journey, the team moves from the cause to a remedy.

DiSC—A profiling instrument that measures characteristic ways in which a person behaves in a particular environment. Four dimensions measured are: *dominance, influence, steadiness,* and *conscientiousness.*

discrete data—Data where all possible outcomes can be distinctly identified as integers (fractional values are not possible). Examples: family size, good/bad, SAT scores, etc. Sometimes known as *attributes data.*

discrimination—The ability of a measuring instrument to respond to small changes in the value of the materials.

dissatisfiers—Those features or functions that the customer or employee has come to expect and that, if they were no longer present, would result in dissatisfaction.

distribution—Describes the amount of potential variation in outputs of a process; it is usually described in terms of its shape, average, and standard deviation.

DMAIC—Pertains to a methodology used in the Six Sigma approach: *Define, Measure, Analyze, Improve, Control.*

drivers of quality—Include customers, products/services, employee satisfaction, and total organizational focus.

E

effect—That which results after an action has been taken. The expected or predicted impact when an action is to be taken or is proposed.

effectiveness—The state of having produced a decided-upon or desired effect. Increased customer satisfaction, increased employee satisfaction, improved supplier relations, cost reduction, increased efficiency, improved timeliness, greater accuracy, and completeness are all contributors to effectiveness.

efficiency—The ratio of the output to the total input in a process.

efficient—A term describing a process that operates effectively while consuming the minimum amount of resources (such as labor and time).

eighty/twenty (80/20) rule—A term referring to the Pareto principle, which suggests that most effects come from relatively few causes; that is, 80 percent of the effects come from 20 percent of the possible causes.

electronic data interchange (EDI)—The electronic exchange of data between customers and suppliers and vice versa; for example, using a dedicated high-speed line, a customer places an order directly with a supplier, and the supplier acknowledges receipt of the order with confirmation of price and shipping date. Some large customers specify that their suppliers must have this capability in order to qualify as approved suppliers.

employee involvement—The practice of involving employees in decisions pertaining to processes, usually within their work units. Such decisions may include suggestions for improving the process, planning, setting objectives, and tracking performance. Natural (work unit) teams, process improvement teams, cross-functional teams, task forces, quality circles, and other vehicles for involvement may be used. Usually participation in decisions related to legal and/or personnel matters is excluded.

empowerment—A condition whereby employees have the authority to make decisions and take action in their work areas, within stated bounds, without prior approval. For example, an operator can stop a production process upon detecting a problem, or a customer service representative can send out a replacement product if a customer calls with a problem.

end users—External customers who purchase products/services for their own use.

error—The degree of variability between estimates of the same characteristic over repeated samples taken under similar conditions.

ethics—An individual or an organization's adherence to a belief or documented code of conduct that is based on moral principles, and that tries to balance what is fair for individuals with what is right for society.

event—The starting or ending point for a task or group of tasks.

excited quality—The additional benefit a customer receives when a product or service goes beyond basic expectations. Excited quality "wows" the customer and distinguishes the provider from the competition. If missing, the customer will still be satisfied.

expected quality—Also known as *basic quality*, the minimum benefit or value a customer expects to receive from a product or service.

expectations—Customer perceptions about how an organization's products and services will meet their specific needs and requirements. Expectations for a product or service are shaped by many factors, including:

- The specific use the customer intends to make of it
- Prior experience with a similar product or service
- Representations and commitments (marketing and advertising descriptions)

external customer—A person or organization who receives a product, a service, or information but is not part of the organization supplying it (*see also* internal customer).

external failure costs—Costs occurring after delivery or shipment of the product, or during or after furnishing of a service, to the customer.

F

facilitator—An individual who is responsible for creating favorable conditions that will enable a team to reach its purpose or achieve its goals by bringing together the necessary tools, information, and resources to get the job done. A facilitator addresses the processes a team uses to achieve its purpose. Specially trained, the facilitator functions as a teacher, coach, and moderator.

failure—The inability of an item, product, or service to perform required functions on demand due to one or more defects.

failure cost—The costs resulting from products or services not conforming to requirements or customer/user needs—that is, the costs resulting from poor quality.

failure mode analysis (FMA)—A procedure to determine which malfunction symptoms appear immediately before or after a failure of a critical parameter in a system. After all the possible causes are listed for each symptom, the product or procedure is designed to eliminate the problems.

failure mode effects analysis (FMEA)—A procedure in which each potential failure mode in every subitem of an item or process is analyzed to determine its effect on other subitems and on the required function of the item or process.

failure mode effects and criticality analysis (FMECA)—A procedure that is performed after a failure mode effects analysis to classify each potential failure effect according to its severity and probability of occurrence.

fault tree analysis—A top-down technique for determining the set of components that could cause a failure in a process. Specifically accounts for both single and multiple causes.

feedback—The response to information received in interpersonal communication (written or oral); it may be based on fact or feeling and helps the party who is receiving the information judge how well the other party is understanding him or her. More generally, feedback is information about a process or performance and is used to make decisions that are directed toward improving or adjusting the process or performance as necessary.

fishbone diagram—*See* cause-and-effect diagram.

fitness for use—A term used to indicate that a product or service fits the customer's defined purpose for that product or service.

five whys—A repetitive questioning technique to probe deeper in order to surface the root cause of a problem.

flowchart—A graphical representation of the steps in a process. Flowcharts are drawn to better understand processes. The flowchart is one of the seven basic tools of quality.

focus group—A qualitative discussion group consisting of 8 to 10 participants, invited from a segment of the customer base to discuss an existing or planned product or service, led by a facilitator working from predetermined questions (focus groups may also be used to gather information in a context other than customers).

force-field analysis—A technique for analyzing the forces that aid or hinder an organization in reaching an objective. An arrow pointing to an objective is drawn down the middle of a piece of paper. The factors that will aid the objective's achievement, called the driving forces, are listed on the left side of the arrow. The factors that will hinder its achievement, called the restraining forces, are listed on the right side of the arrow.

fourteen points—W. Edward Deming's 14 management practices to help companies increase their quality and productivity: (1) create constancy of purpose for improving products and services; (2) adopt the new philosophy; (3) cease dependence on inspection to achieve quality; (4) end the practice of awarding business on price alone, and instead minimize total cost by working with a single supplier; (5) improve constantly and forever every process for planning, production, and service; (6) institute training on the job; (7) adopt and institute leadership; (8) drive out fear; (9) break down barriers between staff areas; (10) eliminate slogans, exhortations, and targets for the workforce; (11) eliminate numerical quotas for the workforce and numerical goals for management; (12) remove barriers that rob people of pride in workmanship and eliminate the annual rating or merit system; (13) institute a vigorous program of education and self-improvement for everyone; and (14) put everybody in the company to work to accomplish the transformation.

frequency distribution (statistical)—A table that graphically presents a large volume of data so that the central tendency (such as the average or mean) and distribution are clearly displayed.

functional organization—An organization organized by discrete functions, for example, marketing/sales, engineering, production, finance, human resources.

G

gage—An instrument or system for testing.

gage repeatability and reproducibility (GR&R)—The evaluation of a gaging instrument's accuracy by determining whether the measurements taken with it are repeatable (i.e., there is close agreement among a number of consecutive measurements of the output for the same value of the input under the same operating conditions) and reproducible (i.e., there is close agreement among repeated measurements of the output for the same value of input made under the same operating conditions over a period of time).

gainsharing—A type of program that rewards individuals financially on the basis of organizational performance.

Gantt chart—A type of bar chart used in process/project planning and control to display planned work and finished work in relation to time. Also called a *milestone chart* when interim checkpoints are added.

gap analysis—A technique that compares a company's existing state to its desired state (as expressed by its long-term plans) to help determine what needs to be done to remove or minimize the gap.

gatekeeping—The role of an individual (often a facilitator) in a group meeting in helping ensure effective interpersonal interactions (for example, someone's ideas are not ignored due to the team moving on to the next topic too quickly).

goal—A statement of general intent, aim, or desire; it is the point toward which management directs its efforts and resources; goals are usually nonquantitative and are measured via supporting objectives.

group dynamics—The interaction (behavior) of individuals within a team meeting.

groupthink—Occurs when most or all team members coalesce in supporting an idea or decision that hasn't been fully explored, or when some members secretly disagree but go along with the other members in apparent support.

H

Hawthorne effect—The concept that every change results (initially, at least) in increased productivity.

histogram—A graphic summary of variation in a set of data. The pictorial nature of the histogram lets people see patterns that are difficult to see in a simple table of numbers. The histogram is one of the seven tools of quality.

house of quality—A diagram (named for its house-shaped appearance) that clarifies the relationship between customer needs and product features. It helps correlate market or customer requirements and analysis of competitive products with higher-level technical and product characteristics and makes it possible to bring several factors into a single figure. Also known as *quality function deployment (QFD)*.

I

imagineering—Developing in the mind's eye a process without waste.

improvement—The positive effect of a process change effort. Improvement may result from incremental changes or from a major breakthrough.

in control—A term that describes a situation in which the variations within a process occur only between the computed upper and lower control limits. The process is considered to be stable and therefore predictable. A process in which the statistical measure being evaluated is in a state of statistical control; that is, the variations among the observed sampling results can be attributed to a constant system of chance/common causes (*see also* out-of-control process).

incremental improvement—Improvements that are implemented on a continual basis. These improvements are typically small steps within the part of an overall process contained within a given work unit.

indicators—Predetermined measures used to measure how well an organization is meeting its customers' needs and its operational and financial performance objectives. Such indicators can be either *leading* or *lagging* indicators. Indicators are also devices used to measure physical objects.

information—Data transformed into an ordered format that makes it usable and allows one to draw conclusions.

information system—Technology-based systems used to support operations, aid day-to-day decision making, and support strategic analysis (other names often used include: management information system, decision system, information technology [IT], data processing).

input—Material, product, or service that is obtained from an upstream internal provider or an external supplier and is used to produce an output.

inspection—Measuring, examining, testing, and gaging one or more characteristics of a product or service and comparing the results with specified requirements to determine whether conformity is achieved for each characteristic.

inspection cost—The cost associated with inspecting the product to ensure that it meets the (internal or external) customer's needs and requirements; an appraisal cost.

intermediate customers—Distributors, dealers, or brokers who make products and services available to the end user by repairing, repackaging, reselling, or creating finished goods from components or subassemblies.

internal audit—An audit conducted within an organization by members of the organization to measure its strengths or weaknesses against its own procedures and/or external standards—a "first-party audit."

internal customer—The recipient, person, or department of another person or department's output (product, service, or information) within an organization (*see also* external customer).

internal failure costs—Costs occurring prior to delivery or shipment of the product, or the furnishing of a service, to the customer.

interrelationship digraph—A management and planning tool that displays the relationship between factors in a complex situation. It identifies meaningful categories from a mass of ideas and is useful when relationships are difficult to determine.

intervention—An action taken by a leader or a facilitator to support the effective functioning of a team or work group.

Ishikawa diagram—*See* cause-and-effect diagram.

ISO—"equal" (Greek). A prefix for a series of standards published by the International Organization for Standardization.

ISO 9000 series standards—A set of individual but related international standards and guidelines on quality management and quality assurance developed to help companies effectively document the quality system elements to be implemented to maintain an efficient quality system. The standards, initially published in 1987, revised in 1994 and 2000, are not specific to any particular industry, product, or service. The standards were developed by the International Organization for Standardization, a specialized international agency for standardization composed of the national standards bodies of nearly 100 countries.

ISO/TS 16949—A set of requirements pertaining to the application of ISO 9001 for automotive production and organizations that manufacture related parts. It is based on ISO 9001, but it also contains requirements specific to the automotive industry.

J

JCAHO—Joint Commission on Accreditation of Healthcare Organizations.

Juran's trilogy—*See* quality trilogy.

just-in-time manufacturing (JIT)—An optimal material requirement planning system for a manufacturing process in which there is little or no manufacturing material inventory on hand at the manufacturing site and little or no incoming inspection.

just-in-time-training—Providing job training coincidental with, or immediately prior to, an employee's assignment to a new or expanded job.

K

kaizen—Incremental improvement; a Japanese term that means gradual unending improvement by doing little things better and setting and achieving increasingly higher standards. Masaaki Imai made the term famous in his book *Kaizen: The Key to Japan's Competitive Success.*

kaizen blitz/event—An intense, short-time-frame (typically 3–5 consecutive days) team approach to employ the concepts and techniques of continual improvement (for example, to reduce cycle time, increase throughput).

kanban—A method for providing material/product to a succeeding operation by signaling the preceding operation when more material/product is needed. This "pull" type of process control employs a kanban, a card or signboard, attached to a lot of material/product in a production line signifying the delivery of a given quantity. When all of the material/product has been processed, the card/sign is returned to its source, where it becomes an order to replenish. The key advantages of this method are that unnecessary buildup of work-in-process inventory is eliminated, space is saved, and the risk of loss due to defective material/product is decreased (less work-in-process inventory is produced before a defect is detected).

Kano model—Three classes of customer requirements as described by Dr. Noriaki Kano: satisfiers—what customers say they want; dissatisfiers—what customers expect and what results in dissatisfaction when not present; delighters/exciters—new or unexpected features that customers do not expect. It is observed that what a customer originally perceives as a delighter will become a dissatisfier if no longer available.

KESAA factors—*See* competence.

key process—A major system-level process that supports the mission and satisfies major customer requirements. The identification of key processes allows the organization to focus its resources on what is important to the customer.

key result area (KRA)—A major category of customer requirements that is critical for the organization's success.

key success factors (KSF)—Those factors that point toward answers to key questions, such as "How will we know if we're successful?" "How will we know when we're heading for trouble?" and "If we are moving away from our organizational strategy and targets, what corrections should we make?" KSFs are selected to measure what is truly important to an organization: customer satisfaction, employee satisfaction, financial stability, and important operational factors.

KJ method—*See* affinity diagram.

knowledge management—Involves transforming data into information, the acquisition or creation of knowledge, as well as the processes and technology employed in identifying, categorizing, storing, retrieving, disseminating, and using information and knowledge for the purposes of improving decisions and plans.

L

LCALI—A process for operating a listening-post system for capturing and using formerly unavailable customer data ("listen," "capture," "analyze," "learn," "improve").[1]

leader—An individual, recognized by others, as the person to lead an effort. One cannot be a "leader" without one or more "followers." The term is often used interchangeably with "manager" (*see* manager). A "leader" may or may not hold an officially designated management-type position.

leadership—An essential part of a quality improvement effort. Organization leaders must establish a vision, communicate that vision to those in the organization, and provide the tools, knowledge, and motivation necessary to accomplish the vision.

life cycle—A product life cycle is the total time frame from product concept to the end of its intended use; a project life cycle is typically divided into five stages: concept, planning, design, implementation, and evaluation and close-out.

listening post—An individual who, by virtue of her or his potential for having contact with customers, is designated to collect, document, and transmit pertinent feedback to a central collection authority within the organization. Such feedback is analyzed for emerging trends or recurring problems, which are reported to management. Preventive actions are taken when the information indicates the need. Positive feedback is passed on to the organizational function or person responsible for a customer's expression of satisfaction.

listening-post data—Customer data and information gathered from designated "listening posts."

lot—A defined quantity of product accumulated under conditions that are considered uniform for sampling purposes.

lower control limit (LCL)—Control limit for points below the central line in a control chart.

M

maintainability—The probability that a given maintenance action for an item under given usage conditions can be performed within a stated time interval when the maintenance is performed under stated conditions using stated procedures and resources. Maintainability has two categories: serviceability, the ease of conducting scheduled inspections and servicing, and repairability, the ease of restoring service after a failure.

management by fact—A business philosophy that decisions should be based on data.

management by walking around (MBWA)—A manager's planned, but usually unannounced, walk-through of the organization to gather information from employees and make observations; may be viewed in a positive light by virtue of giving employees the opportunity to interact with top management; has the potential of being viewed negatively if punitive action is taken as a result of information gathered.

management review—Formal evaluation by top management of the status and adequacy of the quality management system in relation to the applicable standards, and the organization's quality policy and objectives.

manager—An individual who manages and is responsible for resources (people, material, money, time). A person officially designated with a management-type position title. A manager is granted authority from above, whereas a leader's role is derived by virtue of having followers. However, the terms *manager* and *leader* are often used interchangeably.

matrix chart/diagram—A management and planning tool that shows the relationships among various groups of data; it yields information about the relationships and the importance of task/method elements of the subjects.

mean—A measure of central tendency; the arithmetic average of all measurements in a data set.

mean time between failures (MTBF)—The average time interval between failures for repairable product or service for a defined unit of measure, for example, operating hours, cycles, miles.

measure—The criteria, metric, or means to which a comparison is made with output.

measurement—Refers to the reference standard or sample used for the comparison of properties.

median—The middle number or center value of a set of data when all the data are arranged in an increasing sequence.

metric—A standard of measurement or evaluation.

metrology—Science and practice of measurements.

MIL-STD—A military standard.

mission statement—An explanation of purpose or reasons for existing as an organization; it provides the focus for the organization and defines its scope of business.

mode—The value that occurs most frequently in a dataset.

moment-of-truth (MOT)—A MOT was described by Jan Carlzon, former CEO of Scandinavian Air Services, in the 1980s as: "Any episode where a customer comes into contact with any aspect of your company, no matter how distant, and by this contact, has an opportunity to form an opinion about your company."

motivation—Two types of motivation are *extrinsic* and *intrinsic*.

multivoting—A decision-making tool that enables a group to sort through a long list of ideas to identify priorities.

Myers-Briggs Type Indicator/MBTI—A method and instrument for identifying a person's "type" based on Carl Jung's theory of personality preferences.

N

n—Sample size (the number of units in a sample).

natural team—A team of individuals drawn from a single work group; similar to a process improvement team except that it is not cross-functional in composition and it is not usually temporary.

next operation as customer (NOAC)—Concept that the organization is comprised of service/product providers and service/product receivers or "internal customers."

NIST—National Institute of Standards and Technology.

nominal data—Data used for classifying information without an implied order or use of numbers for identification purposes.

nominal group technique (NGT)—A technique, similar to brainstorming, used by teams to generate ideas on a particular subject. Team members are asked to silently come up with as many ideas as possible, writing them down. Each member is then asked to share one idea, which is recorded. After all the ideas are recorded, they are discussed and prioritized by the group.

nonconformity—The result of nonfulfillment of a specified requirement (*see also* blemish, defect, and imperfection).

nondestructive testing and evaluation (NDT)—Testing and evaluation methods that do not damage or destroy the product being tested.

non-value-added—Refers to tasks or activities that can be eliminated with no deterioration in product or service functionality, performance, or quality in the eyes of the customer.

normal distribution—A bell-shaped distribution for continuous data where most of the data are concentrated around the average, and it is equally likely that an observation will occur above or below the average.

norms—Behavioral expectations, mutually agreed-upon rules of conduct, protocols to be followed, and social practice.

normal distribution (statistical)—The charting of a dataset in which most of the data points are concentrated around the average (mean), thus forming a bell-shaped curve.

number of affected units chart (np chart)—A control chart for evaluating the stability of a process in terms of the total number of units in a sample in which an event of a given classification occurs.

O

objective—A statement of future expectations and an indication of when the expectations should be achieved; it flows from goals and clarifies what people must accomplish. An objective includes measurable end results to be accomplished by specific teams or individuals within time limits. It is the "how, when, and who" for achieving a goal. (*see also* S.M.A.R.T. W.A.Y.).

on-the-job-training (OJT)—Training conducted usually at the workstation, typically done one-on-one.

ordinal data—Quantitative data used to put data into order but where the size of the numbers is not important.

organization culture—Refers to the collective beliefs, values, attitudes, manners, customs, behaviors, and artifacts unique to an organization.

outcome—The measurable result of a project, a quality initiative, an improvement, and so on. Usually, some time passes between the completion of the action and the realization of the outcome.

outlier—An observation extremely different in some respect from the other observations in a set of data. More loosely, any extremely different or unusual event.

out-of-control process—A process in which the statistical measure being evaluated is not in a state of statistical control (that is, the variations among the observed sampling results cannot all be attributed to a constant system of chance causes; special or assignable causes exist (*see also* in-control process).

output—The deliverables resulting from a project, a quality initiative, an improvement, and so on. Outputs include data, information, documents, decisions and tangible products. Outputs are generated both from the planning and management of the activity (e.g., project) and the delivered product, service, program, and so on. Output is the item, document, or material delivered by an internal provider/supplier to an internal receiver/customer.

P

Pareto chart—A basic tool used to graphically rank causes from most significant to least significant. It utilizes a vertical bar graph in which the bar height reflects the frequency or impact of causes.

partnership/alliance—A strategy leading to a relationship with suppliers or customers aimed at reducing costs of ownership, maintenance of minimum stocks, just-in-time deliveries, joint participation in design, exchange of information on materials and technologies, new production methods, quality improvement strategies, and the exploitation of market synergy.

percent chart—A control chart for evaluating the stability of a process in terms of the percent of the total number of units in a sample in which an event of a given classification occurs. The percent chart is also referred to as a *proportion chart*.

Plan—Do—Check—Act cycle (PDCA)—A four-step process for quality improvement. In the first step (plan), a plan to effect improvement is developed. In the second step (do), the plan is carried out, preferably on a small scale. In the third step (check), the effects of the plan are observed. In the last step (act), the results are studied to determine what was learned and what can be predicted. The PDCA cycle is sometimes referred to as the Shewhart cycle because Walter A. Shewhart discussed the concept in his book *Statistical Method from the Viewpoint of Quality Control*, and as the Deming cycle because W. Edwards Deming introduced the concept in Japan. The Japanese subsequently called it the Deming cycle. Sometimes referred to as *Plan—Do—Study—Act (PDSA)*.

poka-yoke—(Japanese) A term that means to mistake-proof a process by building safeguards into the system that avoid or immediately find errors. It comes from *poka*, which means "inadvertent error,"and *yokeru*, which means, "to avoid."

policy—An overarching plan (direction) for achieving an organization's goals.

population—A collection or set of individuals, objects, or measurements whose properties or characteristics are to be analyzed. So, if we want to know the proportion of all television viewers who watched the World Series, then the population is all television viewers.

Pp—The ratio of the specification range divided by the natural tolerance range of the process when the process may or may not be in a state of statistical control.

Ppk—The difference between the process average and the closer specification limit divided by one-half the natural tolerance range of the process when the process may or may not be in a state of statistical control.

ppm—Parts per million.

precision—A characteristic of measurement that addresses the consistency or repeatability of a measurement system when the identical item is measured a number of times.

prevention costs—The costs of activities specifically designed to prevent poor quality in products or services.

prevention vs. detection—A term used to contrast two types of quality activities. Prevention refers to those activities designed to prevent nonconformances in products and services. Detection refers to those activities designed to detect nonconformances already in products and services. Another term used to describe this distinction is "designing in quality vs. inspecting in quality."

preventive action—Action taken to eliminate the potential causes of a nonconformity, defect, or other undesirable situation in order to prevent further occurrences.

probability—Refers to the likelihood of occurrence.

problem solving—A rational process for identifying, describing, analyzing, and resolving situations in which something has gone wrong without explanation.

procedure—The steps to be taken in a process. A document that answers the questions: What has to be done? Where is it to be done? When is it to be done? Who is to do it? Why do it? (contrasted with a work instruction, which answers: How is it to be done? With what materials and tools is it to be done?); in the absence of a work instruction, the instructions may be embedded in the procedure.

process—An activity or group of activities that takes an input, adds value to it, and provides an output to an internal or external customer; a planned and repetitive sequence of steps by which a defined product or service is delivered.

process capability—A statistical measure of the inherent process variability for a given characteristic.

process control—The methodology for keeping a process within boundaries; minimizing the variation of a process.

process decision program chart (PDPC)—A management and planning tool that identifies all events that can go wrong and the appropriate countermeasures for these events. It graphically represents all sequences that lead to a desirable effect.

process improvement—Refers to the act of changing a process to reduce variability and cycle time and make the process more effective, efficient, and productive.

process improvement team (PIT)—A natural work group or cross-functional team whose responsibility is to achieve needed improvements in existing processes. The life span of the team is based on the completion of the team purpose and specific goals.

process management—The collection of practices used to implement and improve process effectiveness; it focuses on holding the gains achieved through process improvement and assuring process integrity.

process mapping—The flowcharting of a work process in detail, including key measurements.

process owner—The person who coordinates the various functions and work activities at all levels of a process, has the authority or ability to make changes in the process as required, and manages the entire process cycle so as to ensure performance effectiveness.

process reengineering—*See* reengineering.

producer's risk—For a sampling plan, refers to the probability of not accepting a lot, the quality of which has a designated numerical value representing a level that is generally desirable. Usually the designated value will be the acceptable quality level (also called *alpha risk* and *type 1 error*).

product or service liability—The obligation of a company to make restitution for loss related to personal injury, property damage, or other harm caused by its product or service.

product warranty—The organization's stated policy that it will replace, repair, or reimburse a customer for a defective product providing the product defect occurs under certain conditions and within a stated period of time.

profound knowledge, system of—As defined by W. Edwards Deming, states that learning cannot be based on experience only; it requires comparisons of results to a prediction, plan, or an expression of theory. Predicting why something happens is essential to understand results and to continually improve. The four components of the system of profound knowledge are: appreciation for a system, knowledge of variation, theory of knowledge, and understanding of psychology.

project life cycle—Refers to five sequential phases of project management: concept, planning, design, implementation, and evaluation.

project management—Refers to the management of activities and events involved throughout a project's life cycle.

project team—A designated group of people working together to produce a planned project's outputs and outcome.

pull system—*See* kanban.

Q

qualitative variables—Describes the sample you collected and measures more abstract things. Variables whose values are categories such as man, woman, and child; red, green, and blue; Democrat, Republican, Liberal, Conservative, and independent.

quality—A subjective term for which each person has his or her own definition. In technical usage, quality can have two meanings: (1) the characteristics of a product or service that bear on its ability to satisfy stated or implied needs, and (2) a product or service free of deficiencies.

- Crosby defined quality as "conformance to requirements."
- Deming stated, "Quality should be aimed at the needs of the consumer, present and future. Quality begins with intent, which is fixed by management . . . translated . . . into plans, specifications, tests, production."
- Juran defined quality as "fitness for use."
- Garvin expands the definition to include eight dimensions: performance, features, reliability, conformance, durability, serviceability, aesthetics, and perceived quality.[2]
- Customers define quality as "what I expect" and "I'll know it when I see it."

quality assessment—The process of identifying business practices, attitudes, and activities that are enhancing or inhibiting the achievement of quality improvement in an organization.

quality assurance/quality control (QA/QC)—Two terms that have many interpretations because of the multiple definitions for the words *assurance* and *control*. For example, assurance can mean the act of giving confidence, the state of being certain, or the act of making certain; control can mean an evaluation to indicate needed corrective responses, the act of guiding, or the state of a process in which the variability is attributable to a constant system of chance causes. (For a detailed discussion on the multiple definitions, see ANSI/ISO/ASQC A35342, Statistics—Vocabulary and Symbols—Statistical Quality Control.) One definition of quality assurance is: all the planned and systematic activities implemented within the quality system that can be demonstrated to provide confidence that a product or service will fulfill requirements for quality. One definition for quality control is: the operational techniques and activities used to fulfill requirements for quality. Often, however, *quality assurance* and *quality control* are used interchangeably, referring to the actions performed to ensure the quality of a product, service, or process.

quality audit—A systematic, independent examination and review to determine whether quality activities and related results comply with planned arrangements and whether these arrangements are implemented effectively and are suitable to achieve the objectives.

quality characteristics—The unique characteristics of products and of services by which customers evaluate their perception of quality.

quality circles—Quality improvement or self-improvement study groups composed of a small number of employees—10 or fewer—and their supervisor, who meet regularly with an aim to improve a process.

quality costs—*See* cost of quality (COQ)

quality function—The entire spectrum of activities through which an organization achieves its quality goals and objectives, no matter where these activities are performed.

quality function deployment (QFD)—A multifaceted matrix in which customer requirements are translated into appropriate technical requirements for each stage of product development and production. The QFD process is often referred to as listening to the voice of the customer. Also called *house of quality.*

quality loss function—A parabolic approximation of the quality loss that occurs when a quality characteristic deviates from its target value. The quality loss function is expressed in monetary units: the cost of deviating from the target increases quadratically the farther the quality characteristic moves from the target. The formula used to compute the quality loss function depends on the type of quality characteristic being used. Genichi Taguchi first introduced the quality loss function in this form.

quality management—All activities of the overall management function that determines the quality policy, objectives, and responsibilities, and implements them by means such as quality planning, quality control, quality assurance, and quality improvement within the quality system.

quality management system (QMS)—The organizational structure, processes, procedures, and resources needed to implement, maintain, and continually improve quality management.

quality plan—The document, or documents, setting out the specific quality practices, resources, specifications, and sequence of activities relevant to a particular product, project, or contract.

quality planning—The activity of establishing quality objectives and quality requirements.

quality policy—An organization's formally stated beliefs about quality, how it will occur, and the expected result.

quality principles—Rules, guidelines, or concepts that an organization believes in collectively. The principles are formulated by senior management with input from others and are communicated and understood at every level of the organization.

quality score chart (Q chart)—A control chart for evaluating the stability of a process in terms of a quality score. The quality score is the weighted sum of the count of events of various classifications, where each classification is assigned a weight.

quality tool—An instrument or technique that is used to support and/or improve the activities of process quality management and improvement.

quality trilogy—A three-stage approach to managing for quality. The three stages are quality planning (developing the products and processes required to meet customer needs), quality control (meeting product and process goals), and quality improvement (achieving unprecedented levels of performance). Attributed to Joseph M. Juran.

quantitative variables—Variables whose values are numbers.

quincunx—A tool that creates frequency distributions. Beads tumble over numerous horizontal rows of pins, which force the beads to the right or left. After a random journey, the beads are dropped into vertical slots. After many beads are dropped, a frequency distribution results. In the classroom, quincunxes are often used to simulate a manufacturing process. English scientist Francis Galton invented the quincunx in the 1890s.

R

RABQSA International—A board that evaluates the competency and reliability of registrars (organizations that assess and register companies to the appropriate ISO 9000 series standards). The Registrar Accreditation Board, formed in 1989 by ASQ, is governed by a board of directors from industry, academia, and quality management consulting firms. This body merged with QSA International of Australia in 2004 and continues to co-locate its U.S. headquarters in the American Society for Quality building in Milwaukee, Wisconsin.

random cause—A cause of variation due to chance and not assignable to any factor.

random sampling—A commonly used sampling technique in which sample units are selected in such a manner that all combinations of n units under consideration have an equal chance of being selected as the sample.

random variation—Fluctuations caused by many individually unimportant factors that cannot be feasibly detected, identified, or eliminated. The variability of a process when operating within its natural limits, that is, under a stable system of chance causes.

range—The measure of dispersion in a dataset; highest value minus lowest value.

range chart (R chart)—A control chart in which the subgroup range, R, is used to evaluate the stability of the variability within a process.

red bead experiment—An experiment developed by W. Edwards Deming to illustrate that it is impossible to put employees in rank order of performance for the coming year based on their performance during the past year because performance differences must be attributed to the system, not to employees. Four thousand red and white beads, 20 percent red, in a jar and six people are needed for the experiment. The participants' goal is to produce white beads because the customer will not accept red beads. One person begins by stirring the beads and then, blindfolded, selects a sample of 50 beads. That person hands the jar to the next person, who repeats the process, and so on. When everyone has his or her sample, the number of red beads for each is counted. The limits of variation between employees that can be attributed to the system are calculated. Everyone will fall within the calculated limits of variation that could arise from the system. The calculations will show that there is no evidence one person will be a better performer than another in the future. The experiment shows that it would be a waste of management's time to try to find out why, say, John produced 4 red beads and Jane produced 15; instead, management should improve the system, making it possible for everyone to produce more white beads.

reengineering—Completely redesigning or restructuring a whole organization, an organizational component, or a complete process. It's a "start all over again from the beginning" approach, sometimes called a "breakthrough." In terms of improvement approaches, reengineering is contrasted with incremental improvement (kaizen).

reference material—Material or substance one or more of whose property values are sufficiently homogeneous and well established to be used for the calibration of an apparatus, the assessment of a measurement method, or for assigning values to materials.

registration—The act of including an organization, product, service, or process in a compilation of those having the same or similar attributes. Sometimes incorrectly used interchangeably with the term *certification*. A quality management system for an organization may be "certified" and the organization "registered" in a listing of organizations having achieved ISO 9001 certification. The respective terms for the documents involved are *certificate* and *register*.

regression analysis—A statistical technique for determining the best mathematical expression describing the functional relationship between one response and one or more independent variables.

reliability—In measurement system analysis, refers to the ability of an instrument to produce the same results over repeated administration—to measure consistently. In reliability engineering it is the probability of a product performing its intended function under stated conditions for a given period of time (*see also* mean time between failures).

repeatability—Precision under repeatability conditions, that is, conditions where independent test results are obtained with the same method on identical test items by the same operator using the same equipment within short intervals of time.

representative sample—A sample that contains the characteristics of the corresponding population.

reproducibility—Precision under reproducibility conditions, that is, conditions where test results are obtained with the same method on identical test items with different technicians using the same equipment or procedure.

resource requirements matrix—A tool to relate the resources required to the project tasks requiring them (used to indicate types of individuals needed, material needed, subcontractors, etc.).

right the first time—A term used to convey the concept that it is beneficial and more cost-effective to take the necessary steps up front to ensure a product or service meets its requirements than to provide a product or service that will need rework or not meet customers' needs. In other words, an organization should engage in defect prevention rather than defect detection.

robustness—The condition of a product or process design that remains relatively stable with a minimum of variation even though factors that influence operations or usage, such as environment and wear, are constantly changing.

root cause analysis—A quality tool used to distinguish the source of defects or problems. It is a structured approach that focuses on the decisive or original cause of a problem or condition.

run chart—A line graph showing data collected during a run or an uninterrupted sequence of events. A trend is indicated when the series of collected data points head up or down.

S

sample—A finite number of items of a similar type taken from a population for the purpose of examination to determine whether all members of the population would conform to quality requirements or specifications.

sample size—Refers to the number of units in a sample chosen from the population.

sample standard deviation chart (s chart)—A control chart in which the subgroup standard deviation, s, is used to evaluate the stability of the variability within a process.

sampling—The process of drawing conclusions about the population based on a part of the population.

satisfier—The term used to describe the quality level received by a customer when a product or service meets expectations.

scatter diagram—A graphical technique to analyze the relationship between two variables. Two sets of data are plotted on a graph, with the y-axis being used for the variable to be predicted and the x-axis being used for the variable to make the prediction. The graph will show possible relationships (although two variables might appear to be related, they might not be; those who know most about the variables must make that evaluation). The scatter diagram is one of the seven tools of quality.

scientific management—Aimed at finding the one best way to perform a task so as to increase productivity and efficiency.

self-managed team—A team that requires little supervision and manages itself and the day-to-day work it does; self-directed teams are responsible for whole work processes, with each individual performing multiple tasks.

service—Work performed for others. Services may be internal, such as support services including payroll, engineering, maintenance, hiring, and training, or external, such as legal services, repair services, and training.

set—Collection of objects, such as people or products, described by listing its members. Any portion of a set may itself be a set. Sets that are wholly contained in other sets are known as *subsets*.

setup time—The time taken to change over a process to run a different product or service.

seven basic tools of quality—Tools that help organizations understand their processes in order to improve them. The tools are the cause-and-effect diagram, check sheet, control chart, flowchart, histogram, Pareto chart, and scatter diagram (*see* individual entries).

seven management tools of quality—The tools used primarily for planning and managing are activity network diagram (AND) or arrow diagram, affinity diagram (KJ method), interrelationship digraph, matrix diagram, priorities matrix, process decision program chart (PDPC), and tree diagram.

Shewhart cycle—*see* Plan—Do—Check—Act cycle.

sigma—Greek letter (σ) that stands for the standard deviation of a process.

SIPOC—A macro-level analysis of the suppliers, inputs, processes, outputs, and customers.

Six Sigma approach—A quality philosophy; a collection of techniques and tools for use in reducing variation; a process of improvement.

Six Sigma quality—A term used generally to indicate that a process is well controlled, that is, process limits $\pm 3\sigma$ from the centerline in a control chart, and requirements/tolerance limits $\pm 6\sigma$ from the centerline. The term was initiated by Motorola.

S.M.A.R.T. W.A.Y.—A guide for setting objectives: Specific, Measured, Achievable, Realistic, Time-based, Worth doing, Assigned, Yields results.[3]

special causes—Causes of variation that arise because of special circumstances. They are not an inherent part of a process. Special causes are also referred to as *assignable causes* (*see also* common causes of variation).

specification—The engineering requirement used for judging the acceptability of a particular product/service based on product characteristics, such as appearance, performance, and size. In statistical analysis, specifications refer to the document that prescribes the requirements with which the product or service has to perform.

sponsor—The person who supports a team's plans, activities, and outcomes; the team's "backer." The sponsor provides resources and helps define the mission and scope to set limits. The sponsor may be the same individual as the "champion."

stages of team growth—Teams typically move through four stages as they develop maturity over time: forming, storming, norming, and performing.

stakeholder—People, departments, and organizations that have an investment or interest in the success or actions taken by the organization.

standard—A statement, specification, or quantity of material against which measured outputs from a process may be judged as acceptable or unacceptable.

standard deviation—A calculated measure of variability that shows how much the data are spread around the mean.

statistical process control (SPC)—The application of statistical techniques to control a process.

statistical quality control (SQC)—The application of statistical techniques to control quality. Often the term *statistical process control* is used interchangeably with *statistical quality control,* although statistical quality control includes acceptance sampling as well as statistical process control.

statistics—Descriptive: A field that involves the tabulating, depicting, and describing of data sets. Inferential: A formalized body of techniques characteristically involving attempts to infer the properties of a large collection of data from inspection of a sample of the collection.

statistical thinking—A philosophy of learning and action based on fundamental principles:

- All work occurs in a system of interconnected processes.
- Variation exists in all processes.
- Understanding and reducing variation are vital to improvement.

steering committee—A special group established to guide and track initiatives or projects.

storyboarding—A technique that visually displays thoughts and ideas and groups them into categories, making all aspects of a process visible at once. Often used to communicate to others the activities performed by a team as they improved a process.

strategic planning—A process to set an organization's long-range goals and identify the objectives and actions needed to reach the goals.

stratified sampling—Type of random sampling. It is a technique that can be used when the population is not homogeneous. The approach is to divide the population into strata or subgroups, each of which is more or less homogeneous, and then take a representative sample from each group.

structural variation—Variation caused by regular, systematic changes in output, such as seasonal patterns and long-term trends.

supplier—Any provider whose goods and services may be used at any stage in the production, design, delivery, and use of another company's products and services. Suppliers include businesses, such as distributors, dealers, warranty repair services, transportation contractors, and franchises, and service suppliers, such as health care, training, and education. Internal suppliers provide materials or services to internal customers.

supplier quality assurance—Confidence that a supplier's product or service will fulfill its customers' needs. This confidence is achieved by creating a relationship between the customer and supplier that ensures the product or service will be fit for use with minimal corrective action and inspection. According to J. M. Juran, there are nine primary activities needed: (1) define product and program quality requirements, (2) evaluate alternative suppliers, (3) select suppliers, (4) conduct joint quality planning, (5) cooperate with the supplier during the execution of the contract, (6) obtain proof of conformance to requirements, (7) certify qualified suppliers, (8) conduct quality improvement programs as required, and (9) create and use supplier quality ratings.

supply chain—The series of processes and/or organizations that are involved in producing and delivering a product to the final user.

supply chain management—The process of effectively integrating and managing components of the supply chain.

support systems—Starting with top-management commitment and visible involvement, support systems are a cascading series of interrelated practices or actions aimed at building and sustaining support for continuous quality improvement. Such practices/actions may include: mission statement, transformation of company culture, policies, employment practices, compensation, recognition and rewards, employee involvement, rules and procedures, quality-level agreements, training, empowerment, methods and tools for improving quality, tracking-measuring-evaluating-reporting systems, and so on.

surveillance—Continual monitoring of a process.

survey—An examination for some specific purpose; to inspect or consider carefully; to review in detail (*survey* implies the inclusion of matters not covered by agreed-upon criteria). Also, a structured series of questions designed to elicit a predetermined range of responses covering a preselected area of interest. May be administered orally by a survey-taker, by paper and pencil, or by computer. Responses are tabulated and analyzed to surface significant areas for change.

SWOT analysis—An assessment of an organization's key *strengths, weaknesses, opportunities,* and *threats.* It considers factors such as the organization's industry, the competitive position, functional areas, and management.

symptom—An indication of a problem or opportunity.

system—A network of connecting processes and people that together perform a common mission.

systematic sampling—Type of random sampling. The procedure requires that every kth item is selected after picking a starting point at random.

system of profound knowledge (SoPK)—*see* profound knowledge.

systems approach to management—A management theory that views the organization as a unified, purposeful combination of interrelated parts; managers must look at the organization as a whole and understand that activity in one part of the organization affects all parts of the organization (also known as *systems thinking*).

T

Taguchi method—Taguchi methodology is a prototyping method that enables the engineer or designer to identify the optimal settings to produce a robust product that can survive manufacturing time after time, piece after piece, in order to provide the functionality required by the customer.

tampering—Action taken to compensate for variation within the control limits of a stable system. Tampering increases rather than decreases variation, as evidenced in the funnel experiment.

task—A specific, definable activity to perform an assigned function, usually within a specified time frame.

team—A group of two or more people who are equally accountable for the accomplishment of a purpose and specific performance goals; it is also defined as a small number of people with complementary skills who are committed to a common purpose.

team building/development—The process of transforming a group of people into a team and developing the team to achieve its purpose.

team dynamics—The interactions that occur among team members under different conditions.

team facilitation—Deals with both the role of the facilitator on the team and the techniques and tools for facilitating the team.

team leader—A person designated to be responsible for the ongoing success of the team; keeps the team focused on the task assigned.

team performance evaluation, rewards, and recognition—Special metrics are needed to evaluate the work of a team (to avoid focus on any individual on the team) and as a basis for rewards and recognition for team achievements.

temporary/ad hoc team—A team, usually small, formed to address a short-term mission or emergency situation.

tolerance—The variability of a parameter permitted and tolerated above or below a nominal value.

top management commitment—Participation of the highest-level officials in their organization's quality improvement efforts. Their participation includes establishing and serving on a quality committee, establishing quality policies and goals, deploying those goals to lower levels of the organization, providing the resources and training that the lower levels need to achieve the goals, participating in quality improvement teams, reviewing progress organization-wide, recognizing those who have performed well, and revising the current reward system to reflect the importance of achieving the quality goals. Commitment is top management's visible, personal involvement as seen by others in the organization.

total quality management (TQM)—A term initially coined by the Naval Air Systems Command to describe its management approach to quality improvement. Total quality management (TQM) has taken on many meanings. Simply put, TQM is a management approach to long-term success through customer satisfaction. TQM is based on the participation of all members of an organization in improving processes, products, services, and the culture they work in. TQM benefits all organization members and society. The methods for implementing this approach are found in the teachings of such quality leaders as Philip B. Crosby, W. Edwards Deming, Armand V. Feigenbaum, Kaoru Ishikawa, J. M. Juran, and others.

tree diagram—A management and planning tool that shows the complete range of subtasks required to achieve an objective. A problem-solving method can be identified from this analysis.

trend analysis—Refers to the charting of data over time to identify a tendency or direction.

type 1 error—An incorrect decision to reject something (such as a statistical hypothesis or a lot of products) when it is acceptable. Also known as *producer's risk* and *alpha risk.*

type 2 error—An incorrect decision to accept something when it is unacceptable. Also known as *consumer's risk* and *beta risk.*

U

u chart—Count per unit chart.

upper control limit (UCL)—Control limit for points above the central line in a control chart.

V

validation—Confirmation by examination of objective evidence that specific requirements and/or a specified intended use are met.

validity—Refers to the ability of a feedback instrument to measure what it is intended to measure.

value-added—Refers to tasks or activities that convert resources into products or services consistent with customer requirements. The customer can be internal or external to the organization.

value analysis, value engineering, and value research—Value analysis assumes that a process, procedure, product, or service is of no value unless proven otherwise. It assigns a price to every step of a process and then computes the worth-to-cost ratio of that step. Value engineering points the way to elimination and reengineering. Value research, related to value engineering, for given features of the service/product helps determine the customers' strongest "likes" and "dislikes" and those for which customers are neutral. Focuses attention on strong dislikes and enables identified "neutrals" to be considered for cost reductions.

values—Statements that clarify the behaviors that the organization expects in order to move toward its vision and mission. Values reflect an organization's personality and culture.

variable data—Data resulting from the measurement of a parameter or a variable. Contrast with *attribute data.*

variance—The difference between a planned amount (usually money or time) and the actual amount. (Math) the measure of dispersion on observations based on the mean of the squared deviations from the arithmetic mean. The square of the standard deviation, given by formula.

variation—A change in data, a characteristic, or a function that is caused by one of four factors: special causes, common causes, tampering, or structural variation (*see* individual entries).

verification—The act of reviewing, inspecting, testing, checking, auditing, or otherwise establishing and documenting whether items, processes, services, or documents conform to specified requirements.

virtual team—A boundaryless team functioning without a commonly shared physical structure or physical contact, using technology to link the team members.

vision—A statement that explains what the company wants to become and what it hopes to achieve.

vital few, useful many—A term used by J. M. Juran to describe his use of the Pareto principle, which he first defined in 1950. (The principle was used much earlier in economics and inventory control methodologies.) The principle suggests that most effects come from relatively few causes; that is, 80 percent of the effects come from 20 percent of the possible causes. The 20 percent of the possible causes are referred to as the "vital few"; the remaining causes are referred to as the "useful many." When Juran first defined this principle, he referred to the remaining causes as the "trivial many," but realizing that no problems are trivial in quality assurance, he changed it to "useful many."

voice of the customer—An organization's efforts to understand the customers' needs and expectations ("voice") and to provide products and services that truly meet such needs and expectations.

W

walk the talk—Means not only talking about what one believes in but also being observed acting out those beliefs. Employees' buy-in of the TOM concept is more likely when management is seen involved in the process, every day.

waste—Activities that consume resources but add no value; visible waste (for example, scrap, rework, downtime) and invisible waste (for example, inefficient setups, wait times of people and machines, inventory).

work group—A group composed of people from one functional area who work together on a daily basis and whose goal is to improve the processes of their function.

working standard—Standard that is used routinely to calibrate or check material measures, measuring instruments, or reference materials.

X, Y, Z

X-bar chart—Average chart.

zero defects—A performance standard popularized by Philip B. Crosby to address a dual attitude in the workplace: People are willing to accept imperfection in some areas, whereas in other areas, they expect the number of defects to be zero. This dual attitude developed because people are human and humans make mistakes. However, the zero-defects methodology states that if people commit themselves to watching details and avoiding errors, they can move closer to the goal of zero.

Notes

1. Defined by Russell T. Westcott in *The certified manager of quality/organizational excellence handbook* (3rd ed.). (Milwaukee, WI: ASQ Quality Press, 2006).
2. D. A. Garvin, associate professor of business administration, Harvard Business School, in a paper published in the *Harvard Business Review* in 1987.
3. Westcott, *The certified manager.*

Appendix D
Additional Reading

The following pages list additional resources for readers wishing to gain more knowledge about many of the topics covered in this handbook. The books have been selected from the hundreds of books available. In no way is it implied that any of the books on this list are required reading.

Note: Many of the cited texts are available through ASQ. Call 1-800-248-1946 to request a current catalog, or visit its online store at http://qualitypress.asq.org.

Basic Reference Material

ASQ. *Certified quality improvement associate* (brochure). (Milwaukee: ASQ).

Deming, W. Edwards. *Out of the crisis.* (Cambridge, MA: MIT Center for Advanced Engineering Study, 1986).

Evans, James R., and William M. Lindsay. *The management and control of quality* (6th ed.). (Cincinnati, OH: South-Western College Publishing, 2005).

Juran, Joseph M., and A. Blanton Godfrey, eds. *Juran's quality handbook* (5th ed.). (New York: McGraw-Hill, 1999).

Scholtes, Peter R. *The team handbook* (2nd ed., rev.). (Madison, WI: Joiner Associates, 1996).

Assessments and Auditing

Arter, Dennis R. *Quality audits for improved performance* (3rd ed.). (Milwaukee: ASQ Quality Press, 2003).

Russell, J. P., ed. *The ASQ auditing handbook* (3rd ed.). (Milwaukee: ASQ Quality Press, 2006).

———. *Continual improvement assessment guide: Promoting and sustaining business results.* (Milwaukee, WI: ASQ Quality Press, 2004).

Baldrige Award

Blaze, Mark L. *Insights to performance excellence 2006: An inside look at the 2006 Baldrige Award criteria.* (Milwaukee, WI: ASQ Quality Press, 2006).

NIST. *Baldrige National Quality Program: Criteria for performance excellence.* (Criteria for: Business, Health Care, or Education). Baldrige National Quality Program, National Institute of Standards and Technology, Technology Administration, United States Department of Commerce, Administration Building, Room A600, 100 Bureau Drive, Stop 1020, Gaithersburg, MD 20899-1020. Telephone: 301-975-2036, Fax: 301-948-3716, e-mail: *nqp@nist.gov,* Web site: *http://www.baldrige.nist.gov.* One copy of the criteria appropriate to your organization is available free.

Benchmarking

Camp, Robert C. *Business process benchmarking: Finding and implementing best practices.* (Milwaukee: ASQ Quality Press, 1995).

Spendolini, Michael J. *The benchmarking book.* (New York: Amacom, 1992).

Certification—ASQ

Benbow, Donald W., and T. M. Kubiak. *The certified Six Sigma Black Belt handbook.* (Milwaukee, WI: ASQ Quality Press, 2005).

Benbow, Donald W., Roger W. Berger, Ahmad K. Elshennawy, and H. Fred Walker, eds. *The certified quality engineer handbook.* (Milwaukee: ASQ Quality Press, 2001).

———. *The certified quality technician handbook.* (Milwaukee, WI: ASQ Quality Press, 2003).

Daughtrey, Taz, ed. *Fundamental concepts for the software quality engineer.* (Milwaukee: ASQ Quality Press, 2002).

Westcott, Russell T., ed. *The certified manager of quality/organizational excellence handbook* (3rd ed.). (Milwaukee, WI: ASQ Quality Press, 2006).

Continuous and Breakthrough Improvement

Andersen, Bjørn. *Business process improvement toolbox.* (Milwaukee, WI: ASQ Quality Press, 1999).

Andersen, Bjørn, and Tom Fagerhaug. *Root cause analysis: Simplified tools and techniques.* (2nd ed.) (Milwaukee, WI: ASQ Quality Press, 2006).

ASQ Statistics Division. *Improving performance through statistical thinking.* (Milwaukee, WI: ASQ Quality Press, 2000).

Brassard, Michael, and Diane Ritter. *Memory jogger II.* (Methuen, MA: GOAL/QPC, 1994).

Dettmer, H. William. *Goldratt's theory of constraints: A systems approach to continuous improvement.* (Milwaukee, WI: ASQ Quality Press, 1997).

Escoe, Adrienne. *The practical guide to people-friendly documentation.* (Milwaukee, WI: ASQ Quality Press, 2001).

Galloway, Dianne. *Mapping work processes.* (Milwaukee, WI: ASQ Quality Press, 1994).

GOAL/QPC. *The problem solving memory jogger.* (Metheun, MA: GOAL/QPC, 2000).

Goldratt, Eliyahu M., and Jeff Cox. *The goal* (2nd ed., rev.). (Croton-on-Hudson, NY: North River Press, 1992).

Harry, Mikel, and Richard Schroeder. *Six Sigma: The breakthrough management strategy revolutionizing the world's top corporations.* (New York: Currency, 2000).

Hutton, David W. *From Baldrige to the bottom line: A road map for organizational change and improvement.* (Milwaukee, WI: ASQ Quality Press, 2000).

Imai, Masaaki. *Kaizen: The key to Japan's competitive success.* (New York: Random House, 1986).

NKS/Factory Magazine, ed. *Poka-yoke: Improving product quality by preventing defects.* (Cambridge, MA: Productivity Press, 1989).

ReVelle, Jack B. *Quality essentials: A reference guide from a to z.* (Milwaukee, WI: ASQ Quality Press, 2004).

ReVelle, Jack B., ed. *Manufacturing handbook of best practices: An innovation, productivity, and quality focus.* (Boca Raton, FL: St. Lucie Press, 2002).

Ritter, Diane, and Michael Brassard. *The creativity tools memory jogger.* (Methuen, MA: GOAL/QPC, 1998).

Siebels, Don. *The quality improvement glossary.* (Milwaukee, WI: ASQ Quality Press, 2004).

Tague, Nancy R. *The quality toolbox* (2nd ed.). (Milwaukee, WI: ASQ Quality Press, 2005).

Womack, James P., and Daniel T. Jones. *Lean thinking: Banish waste and create wealth in your corporation.* (New York: Simon & Schuster, 1996).

Customers

Gale, Bradley T. *Managing customer value.* (New York: The Free Press, 1994).

Goodman, Gary S. *Monitoring, measuring, and managing customer service.* (San Francisco: Jossey-Bass, 2000).

Kessler, Sheila. *Measuring and managing customer satisfaction: Going for the gold.* (Milwaukee, WI: ASQ Quality Press, 1996).

Naumann, Earl, and Steven H. Hoisington. *Customer-centered Six Sigma: Linking customers, process improvement, and financial results.* (Milwaukee, WI: ASQ Quality Press, 2001).

Education

Alexander, William F., and Richard W. Seriass. *Futuring tools for strategic quality planning in education.* (Milwaukee, WI: ASQ Quality Press, 1999).

ASQ. *Successful applications of quality systems in K–12 schools.* (Milwaukee, WI: ASQ Quality Education Forum/Division, 2003).

Jenkins, Lee. *Improving student learning: Applying Deming's quality principles in the classroom* (2nd ed). (Milwaukee, WI: ASQ Quality Press, 2003).

Healthcare—Medical

American College of Medical Quality. *Core curriculum for medical quality management.* (Sudbury, MA: Jones and Bartlett Publishers, 2005).

Harnack, Gordon. *Mastering and managing the FDA maze: Medical device overview.* (Milwaukee, WI: ASQ Quality Press, 1999).

McLaughlin, Curtis P., and Arnold D. Kaluzny. *Continuous quality improvement in health care: Theory implementation and applications* (2nd ed.). (New York: Aspen Publishers, 1999).

Ransom, Scott B., Maulik Joshi, and David Nash. *The healthcare quality book: Vision, strategy, and tools.* (Chicago, IL: Health Administration Press, 2005).

ISO 9000

ASQ. *ANSI/ISO/ASQ Q9000-2000 Quality management systems—fundamentals and vocabulary.* (Milwaukee, WI: ASQ, 2000).

ASQ. *ANSI/ISO/ASQ Q9001-2000 Quality management systems—requirements.* (Milwaukee, WI: ASQ, 2000).

ASQ. *ANSI/ISO/ASQ Q9004-2000 Quality management systems—guidelines for performance improvements.* (Milwaukee, WI: ASQ, 2000).

ASQ Chemical and Process Industries Division. *ISO 9001:2000 Guidelines for the chemical and process industries* (3rd ed.). (Milwaukee, WI: ASQ Quality Press, 2002).

Cianfrani, Charles, Joseph J. Tsiakals, and John E. West. *The ASQ ISO 9000-2000 handbook.* (Milwaukee, WI: ASQ Quality Press, 2002).

GOAL/QPC. *Memory jogger 9000/2000.* (Methuen, MA: GOAL/QPC, 2000).

Levinson, William A. *ISO 9000 at the front line.* (Milwaukee, WI: ASQ Quality Press, 2000).

Monnich, Herbert C., Jr. *ISO 9001:2000 for small and medium-sized businesses.* (Milwaukee, WI: ASQ Quality Press, 2002).

West, John E., and Charles A. Cianfrani. *Unlocking the power of your QMS: Keys to business performance improvement.* (Milwaukee, WI: ASQ Quality Press, 2005).

Westcott, Russell T. *Stepping up to ISO 9004:2000.* (Chico, CA: Paton Press, 2003).

Leadership and Management—General

Andersen, Bjørn. *Bringing business ethics to life: Achieving corporate social responsibility.* (Milwaukee, WI: ASQ Quality Press, 2004).

Barker, Tom. *Leadership for results: Removing barriers to success for people, projects, and processes.* (Milwaukee, WI: ASQ Quality Press, 2006).

Bellman, Geoffrey. *Getting things done when you are not in charge.* (San Francisco: Berrett-Koehler Publisher, 2001).

Cartin, Thomas J. *Principles and practices of organizational performance excellence.* (Milwaukee, WI: ASQ Quality Press, 1999).

Harris, Philip R., and Robert T. Moran. *Managing cultural differences: Leadership strategies for a new world of business.* (Houston, TX: Gulf Publishing, 2000).

Miller, Ken. *The change agent's guide to radical improvement.* (Milwaukee, WI: ASQ Quality Press, 2002).

Project Management

Frame, J. Davidson. *The new project management* (2nd ed.). (San Francisco, CA: Jossey-Bass, 2002).

Greer, Michael. *Manager's pocket guide to project management.* (Amherst, MA: HRD Press, 1999).

Harrington, H. James, and Tom McNellis. *The e-business project manager.* (New York: McGraw-Hill, 2002).

Kezsbom, Deborah S., and Katherine A. Edward. *The new dynamic project management: Winning through the competitive advantage.* (New York: John Wiley & Sons, 2001).

Lewis, James P. *Project planning, scheduling and control* (3rd ed.). (New York: McGraw-Hill, 2001).

Lowenthal, Jeffrey N. *Six Sigma project management: A pocket guide.* (Milwaukee, WI: ASQ Quality Press, 2002).

Thomsett, Michael C. *The little black book of project management* (2nd ed.). (New York: AMACOM, 2002).

Westcott, Russell T. *Simplified project management for the quality professional.* (Milwaukee, WI: ASQ Quality Press, 2005).

Quality Costs

ASQ Quality Costs Committee, Jack Campanella, ed. *Principles of quality costs* (3rd ed.). (Milwaukee, WI: ASQ Quality Press, 1999).

Atkinson, Hawley, John Hamburg, and Christopher Ittner. *Linking quality to profits.* (Milwaukee, WI: ASQ Quality Press, 1994).

Software Quality

Daughtrey, Taz, ed. *Fundamental concepts for the software engineer.* (Milwaukee, WI: ASQ Quality Press, 2002).

Statistics

ASQ Statistics Division. *Improving performance through statistical thinking.* (Milwaukee, WI: ASQ Quality Press, 2000).

Crossley, Mark L. *The desk reference of statistical quality methods.* (Milwaukee, WI: ASQ Quality Press, 2000).

Roberts, Lon. *SPC for right-brain thinkers: Process control for non-statisticians.* (Milwaukee, WI: ASQ Quality Press, 2006).

Strategic Management

Chang, Richard Y., and Mark W. Morgan. *Performance scorecards: Measuring the right things in the real world.* (San Francisco: Jossey-Bass, 2000).

Cowley, Michael, and Ellen Domb. *Beyond strategic vision: Effective corporate action with hoshin planning.* (Boston, MA: Butterworth-Heinemann, 1997).

Haines, Stephen G. *Manager's pocket guide to strategic and business planning.* (Amherst, MA: HRD Press, 1999).

Kaplan, Robert S., and David P. Norton. *Balanced scorecard: Translating strategy into action.* (Boston, MA: Harvard Business School Press, 1996).

Supplier Quality

Bossert, James L., ed. *The supplier management handbook* (6th ed.). (Milwaukee, WI: ASA Quality Press, 2004).

Hoover, Bill, Eero Eloranta, Kati Huttunen, and Jan Holmstrom. *Managing the demand chain: Value innovations for supplier excellence.* (New York: John Wiley & Sons, 2001).

Teams

Bens, Ingrid. *Facilitation at a glance!* (Methuen, MA: GOAL/QPC, 1999).

GOAL/QPC-Joiner. *The team memory jogger.* (Methuen, MA: GOAL/QPC, 1995).

Total Quality Management

ASQ Food, Drug, and Cosmetic Division. *Food process industry quality system guidelines.* (Milwaukee, WI: ASQ Quality Press, 1998).

Beecroft, G. Dennis, Grace L. Duffy, and John W. Moran, eds. *The executive guide to improvement and change.* (Milwaukee, WI: ASQ Quality Press, 2003).

Berk, Joseph, and Susan Berk. *Quality management for the technology sector.* (Newnes: Butterworth-Heinemann, 2000).

Besterfield, Dale H. *Quality control* (6th ed.). (New York: Prentice-Hall, 2000).

Crosby, Philip B. *Quality is free: The art of making quality certain.* (New York: McGraw-Hill, 1979).

Deming, W. Edwards. *The new economics: For industry, government, and education.* (Massachusetts Institute of Technology, 1994).

Dobyns, Lloyd, and Clare Crawford-Mason. *Quality or else: The revolution in world business.* (Boston, MA: Houghton-Mifflin Company, 1991).

Feigenbaum, Armand V. *Total quality control* (3rd ed.). (New York: McGraw-Hill, 1991).

Gryna, Frank, Richard C. H. Chua, and Joseph A. DeFeo. *Quality planning and analysis for enterprise quality* (5th ed.). (New York: McGraw-Hill, 2007).

Hutton, David W. *The change agents' handbook: A survival guide for quality improvement champions.* (Milwaukee, WI: ASQ Quality Press, 1994).

Ishikawa, Kaoru. *Guide to quality control.* (White Plains, NY: Quality Resources, 1986).

Juran, J. M. *Juran on leadership for quality: An executive handbook.* (New York: The Free Press, 1989).

———. *Juran on planning for quality.* (New York: The Free Press, 1988).

———. *Juran on quality by design: The new steps for planning quality into goods and services.* (New York: The Free Press, 1992).

Index